Action Learning

THE LEARNED SOCIETY OF PRAXIOLOGY

PRAXIOLOGY:
**The International Annual of Practical Philosophy and Methodology
Vol. 6**

EDITOR-IN-CHIEF
Wojciech W. Gasparski
The Institute of Philosophy and Sociology, Polish Academy of Sciences
Nowy Świat Str. 72, 00-330 Warsaw, Poland

Action Learning

Praxiology: The International Annual of Practical Philosophy and Methodology, Volume 6

Edited by

Wojciech W. Gasparski

& David Botham

Transaction Publishers
New Brunswick (U.S.A.) and London (U.K.)

Preparation of this volume was partly financed by Komitet Badán Naukowych (The Committee for Scientific Research).

Library of Congress Catalog Number: 97-49868
ISBN: 1-56000-371-5
Printed in the United States of America

Library of Congress Cataloging-in-Publication Data

Action learning / Wojciech W. Gasparski, David Botham, editors.
    p. cm. — (Praxiology ; v. 6)
  ISBN 1-56000-371-5 (alk. paper)
    1. Active learning. 2. Praxiology. I. Gasparski, Wojciech. II. Botham, David. III. Series: Praxiology (New Brunswick, N.J.) ; vol. 6.
B832.2.A27 1998
153.1'52—dc21   97-49868
                                               CIP

Contents

Editorial: *Wojciech W. Gasparski* 1

Introduction: *David Botham* 5

PART ONE: The Elements of Action Learning

Fundamental Aspects of Action Learning (with the Annex
by *Reginald W. Revans*): *Albert Barker* 13

The Context of Action Learning: A Short Review
of Revans' Work: *David Botham* 33

PART TWO: Human Action and Learning

Action and Learning: *Timo Airaksinen* 65

It's Not Obvious: How Rational Agents Use Salience:
William Kline 77

Praxiology, Action Research, and Critical Systems Heuristics:
Werner Ulrich....................................... 91

**PART THREE: Learning by Action:
Applications, Techniques, and Case Studies**

Applying Action Learning Principles to Academic Seminars:
A Study in Praxiological Action: *Chris de Winter Hebron*
and *Doreen J. de Winter Hebron* 105

Organisational Learning: A Case Study and Model
for Intervention and Change: *John E. Enderby,
Dean R. Phelan and Greg Birchalll* 129

The Relevance of Action Learning for Business Ethics:
Learning by Solving Ethical and Praxiological Dilemmas
in Business; *Wojciech W. Gasparski* 147

Modifying Group Architecture to Manage Conflict
– the Dance Card Technique, a Novel Methodology
for Managing Group Dynamics: *Gerald M. Levy* 167

Learning by Action. The Case
of the Polish Environmental Movement: *Piotr Gliński*......... 191

The Intellectual Entrepreneur: *Stefan Kwiatkowski* 203

Notes about the Authors 217

Editorial

Wojciech W. Gasparski
Editor-in-Chief

It was 1971 when Professor Reginald W. Revans visited the Department of Praxiology of the Polish Academy of Sciences, Warsaw and when praxiologists learned about Action Learning for the first time.

A manager lives under the constant assault of events; some of these may have no observable effect upon him, some a temporary effect, some an effect that is permanent, or even regenerative. A regenerative effect may be defined as so concentrating his attention that the manager seeks to identify its cause, and thereby to make sustained use of it. He suggests a theory aimed at supporting his practice, and perhaps without realizing it, enrolls in the ranks of the praxiologists thereby. Thus an event, defined very broadly as an opinion or fact expressed in personal conversation in the board room, the logic of a financial report, or even an apparently arbitrary inspiration within the manager's own mind, is postulated as making an impact either upon what the manager already knows, upon who the manager thinks he already is, or upon how the manager already acts. For our present purpose, it is enough consider the impact of the event upon the manager's current activity.

Such activity is probably to find some satisfactory course of action to relive the pressure of the current task, a process of partial escape that some theorists call "problem solving", and the impact of the arresting event upon the manager may be of any order of magnitude. If it is sufficiently striking the manager may pause to note in detail what he finds in it of interest; he may even set out to act upon it at very moment. Managers different widely in their predisposing states of minds towards new experiences of this kind; the power of creativity or of inventiveness seems to be born of the alternatives to notice, and of the curiosity to analyze, unusual events occurring in one's real world. However this may be, we may suppose that the impact of the event upon the previous condition of the manager has produced within him a potentially new condition questioning an old belief, raising a fresh hope, perceiving an unexpected opportunity, finding a hidden resource. This new condition will, to the action-oriented man, suggest some new practice, some different behavior, some fresh line of attack upon a problem, even a change of strategy or of tactics; it may suggest a new relation between things that he had never previously thought of as connected, or that he had always believed to be related in some other way; it may reveal to him fresh explanations for old troubles or unexplored possibilities in stale and accustomed procedures. We may say, in simple English, that the manager has a new idea.[1]

The such introduced concept of Action Learning (AL) was summarized by Revans in a form as a five stage cycle composed of:

- an attention-fixing event occurring within a framework of systematically-classified experience;
- a new constructive relationship perceived, or thought to be perceived, in or around this event;
- a controlled attempt to exploit this relationship for some desired purpose;
- an audit or inspection of the results of this controlled exploitation;
- the incorporation (or not) of the relationship into the experience of the manager.[2]

According to Revans:

The study of achievement, the anatomy of action, the analysis of how things are done, is, or should be, the final task of the scholar and praxiology, the theory of practice, although the most general of all sciences, should also be the most fertile of them. All technologies, all crafts, are but special examples of generalized human action, and all are subjects of the same intellectual queen. When one examines the nature of the dialogue between Man and his environment that is generally regarded as successful progress, it is clear that the growing mastery that Man displays over this environment is not reached by the mastery that he displays over himself. [...]this tragic discrepancy is evidence of an arrested learning process, of a fixation at on ethical level that respects verification but is indifferent to responsibility. But there is evidence that this condition may be historically determined, and there is certainly evidence that countervailing forces are at work to free the younger generation from the scientistic bondage of their parents and their teachers.[3]

This volume[4] proves the prediction and the hope of the author of *Action Learning: New Techniques for Management.*[5] Authors of contributions collected in the book are but a few exceptions representatives of the *younger generation.* Many of them gathered in London for the First International Action Learning Mutual Collaboration Congress, 17–25 April 1995. Maybe not all of them follow the letter of earlier Action Learning definition but for sure all of them – whether from England or Poland, from Switzerland or Australia, from Hungary or USA – share the spirit of the importance of learning through action understood praxiologically.

The first part of the volume to AL preliminaries consists of two papers wrote by Albert Barker and David Botham the devoted guardians of the Revans' intellectual output. Barker introduces basic concepts related to Action Learning characterizing it as applied praxiology while Botham describes history of the approach as it was introduced and developed by Professor Reginald W. Revans.

Philosophical context of the two realms: "action" and "learning" is analyzed by Timo Airaksinen, a Finnish philosopher, who extensively contributed previous *Praxiology* volumes. The essay is followed by William Kline (an American decision theorist visiting Hungary) attempt to show how rationality of human action depends on salience, and by Werner Ulrich (a Swiss system scientist) analysis on other factors of action considered as rational. The three contributions form the second part of the volume.

The third and the largest part of the book is devoted to different implementations of Action Learning. The part begins from a contribution by the experienced followers of the Revans' methodology Chris and Doreen de Winter Hebron. They share with readers of the book the knowledge based on four cases taken from their practice as educators of many learners from numerous countries. And the learners – what is worthy to add – were university faculty members and research institute employees and administrators.

Another case study, this time on applying the AL approach to an Australian hospital, is reported by John E. Enderby, Dean R. Phelan and Greg Birchall. The first two authors are inventors of the *Enderphel* model for organizational learning.

Dilemmas faced by business people whether CEOs, managers or any other stakeholders are of praxiological and ethical nature states the author (Gasparski) of the next contribution. Processes of overcoming them is the true *academy* of Action Learning, one may summarize the message of the paper.

Gerald M. Levy presents – for the first time to the academic communities – the technique based on Dance Card that refers to the formality of social dances and balls of the last centuries. This extraordinary method helps to overcome conflicts through Action Learning suggestion to modify a group structure rather then accommodating behavior to the given structure.

Contributions concluding the volume present new situation in contemporary Poland. Action Learning or learning by action in relation to environmental movement is overviewed by Piotr Gliński, a sociologist. An entrepreneurial capability of intellectuals is surveyed by a management scientist Stefan Kwiatkowski. Both contributors express the belief in the future development of the types of action studied by them and learned by the people they surveyed and interviewed.

It was a real pleasure to meet R.W. Revans and other Action Learning scholars at the London '95 Congress. It was even a greater pleasure to work with these who decided to contribute the book in the period of its preparation. I appreciate very high the efficient collaboration offered by Dr. David Botham, a co-editor of the volume.

Notes

1. Reginald W. Revans, "Action, Creativity and Learning: Some Reflections upon the Nature of Achievement", *Prakseologia* 39/40 (1971): 29–50.
2. Ibid., 33.
3. Ibid., 49–50.
4. The preparation of this volume was partly funded by Komitet Badań Naukowych (Committee for Scientific Research).
5. Reginald W. Revans, *Action Learning: New Techniques for Management* (London: Blond & Bridges, Ltd., 1980).

Introduction

David Botham
Revans Centre for Action Learning
and Research,
University of Salford,
Salford, UK

1. Essentials of Action Learning

Apart from Revans, there have been a number of scholars and practitioners concerned with either a precise definition or a clear understanding of what action learning is.

Take for example Mumford's: *Review of Action Learning* (1985: 1). He begins his article by asking the same question. "What is Action Learning?" before initiating his review of action learning itself. Revans, on the other hand, in his *ABC of Action Learning*, preferred a different approach and wrote a Chapter entitled: *What Action Learning is Not*, which he described as an effort to discriminate between action learning and other approaches (1978: 26).

Although the approaches of Mumford and Revans are different, they attempt in their own particular ways to explain how action learning compares with other approaches to human and organisational development. This concept of learning about something by analysing the difference between that something and something else was central to the way Gregory Bateson was thinking and explaining in his final book *Mind and Nature: A Necessary Unity* (1979: 126). Bateson argued that if the sequence of something is surprisingly different from what is known and established then the experience is truly developmental. Few would argue against the notion that action learning is different, and sometimes surprisingly so, especially for those who anticipate it being a method or technique.

Learning from distinguishable action is even more surprisingly different than learning from a subject expert in human or book form, and for those who have worked with and in action learning, the latest form is always distinguishably different from a former experience.

Revans said of action learning, "It is not new; like most development, it is more the re-interpretations and fresh use of old ideas than any acquisition of additional cognitive knowledge" (1978: 3).

Since the first action learning programme (National Association of Colliery Managers 1952), several re-interpretations of this early programme have taken place by Revans himself , and others, and as such, it could be argued little has changed in terms of the essentials of action learning which are:

(a) that the logical structure (paradigm) of the learning process is assimilated to that of the conscious (quasi-rational) decision; and that both are assimilated to that of the scientific method;

(b) in consequence, there can be no learning unless the participant receives inputs, about his/her own outputs, or feedback about his/her performance; to learn anything the participant must see the effects of using the new knowledge;

(c) participants learn only of their own volition and never at the will of others (unless this is accommodated in the participant's volition for the time being as a bribe, prize or incentive); they are not taught by others, but learn "within themselves" largely by the reorganisation or extension of what they already know;

(d) the volition to learn is most readily engendered by the lure of success or by the read of calamity and the need to solve some problem; such opportunities and such problems must be "real", in the sense that they engage the personal value systems of the learners offering real rewards for success and real penalties for failure;

(e) during the efforts to seize such opportunities or to solve such problems participants may need to be conscious of what they are doing, in the sense of being able to describe their behaviour in words or symbols; what they believe themselves to be doing (such as in defining their objectives) may appear very differently to external observers, and a comparison between the two or more different sets of impressions may (by invoking (b) above) already start the learning process before any visible trial action is taken;

(f) in action learning programmes these external observers are *without exception* other action learners, and the action learning set (that is the cardinal element of action learning) provides that participants learn with and from each other during the nascent interchanges that both precede and follow trial action in the field of the opportunity or of the problem;

(g) the role of the professional teacher in action learning is thus confined to providing (or helping to provide) the conditions in which participants can learn with and from each other; the learning of the subject derives, on the one hand, from the criticism, advice and support of the other and equal participants in the set, and, on the other hand, from the outcome of the real time action taken upon the real world of the problem or opportunity;

(h) action learning has no syllabus, no texts and no experts; it will make use of any existing idea (howsoever absurd) since it seeks one goal only: "Can we do what we set out to do, and by what evidence do we know whether we have done it?" In achieving this the utility (validity) of our ideas are automatically tested, precisely as they are in the application of the scientific method.

2. Implication of Applying Action Learning

Action Learning must be specifically adapted for the chosen field of its application and the following conditions must be observed;

(i) professional practitioners are characterised by their obligation to take responsibility for anticipating and influencing the future; they are supposed to plan ahead and so work in conditions of ignorance, risk and confusion;

(ii) practitioners must, on this account, develop an ability to identify what are likely to be the most fertile questions to ask when nobody around them knows (or can be expected to know) what to do; there is a little evidence to suggest that too great a loyalty to some particular branch of knowledge (or expertise) may inhibit this freedom to choose fresh and unfamiliar lines of inquiry;

(iii) since we do not know how to develop the general capacity to identify what may be useful questions in conditions of ignorance, risk and confusion, we can only proceed empirically, namely, by putting professional practitioners into such conditions to attack real opportunities or problems, and to observe the outcome;

(iv) such a line of support demands that we accept working under the same conditions as those from whom we expect the support; this leads to our having to adopt certain organisational forms into which our learning processes are to fit; these are described as "the learning community, the project, the set, the induction programme" and so forth; it also means the allocation of specific roles to a variety of participants, such as the steering committee, the sponsors, the clients, the fellows, (perhaps, the co-ordinators), the set advisers, and, above all, the initiators;"

(v) within these conditions imposed by the treatment of real world tasks, there is some freedom of design in the project, or exercise to develop the general capacity to pose fertile questions in conditions of ignorance, risk and confusion; since this is an empirical essay set to particular practitioners to tackle some task about which nobody knows what to do (at least at the outset), there are four options open to the designer:

(a) familiar task tackled in familiar setting,
(b) familiar task tackled in unfamiliar setting,
(c) unfamiliar task in familiar setting,
(d) unfamiliar task in unfamiliar setting;

(vii) action learning programmes are not, in general, intended to tackle puzzles, namely, questions to which an answer may be said to exist even if that answer is difficult to find; action learning is intended to help to develop the ability to tackle problems or opportunities, of which different persons, all experienced, intelligent and motivated, might well advocate different courses of action, all reasonable; it is in the set discussions of such differences that the participants are more clearly aware of their own value systems and of their own obliquitys of perception;

(viii) action learning sets are not supposed to be psychotherapeutic sessions, dedicated to self-understanding by self-disclosure (although they are bound to contribute to this); nor are they clinics run partly by the participants, partly by a set adviser, to explain to the practitioners their responses to each other in terms of such-and-such models of individual and group psychology, although they are bound to make each more aware of the impact he/she has upon others;

3. The Revans Centre for Action Learning in Research

Building upon the previously mentioned essentials of action learning, the Revans Centre based at the University of Salford views action learning as a process of inquiry beginning with the experience of not knowing WHAT TO DO NEXT, and finding that an answer is not available from current expertise.

When expertise fails to provide an answer, collaborative inquiry with fellow learners who are undergoing the same experience of questioning what to do next is always available. This PARTNERSHIP IN LEARNING to be effective needs to be both supportive and at the same time, challenging, deeply caring, yet questioning. Such partnerships create themselves when different people with different ideas engage wholeheartedly with each other in order to resolve each others problems as partners in adversity.

This is a profound shift, from dependence on available expertise and pride in the steady accumulation of knowledge, to learning with and from fellow learners, honestly disclosing doubts and admitting ignorance. This process takes place initially in small groups ("sets") but is free to find other opportunities of furthering inquiry. Each question finds possible answers which are tested in action. Those taking part in this process find that they have opened up far more than a useful technique of investigation. They have found a new way of understanding about being responsible for one's own learning in a continuing process of professional and personal development.

A distinctive feature of the Centre is its focus on bringing experienced practitioners to work intensively in small groups on key issues confronting them: learning together from the whole process of research and development and implementation rather than limiting their learning to one phase of the process. As such, the Centre provides a unique resource base for growing global networks of action learning in many fields of endeavour and serves to bring together many initiatives.

4. Action Learning Interfacing with Research

There are few who doubt the important responsibility the Revans Centre has in the development of action learning world-wide. Since the Centre was opened, it has been featured in two major British newspapers and has been the subject of a BBC Open University Programme (B5 738).

The Centre warmly embraced the idea of working alongside fellow colleagues associated with the Learned Society of Praxiology and gave strong support to establishing this particular edition of *Praxiology*.

All of the articles within this volume have been considered and recommended by the Revans Centre as sound contributions to the continuing debate on the processes of learning from distinguishable action. The wide variety of contributions helps to underline this point. However, it needs to be remembered that action learning is both critical and "meta" to its own processes and therefore is constantly developing itself, as the future volumes will aptly demonstrate.

References

Bateson, G. (1979). *Mind & Nature: A Necessary Unity*. Bontam Books.

Botham, D. (1985). *Action Learning: A Confluence of Self and Organisational Development*. Manchester Metropolitan University.

Botham, D. & Morris, J. (1996). Unpublished discussion paper.

Goffman, E. (1974). *Frame of Analysis: An Essay on the Organisation of Experience*. Harper & Row.

Mumford, A. (1985). *Review of Action Learning*. MCB Press.

Revans, R.W. (1978). "Essentials of Action Learning." Unpublished paper. Revans Archive, University of Salford.

Revans, R.W. (1995). *ABC of Action Learning*. University of Salford.

Wilder-Mott, D. & Weakland, J.H. (1981). *Rigour & Imagination (Towards an Ecology of Communication by D.C. Barnlund)*. Praeger Publishers.

PART ONE

The Elements
of Action Learning

Fundamental Aspects of Action Learning

(with the Annex by *Reginald W. Revans*)

Albert Barker
Revans Centre for Action Learning
and Research,
University of Salford,
Salford, UK

The "Necessity for Action" and the "Obligation to Respond" are fundamental precepts of genuine Action Learning. In the following pages they are contrasted with "Sham" and the consequences of listening to "Expert Imposters" – before finally we move on to ponder some implications of genuine Action Learning as we search for pathways to Wisdom and Understanding. Thus we set out to consider briefly five general topics:

1) The Necessity for Action;
2) The Obligation to Respond;
3) Sham ... Manifestations of Deceit;
4) The Legacy of "Expert" Imposters;
5) Of Genuine Action Learning – Applied Praxeology.

1. The Necessity for Action

It is highly relevant that Revans called his work "*Action* Learning" and has insisted all along that ACTION was a key element in Action Learning. He tells us that we can't learn of Action Learning without practising Action Learning. Praxeology similarly focuses upon ACTION and we should note that the 4th century Greek artist Praxiteles was not just a student of sculpture, but was a *practising* sculptor, becoming highly renowned and regarded as second only to Phidias.

Revans often quotes: "One action is worth a thousand words" (Mohammed).

In the *ABC of Action Learning* he reminds us:

> To do a little good is better than to write difficult books. The perfect man is nothing if he does not diffuse benefits on others, if he does not console the lonely. The way of salvation is open to all, but know that a man deceives himself if he thinks he can escape his conscience by taking refuge in a monastery. The only remedy for evil is healthy reality. (Buddha; *Benares Deer Park*)

> One must learn by doing the thing; for though you think you know it you have no certainty, until you try. (Sophocles; *Trachiniae*)

> Be ye doers of the word, and not hearers of it, blinding yourselves with false ideas. Because if any man is a hearer of the word and not a doer, he is like a man looking at his natural face in a glass; for after looking at himself he goes away, and in a short time he has no memory of what he was like. But he who goes on looking into the true law which makes him free, being not a hearer without memory but a doer putting into effect, this man will have a blessing on his acts. (St. James; *CH.1: v. 22–25*)

> It is not enough to know what is good; you must be able to do it. (Shaw; *Back to Methuselah, IV*)

> All meaningful knowledge is for the sake of action, and all meaningful action for the sake of friendship. (John Macmurray; *The Self as Agent*)

Constantly we hear of the need for ACTION and DOING!
To these we could add a few others, such as:

> What we have to learn to do, we learn to do by doing. (Aristotle; *Nichomachean Ethics, Bk 2*)

> Don't listen to their words, fix your attention upon their deeds! (Einstein; *The World as I See It – on theoretical physicists*)

> Is not religion all deeds and reflection? (Kahlil Gibran; *The Prophet*)

> ... as for knowledge, it arises through *experience* only (Immanual Kant)

> Doing is better than saying (Proverbs)

Apart from the above examples there is plenty of evidence from elsewhere too that the essential need to ACT has been advocated down through the ages in all manner of contexts from ethical to metaphysical (as the means of acquiring primary evidence) and in terms of practical application. Since we Learn With & From Each Other – and also from Doing, then it becomes clear that we need to DO TOGETHER in order to learn. Studying together, whilst useful, is not enough – it is necessary but not sufficient. Listening to the advice of others is also not enough, particularly if they too have not been "doing" anything themselves, but only amassing at second hand the second handed experience or theory of others who were also non-practising.

Revans was keen that the Heathrow Congress[1] of 1995 included the words "mutual collaboration" in its title and the project was intended to pursue future practical action as a consequence. Unfortunately the original format, leading towards some kind of delegate determined outcome involving future action, was lost in the enthusiasm for academic analysis using truncated elements of Systems Alpha and Beta to arrive at flip chart resolutions. The attitude "It's done; we've surveyed the problem ($\beta1$) and arrived at a viewpoint ($\beta2$)," seemed to be for many the natural end of the matter (a simple academic exercise involving an Action Learning experience) … whereas without subsequent action, the exercise itself would remain sterile.

The clue lay in the use of the word "Collaboration" and we should note its Latin roots (collaborare/laborare, "to work" – together) indicating the need not merely to talk or consult together (confer/conference – from "conferre"), analyse and exchange, but to act together (involving the performance of deeds) to generate experience through application and experiment ($\beta3$), which could later be reviewed ($\beta4$), and then assimilated as learning ($\beta5$).

We have come to believe that the ability to describe a phenomenon, characteristic or manifestation, thereby renders an understanding of it. It does not. The ability to describe a clock in great detail down to the last measure of any significance at all, does not provide an understanding of the essence of Time. Nor does the ability to describe with great precision the last physical details of the human body bestow upon us a knowledge of Human Nature. We think that once we can describe a thing or have concocted a definition for it, that we then understand it too! Definitions and descriptions do not render understanding.

Sadly, the erroneous idea that understanding comes from the preparation of an identifying account of something, has in many academic minds superseded the need for experiment, experience, action, test or evaluation – indeed the need for any action of any kind whatsoever.

People prepare a definition for "management" (organisational or social, and the more complex, highly structured and jargon-ridden the better) and then presume to know what "management" is all about without any need to engage in it nor even to confer with or listen to those who endeavour to practise it – nor even to those who attempt to respond to it.

The full process of System Beta is too often curtailed. We go straight from β1 (Survey), through β2 (Decision) to assume β5 (Learning), in effect saying "I have looked at the problem and decided – so now we know." The thought that the theory needs also to take account of the reality is anathema. Not all of them but nevertheless too many academics and others are too keen to keep well away from Reality.

Theoretical Economists read and write their books and expound their ideas without much reference at all to those business people, manufacturers, and ordinary folk (imbued with their "animal spirits") who spend the whole of their time living in the day to day world of Applied Economics facing the inescapable realities of daily life; Keynes called the economic experts "madmen in authority."

The Theorists are characterised by their complete disregard for the experiences of those who have to make economic systems work in practice in order to sustain society with the food and goods necessary to support an acceptable standard of living. In the UK, services (such as the NHS) are bedevilled by "experts" from outside who have no practical experience whatsoever of operational responsibility and who have even less inclination to listen to those who have!

Some Action Learning academics and consultants have fallen into the same trap. They can pontificate for hours. create charts and diagrams without end, complicating the simple and making complex the straightforward, without ever entertaining the slightest acknowledgement of the need to engage in that ACTION and DOING which Revans (and others) tell us is quintessential to the acquisition of Learning and Understanding.

We collect and disseminate Knowledge when really we need Understanding. We make a note of "What" happens as a result of pressing the switch – that the light goes on – and are content that this constitutes Knowledge. We stop right there, convinced that we now know about the process. But only when we recognise the "Why" of the light going on, appreciating the basic workings of an electrical circuit, can we begin to aspire to some measure of Understanding.

Our educational systems appear to be more geared to Knowledge than to Understanding. Our Knowledge is witnessed by the awareness that turning on the switch will result in illumination whilst our Understanding will only be demonstrated by creating an operational lighting circuit. Having the answers to "What" questions demonstrates Knowledge, but it is having the answers to "Why" questions which indicates Understanding.

Academe is generally more geared to providing what is believed to be useful knowledge, than to the development of practical Ability, hence the importance of Action Learning and Praxeology when so much emphasis is being placed upon data and theory; unless and until some practical Application is brought about, any Theory will remain a sterile intellectual excursion. An Action Learning based World University or Institution is being researched which will focus upon the pursuit of Ability ("doing") in order to demonstrate Understanding and thus provide the grounds for further Research building upon, rather than simply adding to, the assimilation of information.

He who says "we need a bridge" and walks away, merely articulates an existing problem – this is "Cleverness."

But *he who BUILDS a bridge* demonstrates ability and understanding, also giving service to his fellow beings – this is "Wisdom" ... and it stems from taking Action ... from "Doing."

2. The Obligation to Respond

Simply recognising that something needs to be done and agreeing with Revans and others that people should take ACTION, is insufficient if we fail to realise the personal implications and the need to respond to our own individual moral obligation to undertake practical deeds. The OBLIGATION to act has long been recognised and various justifying circumstances have been suggested – sometimes with references to the consequences should we fail to react.

We are told that "The road to hell is paved with good intentions" indicating that the mere acknowledgement of the obligation is not enough. And what should drive those intentions? What should be the underlying object or motivation behind our endeavours to meet our obligations?

Advice down the ages has been plentiful; some obvious and less obvious examples might include –

> The object of government in peace and in war is not the glory of rulers or of races, but the happiness of the common man. (William Beveridge)

Bonus populi suprema est lex. (Cicero)

Am I my brothers keeper – [Yes] (Genesis)

Just as it is wrong to withdraw from the individual and commit to a community what private enterprise can accomplish, so too is it an injustice, a grave evil and a disturbance of right order, for a larger and higher association to arrogate to itself functions which can be performed efficiently by smaller and lower societies. Of its very nature the true aim of all social activity should be to help members of the social body, but never to destroy or absorb them. (Principle of Subsidiary Function; Pope Pius X)

(So, "Experts" be warned! How far you encroach is a matter of moral consequence.)

I have striven not to laugh at human actions, not to weep *at them, nor to hate them, but to understand them!* (Spinoza)

(And to Understand human actions we must *engage* with them.)

Ethics does not treat of the world. Ethics *must be a condition of the world, like logic.* (Ludwig Wittgenstein; *A Certain World*)

(Hence the need to establish an ethos of moral responsibility.)

And what if we fail our moral obligations?

… we will suffer technological catastrophe unless we learn Morality. (Arthur C. Clarke)

A child becomes an adult when he realises that he *has a right not only to be right but also to be wrong.* (Thomas Szasz; *The Second Sin*)

(So at least if we can learn from our mistakes it is a sign that we are growing up.)

The world's religious leaders and moral philosophers have constantly stressed the urgency of moral commitment and there are thus plenty of admonishments urging us to respond to our ethical obligations. It is simply not sufficient to "Intend to" – we actually have to "Do"! The most significant assessment of our life's worthwhile contribution will centre around not what we talked, wrote or taught about … but what we DID and inspired for accomplishment.

Responsive Action fulfils our spiritual obligation to others – both individually and between societies including our international communities too – be they from Eastern Europe, South America, Poland, Serbia, Ireland, the USA, Africa or wherever.

However, what is needed is exchange from and with people who are practically versed (as opposed to "experts" armed with theories). Collaboration amongst Doers will provide that practical support which can only come through exchange with other practitioners, ie; those who are themselves capable of action, whose understanding originates from deeds (and from failure as much as from success) and not just from theory. If Buddha tells us that the only remedy for the evils of the world is healthy reality (engaging with life rather than just studying it), then we can address this need by adopting the practical approach of applied goodness!

Not only is there a NEED to ACT, but there is also a moral OBLIGATION to act too!

3. Sham ... Manifestations of Deccit

We note that there is a need to Do – and also a Moral Obligation to respond to this need ("Be ye Doers of the Word"). Only by Doing the Word (task, duty) will we Understand it. So how do we recognise the Doers as opposed to the prattlers, scribblers, experts and sundry "know-alls" who will involve themselves in anything whatsoever (including Action Learning) so long as the price is right or the ego-massage and/or personal exposure sufficiently gratifying. Common causes of errors ("Negative deeds" – failures in Understanding) were assessed by Roger Bacon only seven centuries ago; he warns of the dangers arising from the carefully nurtured perceptions people have of some academics and others, ie; the profiles they themselves seek to present. The four basic reasons for causes of erroneous perceptions identified by Roger Bacon were:

1. *Custom*: the traditional assumption that our "betters" actually "know"! We tend to believe automatically what we are told. It is *voluntary acceptance* of the utterances of our mentors. Don't just blame would-be "Divas." It is *US* who make the "Divas"!
2. *Authority*: the declamation of (erroneous) facts'. (False) "Knowledge" asserted and not to be questioned. *Imposed views*.
3. *Majority Opinion*: undue *deference* to the most popular tenets prevailing at the time.
4. *Veneer of Knowledge*: the *pretence* of our mentors that they really understand – and their use of a cloak of cleverness to hide their ignorance.

These are all factors for error inhibiting our learning process. They frustrate our ability to learn at a sufficient rate – and so we become prone to make mistakes. They are occasions of malpractice and not surprisingly they are manifestations of sham "P". Roger Bacon would have lauded the effect of genuine Action Learning in countering these influences through the deployment and use of "Q", and its emancipating effect. Questionable "P" based upon Knowledge alone is dangerous unless fortified by the action of "Q", which leads us to "P" *with Understanding.*

We have plenty of other identifiers and warnings a few of which might include:

> *A musicologist is someone who can read music but can't hear it!* [ie; an "expert" deceiver] (Sir Thomas Beecham)

> The greater the power, the more dangerous the abuse [And this can apply to the influence of "experts" too] (Edmund Burke)

> We trained hard, but it seemed that every time we were beginning to form up into teams we would be reorganised. I was to learn later in life that we tend to meet any new situation by reorganising, and a wonderful method it can be for creating the illusion of progress, while producing, confusion, inefficiency and demoralisation. [So watch out for sham re-organisation by "experts"!] (Caius Petronius; *AD 66*)

> People use the word "guru" only because they do not want to say "charlatan." (Peter Drucker)

> The People must direct the Government and not the Government direct the People. [Which principle also applies to "Experts" too] (Sen. Robert Dole)

And our warnings:

> It is impossible that he should do a thing who is ignorant of how it is done. [If they've not done it, they can't know how – and can't teach others!"] (Arnold Geulinx)

> There was never an age in which useless knowledge was more important than our own. *(*C.E.M. Joad)

> The specialist appears and democracy is half spoilt at a stroke.
> Orthodoxy not only no longer means being right; it practically means being wrong. The modern world is so filled with men who hold dogmas so strongly that they do not even know they are dogmas. (G.K. Chesterton)

> Madmen in authority, who hear voices in the air, are distilling their frenzy from some academic scribblers of a few years back. (John Maynard Keynes)

> They who put out the people's eyes reproach them of their blindness. *(*Milton)

> Gurus of Gobbledygook – what a pity they talk such rubbish. *(*Micklethwait & Wooldridge)

> In Athens we do not say that a man who takes no interest in politics is a man who minds his own business; we say that he has no business here at all. [ie; If

you're not involved – part of the action – then you don't belong here]
(Thucydides; *Words given to Pericles in the funeral oration after the battle of Plataea*)

So Pericles had little use for those not actively involved; Keynes warns us of "madmen in authority"; Chesterton had doubts about specialists, holders of dogma and orthodoxy. We are warned about "gurus of gobbledygook" who talk rubbish and who are called "gurus" because we don't want to use the word "charlatan." They re-organise and direct, they wield power on their own authority and are thus dangerous, they have probably never actually done the task themselves and according to Geulinx must therefore be ignorant about how it is genuinely done. Milton remarks how they baffle and obscure people's vision (with jargon and theory) and then reproach their victims for being blind.

The persistent underlying characteristic about our sham "experts" is their own lack of practical experience. "But we use the experience of others " they may claim. Well, that isn't the Revans style, for he prefers to bring strugglers together in Action Learning fashion letting them "Learn With and From Each Other" whilst others (including some misguided "action learners") are tempted to try to lecture to the world dishonestly, teaching at length from some shaky podium of bogus "expertise." David Botham tells us "They keep trying to make it a science – and it isn't" … "Consultants provide solutions or send managers on courses where they are taught a lot but learn little. Action Learning is about teaching little and learning a lot!"

The shams have an urge to teach a lot (and charge a lot too) for the privilege of having people listen to their a second-hand version of dubious theoretical conjecture – often far removed from the world of hands-on experience. Revans teaches people to learn from each other in the "real here and now" confining himself to empowering and enabling but never engaging in the creation of "client dependency." When someone presents with a problem, Revans does not rush across to bestow voluminous words of structured advice on matters outside his own field of experience, but displays his wisdom by encouraging people to engage with others who have also struggled with one or two problems of their own.

The sham rushes in while Revans simply refers people onwards to others who are struggling too, and may have relevant experience to exchange. He teaches us how to solve problems ourselves and avoids offering prefabricated solutions. He thus gives emphasis to Understanding rather than Knowledge, avoiding Cleverness in preference to pursuing, with others, the goal of Wisdom, through exposing and admitting the nature of our own individual ignorance by having us face what he calls our own individual "Chamber of Horrors" … for which we need each other.

We are more than merely helped by this tribulation for one learns a valuable lesson – that I can learn from people who are ignorant and I can learn from people who are wise … but I can't learn from people who are stupid! But who are the stupid ones? That's easy; they are the ones who think they are "clever" and know all the answers! We can't learn from shams or imposters, for they have nothing worthwhile to impart other than what Roger Bacon called a "veneer of cleverness."

We can detect signs of sham by asking our "experts" and "would-be gurus" what projects they themselves have struggled to complete – not as advisers, consultants, facilitators, report writers, analysers, scribblers or other arms length pontificators, but as real, involved, participants, taking responsibility for consequences and fully engaged in implementation. They can be detected peddling opinions and theories as if they were facts complete with charts and graphs to show how reality can be avoided in a strange world of fantasy and distortion. They are distinguished by the marked absence of any real action or involvement outside of a purely "advisory" function. We should be cautious and note Revans' comments about "For-silly-taters" (Facilitators) and "Sets of Eyesores" (Set Advisors), remembering also his remark "… "facilitation" identified as the apprenticeship to «white collar crime»?" (Golden Jubilee; Page 155). Despite his warnings, people visit him and depart convinced that a programme to give an official blessing of accreditation to training for Facilitators or Set Advisors, would meet with his unreserved approval. Such occasions bring to mind Lord Acton's phrase "accredited mendacity" (The Study of History). Are we now to have "officially licensed" charlatans?

If you ask the right questions, employing a little "Q", the non-practising "experts" will be revealed in all their iniquity as purveyors of gobbledygook, sham and accredited mendacity

And what of the disastrous effects of these "20th century wizards" upon Europe and the rest of the world? Well, don't lose hope. After all, we survived the Black Death … didn't we?

4. The Legacy of "Expert" Imposters

We get dangerous advice from people who make recommendations – but never have to implement them – nor ever personally suffer the consequences. Most management consultants are not managers and typically never have been! They are not corporate or business people and generally never have been!

RWR draws our attention to Nick Cohen writing in "The Independent" in April 1996; he records ...

> The consultants, lobbyists, quangocrats, think-tank staff are coalescing into a new nomenklatura. They are plugged into networks which produce a stream of deals and jobs

... quoting Smith & Young of the Times. Revans also remarks that:

> The fixers can't fix it. A Downing Street review discovered that in 1992, they had received £ 500m of public money for work that generated just £ 10m of savings.

> Management consultancy is a lame duck industry propped up by huge public subsidies.

> The one fix that has not been tried is open government and devolved power. Or real democracy.

Eastern Germany, struggling economically already, saw steady deterioration once the "expert" bureaucrats of West Germany got their hands on the administrative tiller. Eastern European countries, already financially constrained, are burdened with Western European theory from "experts" who think they know the answers to problems they have never even bothered to listen to, from those who not only have to live with them, but with the "solutions" too. In the 1990s the UK, as well, experienced a surge of bureaucratic nonsense that has caused economic havoc in all sorts of industries. A four page euro-Brussels directive on electro magnetic compatibility resulted in 150 pages of DTI regulations and guidelines which even their own officials then struggled to interpret. One book recorded 140 instances of damaging legislative nonsense (including the tropical fish shop which was required to instal a fire extinguisher for every individual fish tank). In FY 1979/80 the UK's National Health Service spent over £ 400,000 on management consultants; by FY 1988/89 the figure had risen to over £ 47 million. In the perceptions of many this increase in the use of consultants also coincided, not with great improvements, but with a steadily deteriorating performance. Some even began to ask if the two occurrences were not perhaps connected?

To Franz Kafka is attributed the remark "Every revolution evaporates, leaving behind only the slime of a new bureaucracy." And what characterises our "expert" imposters and their consequences more than the fact of their remoteness from the scenes of real endeavour, their complete lack of practical engagement or experience, and their total refusal to listen to those most involved? The effects of imposters and sham "experts" from academe and elsewhere detracts from the genuine work of their conscientious colleagues. Let there be no mistaking those we exempt.

We need, and should be grateful for, our conscientious and honest academics, management consultants, lawyers, accountants, business people, etc. Therefore let no criticism herein of the considerable damage inflicted by some of their wayward brethren be allowed to tarnish them all without exception!

5. Of Genuine Action Learning – Applied Praxeology

Considered more fully elsewhere, the benefits of genuine Action Learning come essentially via practice – practical application – which paradoxically engenders more learning. But however brilliant they may be conceptually, solutions left in books "on the shelf" and not implemented, are of little practical use at all. Nor are they of any use if they are inappropriate or removed from reality.

Ross Perot (maverick or not) in the course of his analysis of the problems of America during his campaign to become a reluctant "independent" US President, complained bitterly that the Government machine had analysed every imaginable scenario, had plans for every eventuality, knew the solutions to every problem ... but never implemented any of them! "We have plans for everything," said Perot. "Our problem is not that we don't know what to do, but that we don't DO it!"

Action Learning and Praxeology can only develop as a result of engaging in Deeds and studying the outcome – for the act precedes the theory. The cathonic effect of Action Learning not only fosters Learning based Change in structural and operational approaches (changes resulting from consequential action or implementation – resulting from new learning or understanding), but also engenders the essential personal changes enshrined in what Revans called "System Gamma," the symbiosis of Alpha and Beta. The benefits of Action Learning are thus not confined to changes in the world which surrounds us, but can and must impinge upon us personally too. Action – Change – and Learning, mark our quest for truth. And what of Truth? "There are no whole truths – all truths are half truths" says Revans referring either to Whitehead or Einstein as the mood dictates and revealing his Cambridge scepticism – itself owing much to a long line of contributors from Locke to Aristotle and Plato himself. Despite this we must remember that (in the conventional meaning) two and two make four and therein we have a whole truth! In fact the statement "There are no whole truths ..." is essentially self-destructive in that if it applies universally (and it states "there are *NO* whole truths" – invoking the absolute), then it applies to the statement itself and thus the statement itself is also a half truth, and is therefore not to be taken too literally.

Instead of accepting it literally we should see the statement as an expression of scepticism whereby we take nothing for granted. There ARE "whole truths," but we only half understand them – and that is the message we should hold on to! RWR once remarked "Action Learning teaches us not to be sure we know (understand) anything for certain ... even about Action Learning!"

The Theory of practice has to take account of the Realities of Practice (truth as we experience it). Many who formulate such Theories sadly keep well away from any form of real action and even seem reluctant to liaise as partners with those whose practical deeds demonstrate their experience.

Where does this leave us? With the problem that theorists must either practise themselves or take very close note of those who do. Sadly too many academics and others neither practise themselves nor are inclined to listen to those who do. We want people who can think and DO or else teams of Thinkers and Doers willing and able to work together, Learning With and From Each Other.

Both Aristotle and Locke noted Plato's thinking and the same influence will not be overlooked with reference to the traditions of Cambridge – and indeed, Revans himself. But in what way does Action Learning relate to theories of experiential knowledge and perception? We would certainly not wish to pursue this theme here to the same extent as Ernst Mach whose extreme form of phenomenalistic POSITIVISM suggested that *everything* we know is based on what we EXPERIENCE through our *senses*, following the general line of Hume's empiricist account.

Indeed many are those who have voiced doubts about the reliability of sensory interpretation; the Gestalt School of Psychology founded by Max Wertheimer, Wolfgang Köhler and Kurt Koffka is just one example. A Gestalt is a whole not apparent in the parts (as a melody is to the individual notes comprising it). Elsewhere we suggested that Action Learning leads us to the notion that what is not apparent in the "part," (ie; to the individual), is nevertheless apparent in the whole to our collective insight … leading us to objective knowledge of ourselves and the world through a process of mutual collaboration. Indeed an Action Learning "Set" could be viewed as a gestalt. However, Gestalt psychologists rejected the sensationalist/associationist approach to "Perception" but merely substituted cortically-determined percept for stimulus-determined sensation. Later researchers assimilated a percept to an hypothesis whilst the Gestalt School stayed within the stimulus-response framework. Uncertainty reigns and there are many who warn us that the senses are unreliable.

The Vienna Circle (Schlick and others) explored Mach's ideas further; they were hostile to traditional style metaphysics (despite there being metaphysical features within their own assumptions) and helped develop the debate into the notion of Logical Positivism embodying the view that we must confine ourselves to what is given to us in sense experience as sources of knowledge. Positivism rejects all metaphysical speculation and abstract theorising, even including a critical examination of its own presuppositions. (Which is interesting when we remember David Botham's observation that Action Learning has the ability to evaluate itself!) Note also that when Comte suggested the three phases through which civilisations pass, the theological, the metaphysical and the scientific (or positive), he still harboured reservations about social cohesion in the absence of religion.

Action Learning favours an approach which insists that we ourselves act (do) and thus engender experience through experimentation. It therefore has a positivist dimension, but this is evaluated scientifically rather than sensorily. Furthermore, through b4, (Audit, Reflection, Revue) it also recognises an essential moral perspective. So whilst Comte and others speculated upon the progression of phases, theological through metaphysical to positivism (scientific), Revans' work indicates that these are not sequential but constant … even though the emphasis might change across the centuries; they are distinct but inseparable aspects of our quest and make their contribution in forming our Understanding – which arises out of our practical experience of the world as it actually exists, ie; based upon Reality. We must not try to make a Reality which conforms to the Theory, but instead construct illuminating Theories arising out of Reality itself in order to better understand Reality. (Which may then be changed for the better by those who actually constitute the matter and form, substance and essence of that Reality as part of its inherent dynamic, rather than by further postulating about it.)

It was not science per se which heralded the last stage of civilisations, but the abandonment of spiritual values and moral precepts of earlier recognition once "cleverness" had displaced Wisdom.

We do not therefore reject postulation, theory, or moral precept. We do not advocate positivism to the exclusion of metaphysics. Instead we insist that our efforts include all and are nothing if not based upon Reality, tested by the action of trial and experimentation and scientifically established by mathematics or demonstrable economic and social consequence ... just as much as by chemistry and physics.

It is not "sense-experience" upon which Action Learning relies – but *reality* examined by scientific means. The changes in the Belgian Economy (Inter-University project), the results of the HIC Project, the Manchester Schools study, and other programmes too, are not accounts of "impressions" culled from "sensations" derived from "sense-experience" ... but are true manifestations of reality established by scientific method and owing more to action and intellect than to the senses. The intellectual process is sufficiently an inherent part of Action Learning (analysing experience acquired through Action – System Beta, stages 4 and 5) that the process cannot be said to be based exclusively upon Action alone. For whilst Action is the essential constituent, it is not an isolated element. For this reason the philosophic content suggests that Revans' ideas are also distinct from the Existentialism of Kierkegaard and others ... but without rejecting their ethical concerns either.

So the urge to focus upon Action and Deed when formulating Theory, is not to follow the same path as Mach, Hume, Schlick, and others. The essence of the philosophy of Action Learning is different to these; it is, above all, enshrined in Reality, invoking all the Moral implications too – including personal concerns and regard also – which are enshrined in the need to be Involved and to DO in order to Understand.

Writing about "Management as Creativity and Learning" Revans has this to say:

> The science of praxeology – or the theory of practice – remains amongst the underdeveloped regions of the academic world. And yet it is, or should be, the

queen of all, settling the ancient argument about the relative natures of nominal-
ism and realism ... For successful theory is merely that which enables him who
is suitably armed to carry through successful practice ... to understand an idea
one must be able to apply it in practice, and to understand a situation one must
be able to change it. Verbal description is not comment enough. It is from consistently replicated and successful practice that is distilled and concentrated the
knowledge we describe as successful theory. The process by which one is trans-
formed into the other is the scientific method, and the essence of the scientific
method is the experimental test: "Are the results using the theory in practice
substantially the results we predicted?" ... The essence of the experimental test
is to compare achievement with anticipation; it is the feedback on which the
science of cybernetics is built. Thus, the theory of practice is the ring on which
all the keys of the human intelligence are assembled.

So ... "to understand an idea one must be able to apply it in practice"
– if you can't do it, you don't know it – and the only way you can prove
you know it is to DO it! So studying and writing books about Action
Learning is not enough and proves nothing much at all – only by engaging in Action Learning "hands-on" with others, will the resultant writing of accounts carry the integrity of any true authenticity. We must
endeavour to remember this ... We are unlikely to demonstrate the integrity of our approach by ignoring the very principles we advocate.

Annex by *Reginald W. Revans*

In 1967, shortly after I left my Manchester professorship to practise
with the Belgians an economic idea that had been expressed by Confu-
cius, Buddha and Mohamed sufficiently clearly as to determine the cultures of civilisations historically older and numerically inhabited more
fully than our own, Sir Roy Harrod gave three lectures at this university
in the birthplace of our industrial revolution. They were entitled *Towards a New Economic Policy* and extracts from the first, the middle
and the last pages may suggest why I myself have more than once suggested that Lord Keynes was "morally" right when, in 1936 he published *The General Theory of Employment, Interest and Money*. It was
not any specific suggestion Keynes had made about "new economic
policy" that led me to follow Sir Roy's cautions to what had been established as a new "National Business School," but merely the advice he
gave on his very last two pages about the urgent need of all responsible
authorities to by wary of "academic scribblers." Even three decades there-
after, Sir Roy reinforces the need for all concerned to ask themselves
fresh questions:

page 1: I cannot escape a feeling of uneasiness about the scope and method of economic theory today. It is needful to pay homage to the intellectual distinction of the work of mathematical economists. At the same time I find myself in the awkward position of not having had my understanding of the working of the economies with which we are concerned, whether, for example, our own economy or one or other of those of the less developed countries, greatly enriched, in consequence of this type of work. I am quite ready to admit that this may be because I am incompetent to comprehend it, or because I have not devoted sufficient time to studying it.

page 44: My main objective in these lectures is to focus thought on what system can be devised for, and what principles should govern, domestic economic policy. It does really seem that in recent years we have had no regular system and no regular principles. We have moved from one ad hoc expedient to another. Must we always go on like this? Cannot thought avail to clarify the underlying issues and give us a set of workable principles?

page 70: The burden of these lectures has been that growth, always subject to any desirable increase in leisure, has priority over all other objectives, some of which are often mentioned as co-equal with it. There is nothing new about the concept of "growth"; it is only the frequent use of the word that is new. To give growth top priority merely repeats the ancient view that economic policy should be directed to maximising economic welfare. But in considering how to do this, we have to use the new tools of thought taken from dynamic economics, and not be content with maximising welfare at one point of time only.

And now, three decades after Sir Roy, as he addressed the University of Manchester just three decades after I was at Cambridge and heard much of who was soon to become Lord Keynes, this tract is intended to encourage others from all around the globe to explain how most effectively "to use the new tools of thought taken from dynamic economics," and, most emphatically, "not be content with maximising welfare at one point of time only." Our universal need and our international obligation is to help improve welfare in all places and at all moments the future has yet to bring. What Sir Roy identifies as "dynamic economics" might well have been called *Action Learning* a generation earlier since even before Lord Keynes had pointed out managerial obligation to get subordinates operationally involved, Sir Josiah Stamp, Chairman of London Midland and Scottish Railway, in his article "Some Economic Factors in Modern Life," observed in 1929:

True co-operation should aim at harnessing brains, as well as muscles, and so secure the maximum of effort of men and officers in dealing with the problems that arise from day to day. By such action men gain a more elevated conception of the dignity of their calling, and of what is required from them.

Teamwork, forming more elevated programmes of one's mission, provided all learn with an from each other, is seen today as *Action Learning*. It also inspired Philip Snowden:

> The condition of industry is such that it is imperative that we should get employers and workmen together, that they should abandon their old ideas, that they should realise that they are all partners in industry, and that they should pool their brains and pool their energies.

It is *how* such effective pooling of brains and energies can be successfully achieved that must now become Mankind's first educational objective, and this present manuscript has been built on the morals and the practices of the past five thousand years in the hope that it will encourage employers and workmen, mathematical economists and academic scribblers, men and officers, between different cultures, distant nations, unrelated industries, social services and government bureaucracies, not only to tell each other what they themselves are doing, but also to work upon each others' action learning projects and verify among themselves how deeper self-understanding may most readily arise by seriously overcoming that which, to start with, was totally unfamiliar. Discovering how to ask oneself and one's colleagues intelligible questions about the totally unfamiliar might be how some would interpret the essence of Darwin's *The Origin of Species*, even if the very opening of his *Chapter One* reads:

> When we compare the individuals of the same variety or sub-variety of our older cultivated plants or animals, one of the first points that strikes is, that they generally differ more from each other than to the individuals of any one species or variety in the state of nature. And if we reflect on the vast diversity of the plants the most different climates and treatment, we are driven to conclude that this great variability is due to our domestic productions having been raised under conditions of life not so uniform as, and somewhat different from, those to which the parent species had been exposed under nature.

Plants and animals might not be *asking questions* when suddenly surrounded by different conditions, but are *acting differently* sometimes *more* effectively, sometimes *less*. Those consistently more effective will, in due course, achieve benefits more enduring than others of the same variety, and so, philosophically, become a more lasting and adaptable variety. mankind's most urgent responsibility is to relate our international need for better and more spontaneous adaptability to what has long been known as education, since this exposes our young to "the most different climates and treatment" and may not foresee the need to understand and modify the climate conditions in "which the parent species had been exposed under nature." It was not Lord Keynes alone who urged us all to be so wary of "academic scribblers"; on being asked by His disciples who was greatest in the Kingdom of Heaven, Jesus took a little boy among them and said:

> Verily I say unto you, Except ye be converted, and become as little children, ye shall not enter into the Kingdom of heaven. Whosoever therefore shall humble himself as this little child, the same is greatest in the Kingdom of Heaven.

This may not, from St. Matthew's Gospel, chap. XVIII, vv 2, 3, imply that all experiences after childhood are essentially degrading, but it certainly supports the present moves of teachers in Sweden and South Africa to ask how, by social and parental exchanges wit and among the little children as school-room classes, all may, more deeply and more honestly, begin both to understand themselves and others, and to anticipate how their own beliefs and attitudes will influence tomorrow. And as Mohamed confirmed so long ago, such exchanges must be not of words alone, but also lead to here-and-now activity. His text from *The Koran.* "One action is worth a thousand words!," has not angered our "academic scribblers" alone. After the Israeli invasion of Egypt in 1967 I was asked be the Cairo university to suggest what management education programmes might help those in command of major industries and social services to cope with such emergencies. My idea of *action learning* was to prepare top managers to deal with such *unexpected* troubles as tomorrow's invasion by quarrelsome neighbours by undertaking the definition and solution of *unknown and unfamiliar troubles* handicapping other Egyptian industries or social services; to develop some fresh vision of one's own emergency, actively and determinedly working with new colleagues seriously attacking some totally unfamiliar but desperately urgent strategic problem is the very essence of action learning. Its meaning was given to an international conference in December 1970, by the President of a National Corporation of Egypt; authority throughout the world should now believe and act upon it.

> At first I tried hard to justify myself in rejecting the visiting fellow's report about my company. I thought and how sour were my thoughts! that his criticisms were a spite against us all, against my staff and especially against me. But lows: they are a common feature the one common feature of our entire project. We are all in the same boat. This makes the findings of our fellows very impor-

tant and very relevant; I want to say in public that all of us, whatever our positions, have a great deal to learn from each other. So much of importance, both basic and long term, goes wrong under our very noses, but we must have others to notice it because we ourselves are too easily absorbed in our routines and in our day-to-day problems.

Note

1. First International Action Learning Mutual Collaboration Congress, London 1995.

The Context of Action Learning: A Short Review of Revans' Work

David Botham
Revans Centre for Action Learning
and Research,
University of Salford,
Salford, UK

1. Introduction

It would be incredibly foolish to begin an explanation of something as fundamental as action learning without first paying particular attention to the individual who created and applied it universally.

This paper is a modest review of R.W. Revans' work and his writings. It begins by locating the developments of Revans' thinking and conceptual frameworks within a context built up from his own evaluation.

This is then followed by a brief account of several applications of action learning including the programmes implemented in Belgium, the National Health Service and GEC.

The final section is a brief introduction in Systems Alpha, Beta and Gamma which Revans devised to explain the inter dependencies between planned, deliberate action and conscious human learning.

In October 1945 Revans' concepts of action learning were described in a report titled: *Plans for Recruitment, Education and Training in the Coal Mining Industry*, Mining Association of Great Britain, London, October 1945 (pp. 110–111) But it was much later (in 1983) in another paper titled: *The Validation of Action Learning Programmes*, that Revans reflected back on some of his experiences of these earlier innovator concepts and compares them with similar experiential approaches to management development. (Employing his usual critical eye to anything which claimed to be a "new approach' without acknowledging the form by which it was to be assessed.) In this same article he cited three important dates, or as I prefer, "milestones' in action learning. First, in 1959 the launching of organisation development by proving hospitals to be organic systems for training staff and treating patients. (Revans believed that staff morale was inextricably linked to patient recovery.) Second, in 1963, he posited the concept that "all management development was self-development and not taught but earned by one's own actions."

The third milestone, in 1968, he put forward a structure of action learning which was based on an "indivisible square" consisting of learning, consulting, managing and investigating, along with his uncompromising belief that any degree of splitting between self-development and organisational development, executive action and scientific method was meaningless.

By reviewing his former ideas (first put forward in 1968) Revans in 1983, set out what he called "the prime idea" of action learning, here paraphrased:

(i) It is a learning sequence by which observable behaviour is changed;

(ii) it acts as a transmission between persons offering effective advice; and

(iii) its design and achievement based on rational actions have the same logical structure as that of scientific method (or his System Beta).

2. System Beta

In 1968, Revans revealed his four key aspects which made up his System Beta. These were:

(i) learning as the accession of knowledge;

(ii) consultation as the communication or exchange of opinion;

(iii) deliberate action as the fulfilment of identifiable desire;

(iv) scientific research as the quest for deeper understanding.

He also claimed that most fundamental changes in human relationships consist of:

(i) learning, or seeing one's work in a new light;

(ii) counselling, or effectively changing the perceptions of a neighbour;

(iii) achieving, or beneficially changing the externals by which one is surrounded.

Moreover, he believed that such changes were universal linguistic elements of first, second and third persons and of which any formulation of human purpose starts. Revans synthesised his ideas in a conceptual framework called the "Action Learning Table," which of itself was built up from his System Beta comprising fifteen descriptive cells. (An example of this table originally published in 1983a: 208–11 is set out in Figure 1).

FIGURE 1.
The Action Learning Table

Linguistic element	FIVE STAGES OF SCIENTIFIC METHOD					
	(1) Survey or observation	(2) theory or hypothesis	(3) test or experiment	(4) audit or evaluation	(5) review or control	Apparent human process
first person	admitting one's own ignorance	guessing at likely knowledge	referring to reliable authority	assessing measure of agreement	rememebering or forgetting guesswork	learning
second person	admitting need for support	discussion with likely supporter	co-operation in realistic realistic rehearsal	interpretive exchanges consequences	enhancing ending alliance	advising or being advised
third person	gathering relevant clues	suggesting provisional strategy	pilot text with strict control	comparing test outcome with target	verifying adjusting or dropping strategy	achieving by deciding

In this Table the three rows represent the relations, P, of the person (manager) to (i) him/herself; (ii) colleagues; (iii) the operational environment; the five columns represent S, the scientific method. Row-Column interactions are represented by Revans' Equation and determine the value generated by the action learning implied.

I feel that it is important to point out that this table along with the rest of Revans' argument within this particular paper seemed to be designed to test out and perhaps refute any other form of experiential learning which could not be evaluated against his scientific method.

Also, again in this same paper, he launched the first version of his Learning Equation. This was put forward as a functional equation relating the benefits of action learning – what he called V. The extent and motive of the involvement of the three row elements shown in the Action Learning Table he called P. The five steps of stages of the scientific method he called S. Thus the Revans' Equation was:

$$V = F (P,S)$$

or

The benefits of Action Learning are equal to:
- (i) the functional relationships of the first person learning using the five stages of scientific method;
- (ii) the second person advising or being advised;
- (iii) and the third person achieving by deciding.

Later (1983) in his ABC of Action Learning, Revans developed his Action Learning Table and attempted to clarify what he had previously meant by personal relationships and terms referring to first, second and third persons. His view, by now was that this nomenclature was something common to all languages by the nature of the language itself: person(s) speaking, person(s) spoke to, and person(s) or thing(s) spoken about. His argument was that language may be taken as a model of awareness: awareness of self, awareness of companions, awareness of third parties and of the external world along with a model of influence upon self, companions and upon third parties.

System Beta and Revans' reviews of System Beta[1] suggests that he had found it necessary to establish a closed and self-evaluating system which was both scientifically rigorous and humanistically complex, in order to defend his position and fend off his critics. Moreover, this system provided Revans with a powerful intellectual fortress on which he could challenge those who had claimed that experiential learning and action learning were one of the same.

Reg Revans has always been consistently eager to point out that five stages of the scientific method in his System Beta were derived from Roger Bacon's thesis on scientific method and controlled experiment (c.1292). See the Origins and Growth of Action Learning (1982: 502).

3. Borne in a Laboratory and Tested in Industry

During the 1920s Reg Revans worked as Research Fellow in the Cavendish Laboratories, Cambridge, with no less than ten Nobel Prize winners. Every Wednesday afternoon Revans and his fellow research scientists attended a seminar with their Director, Lord Rutherford. Rutherford had determined that each scientist was to open the seminar by openly confessing what had gone wrong with his own experiments: for Rutherford, it was crucial for every practising scientist to discover how he explored his own ignorance.

This inward-looking approach steeped in a human beings self-confessed honesty as the gateway to learning impressed Revans so much that it became crucial to his questioning approach in later examples of action learning.

The exploration of one's own ignorance by open discussion with others equally discussing their own ignorance in the Cavendish laboratories in the 1920s was the first prototype action learning set, later to be discovered and named so.

After spending three and one quarter hours of one such discussion, Rutherford claimed that what had impressed him most was the level of his own ignorance. But then asked the stunning question: "How does yours look like to you?"

These insights into Revans' experiences as a young Research Fellow in the 1920s suggest that he discovered the penetration power of questioning which powerfully influenced his attitude toward learning and human development. What follows describes what he did with his discovery and how it became action learning.

In 1935 Revans left Cambridge to work with Sir John Sargent, Director of Education to the Essex County Council. (His first published reference to action learning was October 1945).

Revans worked on the development of technical education; "the unprecedented migrations from London along the north bank of the Thames had opened industrial estates offering employment to engineers and technologists that demanded new forms of secondary and higher education such as the then grammar schools could neither provide nor anticipate." (p. 18)

It will be of interest to note that Revans spent his whole life, after his "apprenticeship" with Sir John Sargent, struggling to adapt the British educational system to the social and economic needs of change both

inside the education system itself and in industry and claimed that action
learning was borne out of these unending challenges: (p. 21)

> When leaders are needed in industry and commerce and when the education
> system in its manifold forms is quite unable to provide (as Manifesto for Change
> (3) suggests), then those in industry and commerce must find them from within
> their own resources and by their own methods. Among these is action learning,
> whereby managers, indeed, leaders of many descriptions, learn with and from
> other managers and other leaders in the course of doing what they are employed
> to do, namely, to manage to lead.

Revans (1982: 30–31, 1984) has been consistent in his claims that
action learning came into one most important stage in 1945. As Director
of Education for the Coal Industry, Revans' brief was to find a group of
managers to run a thousand collieries within a time scale of three months.
One of Revans responses was to propose the establishment of a Staff
College for the Mining Industry. The following is a commentary from
a report titled: "Plans for Recruitment, Education and Training in the
Coal Mining Industry" published by the Mining Association of Great
Britain, October 1995.

This report, apart from its unquestionable significance concerning
Revans' unique approach to education and training, has a further significance, for this paper. For it stands as Revans' first explicit statement
of what was later called "action learning." Moreover, it has within its
context the fundamental principles which he used, on the one hand, to
hold action learning and education together, and on the other, prise them
apart in a dialectical relationship often well out of the reaches of professional consultants, educators and trainers. A summary of these challenging and contentious principles suggest that:

     (i) the "syllabus" is the manager's here-and-now troubles which
          have to be dealt with;

    (ii) the tutors are other managers tormented by similar afflictions;

   (iii) the "campus" is partly the college (depicted here as the Staff
          College previously alluded to) but mainly the pits that re-
          quire putting right;

   (iv) the learning is to come by posing of questions made relevant
          through the advice and criticisms of other managers going
          through many of the same uncertainties.

From this it can be assumed that Revans' proposed action learning
would be vastly different from expert-led approaches to training and
development – an approach Revans was well acquainted with. Revans'

concept of the Staff College for the Mining Industry was vastly different from that of British Colleges and Universities. He viewed it as an environment wherein conditions of confusion could be created so that individuals could concentrate on change – both personal and organisational.

The Staff College was delayed because the coal industry was taken into public ownership. Instead, Revans modified his plans and focused on establishing a number of action learning sets made up from twenty-two colliery managers. In 1954 the very first action learning sets – composed of four or five managers – met close to their respective pits so they could arrange visits to each others workplaces with the intention of looking at problems first-hand and using their own eyes, they could ask questions about what they had seen. (1983: 56; 1982: 39; 1984: 8)

Revans claimed that such encounters had dramatic effects on the managers' behaviour. For example:

    (i)   they began to think in fresh ways about their own past experiences;

    (ii) they recognised how they had viewed their own jobs;

    (iii) how they saw their subordinates and

    (iv) how they saw themselves.

Further, two of the original twenty-two tried the action learning concept out with their colleagues in three neighbouring pits and as a result, Revans claimed that an increased output of 30% per person was achieved.

Perhaps more importantly for Revans (pp32–38) was that this analysis had been made from the statistical incidences in respect of mining accidents. Revans sent his report to the scientific department of the National Coal Board in 1954, claiming that the improvements were by-products of the first action learning programme. Moreover, Revans suggested that the improvement of mining accidents were directly linked to improvements in morale, communications, sizes of working groups and managerial awareness (1953).

In his chapter: "Group factors in Mining Accidents in The Origins of Growth of Action Learning" (1982), Revans depicts and structures his analysis and presents them in sixteen qualitative summaries with a further five explanations derived from summary sixteen. In all, Revans makes some well argued claims that the first action learning programme had, (perhaps indirectly) changed the general attitudinal behaviours of the miners themselves. To quote from paragraph A:

> The factors that account for these differences between comparable pits and between years in the same pits may be looked upon as group factors or social

factors ... They exist in some ways in the body of the men as a whole; they are, in other words, specific attributes of the particular communities of men making up particular pits.

4. A Closer Analysis
of the First Ever Action Learning Programme

This first action learning programme ran from February 1954 to November 1956. In essence, twenty-two colliery managers met regularly to "receive reports upon their own operations and those of their colleagues" (1956: 39). In Revans' words "... (it) was a practical expression of the proposals made in ... (a Staff College for the Mining Industry, some nine years previously) ... that active managers would learn most with and from each other while working on the here-and-now of their own problems." (1982: 37)

What figures here is that this above statement made in 1956 was in a way Revans' hypothesis or stage two in his System Beta and stands as an example of his positivistic approach to organised and organisational learning, if we consider that he completed stage one of System Beta, that is, his surveys described in the quotation extracted from the document first published in 1945. His System Alpha paradigm concerning objectives and strategies were encapsulated within the investigatory lead-up to the launch of the very first action learning programme and stands as a testimony to his scientific rigour. Despite what others have written, acted out and/or professed, and there have been many since, it seems that no-one else has matched the ingenuity of this unique individual in implementing one of the most important projects in the field of management development.

In 1955, Revans was appointed as the first-ever Professor of Industrial Administration at the University of Manchester. During this time he wrote and had published several papers on the virtues of small working groups and established his theory that:

(i)   members of small working groups learn quickly from each other and

(ii) they support each other in the tasks of getting the job done. (1982: 76–78)

However, this experience and especially his criticism of University life, documented fully elsewhere, tend to suggest that the interface, or indeed the lack of it, seemed to have a major impact on his relationship with some of his fellow academics.

The following illustrates this point:

> For about a year I was resigned to writing papers about management and productivity rather than being involved first-hand with a score of practical men striving to get more coal up the shafts of their pits and to see fewer of their miners suffering injury. (1984: 9)

As I have indicated, Revans was in every sense of the term a man of action and has continuously been anxious about being excluded from the "pit face" action where the outcome of doing can be not only observed but statistically measured – homogeneously.

Accordingly, it is hardly surprising that in 1958 Revans made his first links with the National Health Service and was invited to help tackle the problem of retaining qualified nurses in one of our leading teaching hospitals, namely The Manchester Royal Infirmary.

The full experiences and results of Revans' studies are recorded elsewhere (1982: 124–132) but in summary his research revealed that in larger hospitals student nurses were forbidden to ask questions because there was a strong chance they would disturb their seniors. By contrast, however, other student nurses working in smaller hospitals "were encouraged to find answers to question and helped to find new ones'.

Revans' inquiries revealed that experienced nurses were also treated in much the same way; during interview both Sisters and Deputy Matrons stated that is was easier to adjust when the duties and functions of others were easier to interpret. Such interpretations were more readily accepted in smaller hospitals and therefore nurses were more inclined to stay longer. Revans called this phenomenon: "Small is dutiful" based on his conviction that:

> One knows one's duty to others when there are only few working together.

This view of group size affecting behavioural responses, shown here from an extract of his published work in 1959, has very strong parallels with the way he viewed sets. He preferred four or five members whereas others have worked with nine and sometimes ten.

Later Revans in his own unique way linked the relationship of hospital size and the freedom to question as a way of learning with actual patient recovery. He postulated the notion that:

> Might not similar patients recover more quickly in hospitals in which nurses learn more readily, and more slowly in hospitals where nurses learn only with reluctance. (1984: 10–12)

Revans' research[2] tried to establish a clear link between patient recovery times expressed in period of stay in hospitals with nurses learning by finding answers to questions themselves interlinked to managing their own problems. An analysis of this research would suggest that as action learning takes place in the wards by nurses raising questions and finding their own solutions, their stay in the organisation increases, patients indirectly benefiting from the results of action learning, stay less.

5. Further Contributions by Revans to Action Learning

Revans, in 1964, expanded his concepts of learning, morale and their effects on patient recoveries (1984: 11) and formed a special consortium, involving ten London Hospitals, to work on Health Service problems. Each hospital had an "organic team" comprising doctors, nurses and administrators (now called managers) to represent them in the consortium. The organic teams met for about four years and worked through forty or so projects, ranging from improving relationships between nursing staff and social workers to more efficient uses of operating theatres. This was Revans' famous HIC project or more specifically his Hospital Internal Communications Project.

According to Revans this was an important turning point in the development of action learning. His original view, focused on a small group of managers forming learning partnerships called sets, was considerably expanded and embraced the notion of the complete institution as a set; realised as a hospital employing two thousand people acting as a large learning community.

Fierce critics of the project, such as Klein (1972) reviewed it as:

> ... a highly instructive failure though whether the instruction gained represents an adequate return on the investment is very doubtful: a rough guess suggests that the real cost of the project – which involved the time of nearly a hundred, sometimes highly paid, NHS employees – may have been something like double the £62,000 grant from the Department of Health and Social Security.

Klein attacked the purpose of the project and claimed that it was a kind of "curious moral evangelism of those who see better communications as being an end in itself." Klein concluded that the HIC project was "doomed from the start because of its lack of clearly defined aims."

By contrast, Wieland (1981) commenting some ten years after the evaluations of the HIC project was completed, viewed the project very differently from Klein:

> Perhaps the most important outline of this evaluative study is the demonstration that Revans' self-help approach to management improvement is indeed effective ... hospital management efficiency can be systematically improved no small matter in these times of spiralling health care costs ... Thus, during the five years after the project (1969–1973) ... medical and surgical patient yielded a total saving of £5 million. This is impressive, since there were no project activities aimed specifically at this criterion. In short, these demonstrated effects and efficiency of patient care are probably only the tip of the iceberg as far as the HIC Projects are concerned ... Revans emphasised that only the hospital staff knew their own problems and could solve them and having said this he withdrew from active management of the project. (1984: 12)

Revans viewed criticisms and commentaries differently; he viewed them as "obscurely complimentary" to his work, believing that the more important the issue or project the more it would be attacked by opponents. Further he sarcastically linked the behaviour of his critics with their own personal states of insecurity:

> ... that even professors of social administration are human, and do not like the suggestion that their services may not be called upon ... Such professors who live, not by taking action but by talking about others taking action, are unlikely to learn a great deal from what they do. Hence it is that the universities have become the marmoreal institutions of the age, their staffs are not menaced by reality, (1984: 13)

are (somewhat) typical of his way of launching counter-attacks.

Going back to the fundamental principles of action learning for the benefit of staying with this theme, action learning has now been recognised as the logical unity of four activities:

(1)	Hearing	encountering changes in the managers perceptions of his or her world;
(2)	Counselling	exchanging information, advice, criticisms and other forms of influence;
(3)	Managing	taking action upon the world in accordance with plans deliberately designed (or System Alpha);
(4)	Authentication	following the five stages of scientific method (System Beta).

Revans has argued that the first three stages are "inextricably mixed up in all action learning exercises" because they are expressed in the language or communication which takes place when managers try to deal with problems or exploit opportunities resulting in the managers own perceptual change as he or she tries to influence fellow set members, or as Revans says:

> One has to expose one's perceptions (values, knowledge) to the impartial and of merciless criticism of others out of which one may learn to shift that perception. One has to influence one's colleagues in the set, or be influenced by them – even to be involved both ways. (1984: 14)

During his ten years, from 1955 to 1965, spent at the University of Manchester, Revans produced a hundred or so papers which included expositions of his learning equation and managerial learning – later known as systems alpha, beta and gamma (1984: 18; 1959: 28 ff, "The Hospital as an Organism" proceedings of the September 1959 conference of The Institute of Management Sciences, Paris).

In 1965, Revans and action learning was "taken away from Manchester" and placed under the protection of the "Foundation Industry – University of Belgium."

This was a joint venture of Belgian businessmen and five major universities . Because both these joint partners realised their needs to raise management standards to the highest possible level, "action learning came into its own" (1984: 19). Not only was this confluence of action learning of great significance to Revans, but equally he recognised that the intellectual calibre of the participants themselves far excelled those he had worked with at the Coal Board and the Health Service.

In June 1967, at a conference in Barcelona to set up a doctoral programme Revans recorded the references made by Dr George F F Lombard, the Associate Dean of the Harvard Business School, to his earlier work with the Coal Board and the Health Service's HIC project and Lombard's enthusiasm for similar approaches to be encouraged at Harvard. But alas the response from this University was less than expected.

Nonetheless, Revans in his writings concentrated on statistical evidence drawn from the growth in the Belgian economy in order to support the Inter University Project.

It was during the Inter University Project that Revans developed his two-by-two model based on four possible variable combinations for both managers and their problems. More explicitly:
   (i) Familiar problem in familiar setting;
   (ii) familiar problem in unfamiliar setting;

(iii) unfamiliar problem in familiar setting; and
(iv) unfamiliar problem in unfamiliar setting.

As he put it in *The Sequence of Managerial Achievement* (1984: 36):

> To get real managers at work on unfamiliar problems in unfamiliar settings, such as the logistics analyst of an international company helping to clarify the long-term development of problems of an international bank, or the marketing director of a chain of department stores to standby the research and development troubles of a major steel concern, I was obliged to go to Belgium, where I had the unswerving support of Gaston Deurnick, Managing Director of the Foundation Industry – University … was the start of real action learning, and still remains, 15 years later, its most powerful application.

Perhaps one of the most important of Revans' programmes to be launched in Great Britain was the General Electric Company Programme (GEC) established in 1975. (1980: 61–68; 1982: 278).

Sir Arnold Weinstock, Managing Director of the General Electric Company of England, as he then was, having listened to Revans on BBC TV (late 1973), invited him to a meeting with a view to invite Revans to set up action learning throughout the entire company.

Initially, Weinstock invited Revans to work within GEC for ten years, but characteristically Revans refused.[3]

> … I asked that any agreement into which I entered with the company specifically stated that in no conditions would I be asked to run a second programme. … if my ideas upon how an organisation learns from the study of its own treatment of its own problems could not be grasped by the officers of the company within twelve months, I saw no virtue in staying with it. (1980: 62)

This typical, honest and somewhat paradoxical behaviour, where on the one hand, Revans had convincingly demonstrated his mastery and his unquestionable expertise, and on the other, refused to become type cast as an expert consultant with ten years of programmes, of one sort or another, in his brief-case, convinced Weinstock of Revans' honesty and genuineness. This resulted in a most remarkable and long lasting friendship, almost made instantly.

Revans agreed to implement one action learning programme based on the conviction that managers themselves must carry the concept forward. The GEC action learning programme, therefore, was developed from one national consortium consisting of twenty (20) of the GEC companies.

The design of this programme was such that it upheld a good deal of the work already well established beforehand in Belgium and offered exchanges both within and between each GEC enterprise and with other companies and public sector organisations like the Civil Service (1983: 58–59).

Rushton Gas Turbines of Lincoln, has been cited by Revans as an example of the effectiveness of the GEC action learning programme. After first taking part in the original consortium with Revans between 1975 and 1976 the managers continued to run their own internal programmes which incorporated other companies from the same area including the Local Education Authority and Constabulary. Revans reviews and evaluations of such programmes described in *Confirming Cases* published by Revans Action Learning International (1985: 15–16) have always been at pains to point to the statistical evidence gained as a direct result of using action learning against the background which had been disturbed by his sensitivity to the scathing attacks and harsh criticism of Klein and Jacques et al.

The beginning of this example demonstrates this:

> There may be those who see this campaign (referring here to the Rushton Programme), not as serious and dispassionate analysis of the total activity in which this high technological enterprise is engaged, but as an emotional crusade, fervently evangelical in character, with slogans and banners aloft on the flagpole ...

6. Analysis

David Sutton, in his chapter on "A Range of Application" in Action Learning in Practice (1983: 65–72), has placed Revans' GEC Programme in a context alongside others, and in so doing, has drawn out a number of useful points:

(1) Each action learning programme that has operated within the U.K. from 1973 onwards was progressively different from the original, that is, the GEC Programme.

(2) The very nature of action learning itself is iterative therefore it can not easily replicate itself on a continuous basis.

(3) Novelty and newness hold juxtaposition, within the areas allocated to action learning, as an acceptable feature and the required objectives which relate to organisational need as well as the development of the action learning process.

Sutton (1983: 69) has cited examples of the above in areas such as small organisations through to large nationalised organisational and public sector services to demonstrate both the range and flexibility of the approach.

A brief survey of these emergent pieces of action learning, adapted from Sutton's work includes:

GEC Action Learning Programme:

Objectives:	To develop Senior Managers (one level below Chief Executive) of member companies of GEC Ltd.
Structure:	Six months full-time secondment, including six weeks working as one group.
Number & Size of Sets:	Four sets each of five members.
Problem Type:	Unknown environment and job, individual project.

E W Andrew Ltd Action Learning Programme:

Objectives:	To build a team of Junior Production Managers; develop individuals; tackle small-scale problems in a field of activity.
Structure:	Ten day teaching programme over twenty weeks (half day per week) throughout a six month project period. Set meetings after the first six weeks.
Number & Size of Sets:	Two sets each of five members.
Problem Type:	Own environment, own job, individual projects.

Action Learning in Hospitals for the Mentally Handicapped:

Objectives:	To improve the service locally; provide information and ideas for general use; develop individuals at all staff levels.
Structure:	Twelve months part-time with monthly set meetings.
Number & Size of Sets:	Seven sets ranging in size from six to ten members.
Problem Type:	Own job and environment, group projects.

Sutton has listed and commented on three additional programmes in his chapter which looks at the range of applications for action learning and has concluded that the approach itself can lead to "mental re-organisation" and the re-examination of one's own experiences as one's most valuable learning asset. He goes on to suggest, however, that experience itself, rather than leading to new learning is in fact a major barrier and posits the idea that "new learning ventures take the form of attempts to escape from the constraints of old experiences." This is an interesting paradox and one which reminds us that we cannot rely on experience as the effective teacher and reinforces Revans' view that set members themselves should and do often act as tutors.

But it has to be noted that although variation and modification are the key outcomes of an action learning programme, in the sense that those which have followed on in the UK since the GEC Programme (1973) have been different both from the original and from each other, they have nonetheless, had three elemental characteristics which have distinguished them from other similar approaches to management development, such as, action centred learning, self-managed learning and action research/project groups. These elements have been:

(1) A real organisational problem as the basis of a personal project for one or more managers which has demanded deliberate action from managers and in some cases his or her colleagues.
(2) A personal learning experience which was describable to others.
(3) A set consisting of a small number of managers who met on a regular basis to help solve/tackle each others problems.

Before leaving this review which has in the main focused almost entirely on this pioneering work of Reg Revans, I will outline a small number of his projects which were implemented since the initiation of the Rushton Project (1976–1981). These have demonstrated without question the variable nature, variety of application and the multi-diversity of action learning, yet at the same time stand as attributes to the consistent claim that it is possible to get real organisational problems solved by using the internal expertise of existing managers and at the same time fully expect each manager to develop himself/herself as a direct consequence.

In 1978, Foster Wheeler Power Products (FWPP), a leading designer and manufacturer of large scale boilers and similar power plants were, according to Revans (1985: 4–5), "seeking an effective means of accelerated management development," and as such, were attracted to his concepts of action learning. FWPP, joined ALP International – a consortium of companies committed to action learning and a forum for exchanging managers between members of the consortium for six months with the intention of tackling and implementing solutions and pre-existing problems within a limited time-scale.

It is important to note that Revans used these elements of reality and stress to differentiate his concept of action learning from that of the case study approach to manager development and believed with uncompromising conviction that trying to change existing organisational approaches to problem solving by first convincing the "self" before trying to convince others was the key to learning and development both for the manager and for his/her own organisation.

From the ALP International Consortium, Tony Benning was sent from Foster Wheeler to tackle a project in Courage Breweries and Foster Wheeler received in turn Bruce Holding – a senior manager from Cable and Wireless.

The brief Holding was given was:

> ... to examine the potential market for automatic welding equipment originally developed by Foster Wheeler for this own specialist use. (1985: 4)

In his evaluation of this project, Revans confirms that:

(1) "Action learning can be particularly effective to problem solving because participants (managers) who come into another company to help solve its problems are not experts selling any preconceived solution."

Revans has always maintained that one's acknowledged ignorance is the friend of gaining new insight and learning, a lesson he learned from his experience of working with Rutherford in the 1920s in the Cavendish Laboratories coupled with his later expositions of Socratian paradoxes: (see *Early Socratic Dialogue* 1987: 145–151).

(2) An ignorance of knowing nothing about their host company and its problems forces the participant – manager into a questioning procedure, which in turn, becomes a learning experience for both the individual with the host company and the visiting manager.

(3) Because of the "unknown" working environment, the manager gains in both competence and confidence and hence human development.

Revans has supported the conclusions in the Foster Wheeler case, commenting on the fact that Holding, the visiting manager, "quickly discerned that the real problem was only minimally about welding, and was actually about markets, expertise and profit, managing to subject the real problem to the following simple question:

(a) What are we seeking to achieve?

(b) Is there a market for these goods and services?

(c) What resources would be required to enter that market more positively? and

(d) What is the competitive environment?"

Revans has claimed that the seeking of answers and facts to such questions helped Foster Wheeler to establish a new company: Foster Wheeler Automated Welding Limited, one year after the project was actually started, and offering a complete range of design and manufacturing services along with specialist consultancy advice for fully automated and programmable TIG welding systems.

Holding's own analysis of his experience concluded:

> I knew nothing about Foster Wheeler or their business, so, whatever I may have contributed, it certainly was not professional advice. However, ... the programme ... became a "live issue" (for the Foster Wheeler Board), ... a time-frame for consideration of the question ... and a feeling that if a decision was not reached ... then it was unlikely that the opportunity would never recur.

This organisational transformation from the old established Foster Wheeler to the new Foster Wheeler Automated Welding Ltd, supports the Revans notion that a questioning approach aimed at a set of "here-and-now" problems always has the potential to change the questioners themselves and their organisations.

Another example of an action learning programme which clearly belongs to Revans' post Rushton era, was one described by Dr Roy V Gilbert in Human Resource Management, Australia, 1978.

Revans called this: "Action Learning in Government, or Australia Shows How" and could at first sight read like a piece of deliberate propaganda designed to embarrass those who had chosen to ignore Revans' ideas. But on closer scrutiny, Gilbert's own paper addresses issues concerned with:

(1) differences and tensions between training and development;

(2) the need to identify management problems in large bureaucracies;

(3) performance improvements against staff appraisal; and

(4) action learning as a way of solving of management problems by "encouraging public servants and private sector managers to take part on an exchange programme."

The first action learning programme at top level in Australia was initiated by Gilbert and consisted of four senior officers. This "quartet," as Gilbert had called it, provided the forum for the officers to be involved in problems that were foreign to their previous training and experience.

A Meteorologist, for example, from the Commonwealth Department of Science worked in the Premier's Department of Victoria to improve co-operation within the State Co-ordination Council. Another, a Surveyor from the Commonwealth Department of National Resources, tried to reduce the delays in supplying furniture and equipment to client departments of the Victoria Public Works Department, and to complete the exchange between members of this quartet, a Civil Engineer from the Public Works Department attempted to improve the management in the weather forecasting and warning services in the Regional Forecasting Centres, and a Senior Research Officer of the Victoria Premier's Department investigated the selection policies for promotion and transfer in the Australian Public Service (1985: 20–7).

A further example was the action learning programme described by Revans (1985) in co-operation with William Precious, the former Managing Director of F Hills and Sons of Stockton-on-Tees, a Bowater company engaged in making doors and door sets, and described by Precious in Management Education and Development Vol. 13 Pt, 1983: 89–97.

The first action learning programme at Hills ran from January, 1980 and began by analysing and categorising existing problems for the company. The factory supervisors were invited to choose one of the problems to work on as a personal project. Middle managers were then asked to choose a set, and become the set adviser. Individual members of the senior management group took responsibility for the set specifically dealing with their functional area, committing themselves to accepting the recommendations made by set members or at least, to give sound reasons for not accepting such recommendations.

Features of the programme:
(1) Sets met regularly for three months in the supervisors' own time because they claimed this helped them speak more freely of criticisms.
(2) Real problems of the organisation were solved.
(3) They recognised that many of the problems reflected the organisation's position in relation to the changing environment.
(4) The multi disciplinary composition of sets improved the participants understanding of roles and relationships and as a consequence removed a number of interdepartmental barriers.
(5) Attitudinal problems improved in the sense that the managers gained a greater level of commitment to the organisation.
(6) The environment of the set allowed formal self-expression from which personal development flowed.

(7) Some middle managers acting as set advisers dropped out because they found the role too much.

(8) Some senior managers acting as clients were very open to criticism and disliked the experience.

From this initial programme review and evaluation of the Hills programme a second action learning programme was launched in September 1980.

This time, however, the six sets were:

    (i) composed of middle managers and supervisors, mainly self
    selected;

    (ii) advised by senior managers with each set choosing its own
    set adviser and his or her role within the set; one set chose to
    have no set adviser only a chairman co-ordinator for their
    different sub-tasks;

    (iii) allowed to form a number of sub-sets with the intention of
    working on specialised problems.

In addition to these modifications, the set advisers themselves formed
a set of their own.

Revans (1985: 37) claimed that both programmes were effective in
that they treated the company's problems, and at the same time, developed the staff involved, or as he put it: "Enterprise and individual grew
in step," and unlike the previous programme the middle managers acting as set advisers were treated as equals by the set membership. Revans
described this rather prophetically as: " … a good example of participation at work, and that action learning might well become an effective
form of industrial democracy." (1985: 37)

The fourth and final example of Revans' action learning projects in
this paper is the programme devised for a particular Division of Dunlop:
1981–82. Unlike the three former examples, this programme was designed to solve – partly or fully – problems associated with training;
namely, that techniques taught on management courses were not easily
applied when the manager returned to his/her job; that the manager's/
/participant's boss is often reluctant to become involved so that any new
development and/or learning was rarely implemented; that specific learning needs by managers/participants could not be met on standard courses;
that the costs of running external courses especially in residential set-
tings was ever increasing.

Revans' response to these problems were consistent with his former
arguments and reflect what I have remarked on elsewhere in this chapter.

The action learning approach to management development immediately gets to grip with some of these training problems. From the outset, the sponsoring manager is involved in the training process. He is asked to consider the strengths and weaknesses of his delegate manager, and, in conjunction with the Company Trainer, to establish learning aims. The next step is to select a project which will give scope for the achievement of these aims. This stage demands a lot of thought if it is to be successful"

From the delegate's viewpoint, the learning aims can be seen to be achievable and he responds favourably to his training. He enjoys this learning-by-doing approach and becomes open to listen to new ideas. He is also more amenable to taking risks, since mistakes (that open up real learning chances) can be made in the action learning set without loss of face. The learning is also spread over a relatively long period and the Company Trainer is able to ask questions about the delegate's progress without creating any formal de-briefing. The sponsoring manager also has the opportunity at the end of the training period to help the delegate with any real weaknesses that may have come to light, and this is easier to do in the training context than in any appraisal interview. (1984: 32–33)

As an aside this lucid summary given as a response to the training needs of Dunlop, part Rogerian in style and arguably far-reaching in approach, had close parallels with training problems within the NHS, although at the time Individual Performance Review for Health Service Managers had not been invented nor the three action learning programmes studied here in the main body of this paper. Also, the review of the Dunlop Programme had led to a clear understanding of the problematic nature of action learning and the need to establish firm criteria as a basis for running programmes based on this approach.

Revans summarised:

"We are now convinced that the concept is good, but have also learned that benefits can be partially, or even wholly, lost by lack of attention to any one (or even all) of three things; these are:

(1) The group mix; Revans had established that the delegates should be of similar status and experiences but from different organisations and disciplines. Also, each delegate should be able to demonstrate his/her commitment and his/her boss's commitment.

(2) The choice of project; he had established the need of a well-considered project based on a real problem which had already "been the subject of initial examinations." Equally, he had emphasised that the problem itself should be serious and worthy of the efforts of set members, yet at the same time, have a fair chance of a conclusion within a reasonable time-scale (he actually specified six months, page 34).

(3) The ability of the person chosen Revans' descriptions of this role give use as the group adviser; ful insight.

The group (set) adviser is a key figure in the learning process. He (she) should be more than an organiser or administrator, or even an "adviser." He (she) should be capable of turning the behaviour of individuals, and of the whole group, into a learning process

> If, for example, one member of the group (or set) is perceived, to contribute little, the adviser should ask the group why they are allowing this to happen.

7. The Alpha, Beta and Gamma Paradigm

It has been pointed out elsewhere in this paper that System Beta can be viewed as the five stages of scientific inquiry, as Lessem reviewed it. Nonetheless, my view is that Revans placed these five stages in a matrix between the "procedural" world of the scientific method and the "processual"[4] world of an individual manager's behavioural responses to both himself/herself and his/her fellow learners.

From this, he developed his relationship matrix incorporating important epistemological argument. For example, his Beta model can be viewed as an emergent system which dominates his entire work in a way which is totally unique to Revans himself, treating Systems Alpha and more so Gamma, with less significance.

System Beta attempts to separate out and solidify a complex within a scientific context for thinking (five stage), thus presenting every working manager with a (the) methodological framework for evaluating his/ /her actions and resultant learning. To my mind, this is a mechanistic way of providing a workable "do-it-yourself kit" which cuts out the professional consultant, academic or management tutor from interfering with a process known only to the principal actor/manager.

I would conclude from that Revans has been largely concerned with communicating System Beta throughout his long life. Always remaining loyal to his earlier scientific roots and viewing all behavioural change within a framework matrix built around

"Survey – Hypothesis – Experiment – Audit – Review." (See Figure 2.)

Indeed, in Origins and Growth of Action Learning, he excludes any notion of psychotherapy or reliance on practising therapists within his system – critically reviewing the work of Professor Carl Rogers

(1982: 635–637) and pointing to the questionable necessity of a therapists professional status within any close analytical relationship:

> Professor Rogers seems, however, to focus upon the sincerity in the therapist by first assuming that he is (and perhaps must necessarily be) a participant in the dialogue categorically different from his client. Although expected to be "warmly human and genuine" (by ensuring that "he must use the knowledge only to enrich and enlarge his subjective self, but a professional who earns a living in pursuit of these exalted aims.
>
> My thesis (Revans') is that, even though it has taken the laborious and insightful researches of Professor Rogers and his fellow professionals for us to know the dungeons of our secret selves – although St Luke, himself a physician, was making many of the same points two thousand years earlier – there remains much scope for ordinary persons to help each other.

I have used this rather long quotation to illustrate here that Revans has been consistent in his scepticism concerning professional helpers – even in the very broadest sense – because the "professional this or that" always seems to cut across learning operating in a System Beta Matrix.

> My experience (Revans') of action learning suggests that when four or five comrades in adversity are able to work closely together, not only upon each others' problems in the responsible Me Here   and Now, but also upon their own inner and personal hang-ups behind which those problems are obscured, they have less need of professional counselling than might be imagined. When there are neither Chiefs nor Indians, each may, in seeking to enrich and enlarge his own subjective self, reciprocally help to enrich and enlarge the subjective selves of his fellows ... I am totally opposed to any suggestion that the exploration of the subjective self, at least that of the ordinary line manager, should be through his one-to-one correspondence with some professional therapist, howsoever warmly human and genuine.

I do not believe it was by accident that Revans after mounting his objection to professional therapists and counsellors interfering with his ideas of action learning, counters and tempers the proposition within the next section dealing with a further development of System Beta (1982: 637). Revans, in my view, infuses his five stages of the scientific method with a behaviouralistic taxonomy which talks back to the manager as he//she works through each stage:

> (i) a stage of being aware, of survey, of observation, of data (including opinion) of collection, of recognition, input, search, fact finding, investigation and so forth: ...
>
> (ii) a stage of speculation, of insightful guesswork, of theorising of conjecture, of invention, of pattern formation, of provisional design, of hypothesis, trial decision and so forth: ...

    (iii) a stage of test, experiment, of trial in which the pattern, theory, hypothesis, supposed relationships or order is subjected to the independent or impartial test: ...

    (iv) a stage of audit, inspection, verification, scouting, cross questioning, inquiry and so forth: ...

    (v) ... a stage of control, assessment, review, conclusion, sentence, decree, adjudication and so forth: the subject having weighed the evidence at the audit stage between what was forecast by the supposed relationship or hypothesis (against that) which was achieved by the test or experiment, (may suggest that the hypothesis may well be worth further thought (along with) fresh data. But if they contrasts between, i.e. what was achieved and what was forecast were so small that the provisional hypothesis can be taken as not disproved, and can therefore be employed in further attempts to advance the particular activity of the subject: (additional) attempts may show that the hypothesis, while not disproved by the first experiment, is nonetheless incomplete and requires extension.

This way of seeing individuals working with problems, both organisationally and personally, is at the heart of System Beta and if accepted, is a way of holding the complexity of action learning together. In fact Revans looked upon System Beta as "The Paradigm of Wise Counsel" – a title used later (1982: 648), which like his other writings creates a high degree of distance between professional help and managers understanding their own problems and development as they follow Revans' Beta Matrix.

Revans advocates (1982: 96–7) that the scientific method which structures the manager's own behavioural responses can be simplified and used as a way of analysing action:

    (i) find out what needs to be done;

    (ii) decide what to do;

    (iii) do it in what seems to be the best way;

    (iv) test out how well it has been done; and

    (v) either review the original field or modify the decisions about what to do.

8. System Alpha

This opens up the appropriate fields of survey (Revans 1982: 342) and the discussion notes to check the appropriate validity.

Lessem (1985: 11) has argued that System Alpha is concerned with the managers' use of information in designing objectives or strategies, whereas Revans' examples of System Alpha Paradigm (See Figure 3) shows his design of a management decision or set of potential decisions as a strategy requiring (demanding) information about three critical elements:

(1) A value system of the manager (Revans' universality of System Alpha shows different values for different roles except for that of the manager).

(2) The external system that managers exploit.

(3) The internal system by which exploitation takes place, System Alpha is the structural interlay of these three elements.

FIGURE 2.
System Alpha

Design Element	Factory Worker	Factory Owner	Opera Singer	Board of Directors	Growing Nation	Research Laboratory
Values	Own earbubgs	Profits: Honours list	Fame	Dividens growth	Imperialist ambition	Scientific reputation
External system	Labour market	Customer needs: Political machine	Audience: Critics	Market	Weak neighbours	Unsolved problems
Internal system	Craft skills: Trade union	Men and machines:	Voice: Publicity	Assets: take-over	Superior armaments	Skills and apparatus

FIGURE 3.
System Beta

β_1 survey	β_2 decision	β_3 action	β_4 inspection	β_5 control
market lntelligence	manufacturing policy	optimal resource allocation	standard cost accounting	
sales demand	princing policy	specification	auditing	
feedback from former operation	distribution and service policy	process design and operation	quality control	confirmation amendment, or rejection
own research	design policy	method improvement	safety	of first decision in light of
information retrieval	investment and growth policy	purchasing and store keeping	field tests of performance	action experience
expert advice subjective judgement	staffing policy expenditure on research	staff sheduled replacement	stock recording variance analysis around budgets	

The activities listed in each of the first four columns are professional tasks strongly loaded with the factor mentioned at the head. Each task, in turn, must observe the cycle of System Beta; the auditor, for example, must begin with a survey of the facts; form a first hypothesis (that there are – or are not – discrepancies revealed by the survey); take trial action by following his suspicions elsewhere; assess carefully the results of this further search; and draw his final conclusions.

9. System Gamma

... we must ask how he interacts with the two systems and affects their joint output.

Revans has claimed (p. 345) that System Beta is the "logic of the scientific method and of the learning process." Thus the decision-taker, following the cycle of System Beta, is not only helping to change the actual state of affairs – he is continually checking his expectations of what will happen against what he observes to happen.

System Gamma, is therefore, a learning process based on the changes he or she experiences within himself/herself and observed and tested using System Beta.

Revans has asserted that the key element in this symbiosis (a dependence on the organic partnership with its other partners) is the ability of the manager to listen and then to change his or her behaviour as a result of what has been said.

Self-image and the preservation of such, according to Revans' theories, impede and inhibit this degree of insight.

> In the action learning programmes within which I have been concerned, alike in Europe and India, .. the managers (help) one another and recognise the knowledge each has stored in his consciousness.

> They learn, with and from each other as they work together upon their common problems, to reinterpret their remembered experience and, thereby, to recall and employ that which is most appropriate even if it has been forgotten. (1976a: 11)

In this statement, Revans has compared his analysis behind his own evaluative thinking with that of the Buddha 518 BC, and building on the premise that it was he who probably taught that salvation or at least the deliverance from adversity must be achieved by each individual by his own actions, brought his symbiotic Gamma Systematic thinking into play and concluded that learning which is manifested by and with observable changes in behaviour relics entirely on the effects it has on others.

A year later (1977) Revans concluded that his Inter-University Programme of 1968–69, generated three important ideas which must be incorporated in any action learning programme:

(1) True learning – in the sense of being accompanied by some observable change in activity or behaviour that could not have been achieved otherwise, demands that the subject sees the practical outcome of applying in the real world what he believes himself to have understood during the learning experience.

(2) Sufficient risk or failure or sufficient load of responsibility – to concentrate the attentions of the subject upon his own system be-

liefs and values; behavioural change is unlikely to occur in the absence of fresh self-recognition.

(3) Self-recognition – powerfully assisted by the continuous support and criticism of others who seek it for themselves. Managers, in other words, learn behavioural change calculated to improve them as managers and from each other during their simultaneous and continued efforts to improve themselves as managers; in practise this implies that they meet over substantial periods both to give and to accept support and criticism to and from each other.

In reviewing a limited selection of Revans' work, I have attempted to highlight some of the more significant points he has raised about his own work so that others might learn from them and develop similar processes for themselves.

There is little doubt amongst serious practitioners and scholars that Revans is a unique and vigilant researcher. His entire work upholds the conviction that action learning stands for distinguishable human and organisational change (see Disclosing Doubts: International Congress on Action Learning 1995). Which leads us to conclude that he is one of the greatest praxiologists of all time.

Notes

1. Ronnie Leesem has commented on Revans System Beta and its relationship to David Kolb's Learning Cycle, in *The Origins and Growth of Action Learning* (1982: 10–11).
2. Revans Chapter devoted to the study of patient cure and general morals of nursing and other hospital staff reveals an example of the scientific method he employed throughout his research. This can be found on pages 123 to 132 inclusively in *The Origins and Growth of Action Learning* (1982).
3. The main theme and wording of the above was taken from a personal conversation with Reg Revans 28/04/92.
4. The term processual means evolving in nature. Strauss and Corbin have argued in: "Basics of Qualitative Research" that processual notes can be studied in terms of sequences of movement of change over time. (P104)

References

Botham, D. (1985). "What is Action Learning & How Can We Implement it." A seminar paper (unpublished).

Chappell S. (1987). "A Reflective Document." Diploma dissertation (unpublished).

Cunningham I. (1986). "Developing Chief Executives: An Evaluation." Report Ashridge Management College.

Eraut M. (1985). "Knowledge Creation & Knowledge Use in Professional Contexts." *Studies in Higher* Education Vol. 10 No 2: 132–77.

Gill J. (1987). "Action Research & Action Learning in Management Development." A conference paper.

Harrison R. (1983). "Strategies for a New Age." *Human Resource Management* Vol. 22 No 3: 209–35.

Leesem R. (1985). "The New Paradigm: Work as a Means of Personal & Community Fulfilment." *Bacie Journal:* 7–10.

Logan A. & Stuart R. (1987). "Management Development & Action Learning: Current States & Future Possibilities." A conference paper.

Morgan G. & Ramirez R. (1984). "Action Learning: A Holographic Metaphor for Guiding Social Change." Paper delivered in Tavistock Institute of Human Relations.

Morris J. (1986). "The Learning Spiral." In *Handbook of Management Development*, edited by A. Mumford.

Mumford A. (1985). "A Review of Action Learning." *Management Bibliographies & Reviews* Vol. 11 No 2: MCB University Press.

Mumford A. (1989). "Management Development: Strategies for Action." In *Institute of Personal Management.*

Mumford A. (1991). "Learning Action." In *Personnel Management.*

Revans R. W. (1967). "Tomorrow or the Worst Efficiency of the Bad Manager." Unpublished paper.

Revans R. W. (1970). "Action Learning Itself as a Theme for Doctoral Dissertations." (Unpublished)

Revans R. W. (1972). "The Evaluation of the (Proposed) British Inter-University Programme." Unpublished.

Revans R. W. (1976). "Past, Present & Future: Evidence of Action Learning." Unpublished paper.

Revans R. W. (1976a). "The Immemorial Precursor: Action Learning, Past & Present." Unpublished.

Revans R. W. (1977). "On the Necessary Assumptions of Action Learning." Paper presented to the College Interuniversataire D'Etudes Doctrales Dans Les Sciences Du Management.

Revans R. W. (1980). *Action Learning: New Techniques for Management.* London: Blond & Briggs Ltd.

Revans R. W. (1982). *Origins and Growth of Action Learning.* Chartwell-Bratt Ltd.

Revans R. W. (1983). *ABC of Action Learning.* Chartwell-Bratt Ltd.

Revans R. W. (1983a). "'Ex Cathedra': The Validation of Action Learning Programmes." *Management Education & Development* Vol. 14: 208–11.

Revans R. W. (1984). *The Sequence of Managerial Achievement.* MCB University Press.

Revans R. W. (1985). *Confirming Cases.* Revans Action Learning International.

Revans R. W. (1988). *The Golden Jubilee of Action Learning.* Manchester: Malex.

Revans R. W. (1989). "Management, Talent & Society." Paper presented to Manchester Business School, 8 February 1989.

Revans R. W. (1990). "The Hospital as a Human System." *Behavioural Science* Vol. 35.

Rugina A. N. (1991). A Personal Letter Written to Professor Revans from the International Society for the Intercommunication of New Ideas Inc.

Sharman D. (1983). "Levels of Action Learning Philosophy." M. A. thesis, University of Bath.

Wallace M. (1990). "Can Action Learning Live Up to Its Reputation?" *Management Education and Development* Vol. 21: 89–103.

PART TWO

Human Action and Learning

Action and Learning

Timo Airaksinen
Department of Philosophy,
University of Helsinki,
Helsinki, Finland

1. The world can be divided, according to an Aristotelian philosophical dogma, into two realms, theoretical and practical. It is also tempting to say that both require their own, typical principles of learning. One learns *that* something is the case, a fact, which means that the learner is dealing with theoretical things. He learns that the Earth is larger than the Moon. He believes that all crows are black. But one may also know *how* to play football. One may also know how to cheat with taxes. This is a practical achievement (see Airaksinen, 1990: 35–46).

The distinction between "knowing how" and "knowing that" was made popular by Gilbert Ryle in his classic *The Concept of Mind* (1949, Ch. VI). After that, as it seems, this important distinction has not been as visible in philosophy as it should be. Therefore, Professor Revan's concept of action learning deserves our close attention, as simple as its main principles may seem. In this paper I try to analyze some of the philosophical implications of his ideas. I do not say anything about their practical applications to business and management. This is beyond the scope of philosophy.

2. First we notice that the epistemic context where we use "knowing that" is much richer than that of "knowing how." This is easy to verify:

(i) I know/believe/trust that she is faithful.

(ii) I know how to kill a cat painlessly.

One cannot say, for instance, "I believe how to kill a cat." One can say:

(iii) I know a method of killing a cat

but because one may not be capable of using the method, this is really a masked instance of "knowing that," namely,

(iv) I know that there is a method that can be used to kill a cat.

Therefore, "knowing how" seems to require that the agent is able to do something, but this ability is not specifiable. It remains as an umbrella under which a number of methods and other practical entities may find their home. In the case of "knowing that" we seem to be both willing and able to specify exactly what kind of "knowledge," or epistemic attitude we have towards the proposition that follows it. There are many epistemic and only one practical attitude. Intuitively, an action is just that, an action, and not another thing. One may wonder why this is the case. Of course one may say

(ii*) I possess a method of killing a cat painlessly.

But the respective meanings of (ii) and (ii*) are identical. Compare this to the case in which one believes, knows, or trusts something: the meanings are different.

There is, however, a feature of (ii) that captures one's attention, namely, the fact that the in (i) we find always the same thing after "know that," namely, a proposition, never anything else. But in the case of (ii), after "know" we can find a variety of things: a method, skill, act, project, language and so on:

(v) Richard knows how to tell a lie/kill/do research/sing/speak Finnish.

Of course one may suggest, simply, that "knowing how" is always associated with an act, just like "knowing that" requires a proposition. This may simplify the situation too much because in this case the word "action" is very general indeed, unlike the world "proposition" which is a technically specific problem. And this was exactly the interesting difference between (i) and (ii).

To make this more evident let as ask whether, in (v), killing and telling a lie are actions in the same sense. They are not because killing, unlike telling a lie, is achievement verb. To lie is just to do it but if you kill someone you must also succeed, and therefore the meaning of "kill" requires a reference to an act and its required results. Moreover, in (v), singing is not only an act but also a skill. To be able to sing is to have a talent, as shown by a paradox presented by Sartre: She is wonderful singer although she never sang. It is indeed possible to be a singer or a Finnish speaker who does not act by singing or speaking Finnish. The conclusion is that the practical side of human abilities and actions is much richer than their theoretical counterpart.

It follows also that the richness of "knowing how"-expressions does not depend on how one knows but what one knows, unlike in the case of "knowing that." In this way both these expressions are different which offers a reason to be skeptical about any thesis which treats them as somehow parallel cases. They are not because in (ii) the word "know" does not specify a linguistic or mental entity. On the contrary, it covers a wide variety of different practical meanings, and this fact can be used to explain why the right side of (ii) is so rich.

3. What has this semantic analysis to do with the problems of learning? First of all, it shows that within the realm of "knowing how" a wide variety of cases exist which we need to consider. But if we are interested in "knowing that" the method of learning is simple. Because this is a learning context, we are interested only in one special propositional attitude, knowing. This decision simplifies (i) to the extreme because the left side is now simple, and the right side has always been simple. The only thing which we need to do is to provide the fact which corresponds to the proposition in (i) to the learner. If we want S to know that this is a horse, we only need to show a horse to S so that he can learn it. Theoretical learning is so simple that it is no wonder that philosophers have paid not much attention to it.

However, some difficulties exist even here. Consider the following:
(vi) John doubts that his wife is faithful.

Here John may want to know about his wife's behavior but we want to teach John how to doubt. And as it is easy to see we cannot teach this by simply presenting sufficient evidence for his wife's affairs. This indicates that doubt is a practical skill which is different from "knowing that." Doubt is induced by denying knowledge, or by presenting conflicting evidence. And one learns how to doubt by confronting a series of cases in which he wants to know but has no sufficient evidence. Now John knows how to doubt.

Here we have a case in which theoretical learning may present difficulties because its complexity. Practice is needed and then the learning situations become difficult to organize and understand. This happens simply because doubt as an attitude does not focus on the actual world of facts but on various possible worlds. Doubting requires a skill by means of which such comparisons can be made. This shows that the practical and theoretical realms are not mutually fully independent. But most of all it shows that when the practical learning cases are introduced the situations become more complicated than what would otherwise be the case. Proposition (vi) also suggests that practical learning has priority over theoretical, epistemic attitudes. One needs practice in order to be able to know, believe or doubt.

It seems natural to suppose that when one learns practical things some theoretical knowledge is needed as well. But it is also possible to suggest that the theoretical part is a simple one, namely, the teacher simply provides the fact which induces knowledge. Any complications which arise in such cases are practical by nature; therefore, practical learning is what we are interested in.

4. When one learns practical things, or "knowing how," its various cases are complicated. Let us distinguish between learning an action, method, and skill or ability. We need to keep in mind the distinction between process and success verbs. Also we need to distinguish between the case in which someone knows how to act from those cases in which no one knows. For instance, no one knows how to achieve the perfect accuracy when shooting arrows, although it can be learned. But many people know how to build a boat. Notice that it does not follow that a success verb implies that one knows how to do it. I may have killed the cat although I have no idea how I did it. The fact is that the cat is dead – but that is all. I cannot explain the fact, nor can I repeat it. I may have scored a goal although it is true that I do not know how I did it.

What is the logic of learning practical things? We may narrow down the context so that there are only three elements: actions, methods, and skills. We may then follow Professor Revans's suggestion that we learn by action. This is action learning. But it also presupposes that we are already able to act, although this is not to say that we could not learn how to act by acting. By performing action A we learn action B. This idea is worth stating only because it is not the only possibility. We can learn how to act without acting. In other words we confront X and thereby learn action B, but X is not an action. Let us consider this possibility because it may help us understand the more restricted idea of action learning.

Suppose agent S walks on thin ice which covers a lake in wintertime in Finland. He stops in order to rest a little bit but this puts some extra pressure on the ice which breaks so that S falls through it. He fell because he stopped, or because he rested. He fell also because he was too heavy. Of course it is true that his stopping was a necessary condition of plunging into the water, but if he was so tired that he could not continue, his stopping was not an action; it was involuntary cessation of action.

In this way an event, falling, which is not an action, taught S a lesson, namely, do not stop when ice is too thin. We instantly notice another presupposition: cold swim is not something S is indifferent to, therefore he learns from his experience. A value component is needed if learning is going to take place. This is self-evident, however. We may suppose that S is able to learn from one-item induction, which is to say that we do not suppose that he either needs or wants to iterate his evidence. In most cases, of course, S would need a series of events which teach him a response to those events. All this seems clear.

Let us take seriously the restriction according to which we learn from action or by acting when the items to be learned are actions, skills or methods. We exclude the cases in which something merely happens to S. This same point can be expressed in terms of the so-called hermeneutical circle: an agent learns on the basis of what he already knows; the same idea was already expressed by Plato in his *Meno* where a young slave solves a geometrical problem independently of explicit teaching. Here we need to apply the same idea to practical learning: S's skill or method is always based on S's abilities, especially his previously mastered actions (cf. Hamlyn, 1978: 147).

Such an application of hermeneutics to the practical realm suggests the following idea, namely, the relations between actions and skills or methods is internal and not external. Somehow the actions entail the skills and methods in questions, which is impossible if actions are just external means of bringing about certain causal consequences. In other words, the action which S, as an action learner, uses has the power to induce learning. Such an idea requires elaboration.

5. Practical or action learning is always problem centered, unlike theoretical learning. But in order to have a problem, the agent must consider his values which he wants to protect or realize. In order to find a solution he may apply a method or possess a skill. These are two different things because a method is an intersubjective and skill a subjective thing. Many people can use the same method, unlike a skill. Method is a rule which leads an agent from its antecedent conditions, once they are realized, into a desired endstate. A skill requires an ability to produce the endstate which no one else can produce in the same way. A mathematician uses the method of arithmetic when he produces the result that 2+2 is 4. But an opera singer utilizes her skill in order to produce an interpretatioin of an aria that belongs to *Tosca*.

It is important to notice that the concepts of skill and method provide the link between acting, problem solving, and learning. To this we need to add the idea of the internal relation between action and learning and, finally, we need to introduce the idea of a feedback loop which is the prototype of practical experience.

Action, skill, method, problem, feedback, and experience are the key words by means of which we try to understand practical learning. To put it simply, agent S performs an action according to a method in order to solve a problem, which is a problem because of his values, and this provides him experience according to the feedback loop at his disposal. To create an efficient learning situation one needs to take care of the realization of all these various conditions. For instance, it may not be easy to construct a reliable feedback loop. After the action has been performed S may be in a position where he relies on other agents as informants. If their values are sufficiently different from S's values, they may not share with S the characterization of the problem, after which it is not to be expected that their feedback responses are reliable. This indicates why and in which sense the whole chain of conditions must be designed, constructed and maintained with care. Much can be said of such a procedure but, perhaps, not from the philosophical point of view.

The main philosophical problem is related to the practice-internal loop between action and learning. This allows us to say that S learns on the basis of what he is already able to accomplish, via actions. Let us call the following the law of action learning, when C refers to the chain of conditions mentioned above:

(L) If S acts under conditions C he learns from his own actions.

This law specifies in what sense actions and learning are internally related. Next it is important to specify the concept of learning in (L). Perhaps we should write this law as follows:

(L1) If S acts under conditions C he learns how to act from his own actions.

This is to say that the objects of learning are further actions, which is a natural point when we discuss action learning.

As an abbreviation of (L) we can say that acting is learning. Here we can use an analogy to theoretical learning, or to "learning that." In that context it has been suggested that perception is at the same time a judgement. When S perceives a horse he acquires the corresponding belief that there is a horse, and the belief logically entails the judgement. We can say that S has acquired (theoretical) knowledge. In the same way, when S acts he learns: if action and perception are the starting points, the results are action and judgement. As we can see, the analogy is not too informative, simply because in action learning one action leads to another action, unlike in theoretical learning where perception leads to judgment. The latter case is informative, unlike the former one

Let us try again. An action is, by definition, free, intentional, and based on knowledge. S can do what he wants and he knows what he is going to do and where he is. Suppose further that S has no source of knowledge available to him such that he could base his learning on this knowledge. He must rely on his action. This is the same as saying that no propositional knowledge may help him when he tries to learn, not even those propositions which can be derived from his own actions and his experience of them. Therefore he can rely only on his actions to teach him about some further actions, skills, and methods.

For example, suppose S wants (or intends) to organize a philosophy conference. This is an intention to act so that the successful endstate is a temporary social organization, a conference. But S has no direct intention to learn how to organize conferences (a method) or how to make a conference successful (a skill). After he has organized the conference we can say that he knows how to organize a conference. This simple example shows once again in what sense learning is internal to action. Action is learning, just like perception is learning but the case of action is more difficult to comprehend because of its simplicity which sounds like a tautology: an action is learning by acting.

The main point here is that it is not easy to act. But once one acts one learns how to act. An action just makes this learning explicit and, when it is iterated, reinforces learning. As such the idea of action learning may look tautologous, circular, and ad hoc. It seems to skip the question because once S acts he knows already how to act, and then learning was never a problem.

6. This criticism can be shown to be misleading once we turn to the learning of skills and methods. Let us take the case of skills first.

As we said above, a skill is a personal ability to achieve a goal which is variably instantiated, often in difficult or non-standard conditions. Here we are interested in goals which are open problems, in the sense that their solution is not knowable in advance. This last condition is important because then we can say that a skill-based solution is creative. The solution which was not available earlier becomes now available because of the actions based on the agent's skill.

Let us suppose that S wants to learn the skill of organizing all kinds of conferences in different social-historical situations. First he must be able to act, or in other words, he needs a pre-acquired list of actions. In this case it is not enough to pick one item from this list, like in the simple case of learning how to act. In the present case there is no action like "organizing a conference." Instead S's list of all available actions must be activated under the intention "organizing a conference." After this happens there are two possibilities: S may simulate the organizing activity or he may actually try to organize an event. In many cases the latter alternative is too costly, unethical or otherwise impermissible. Social experiments may require changes in the lives of people which they may be unwilling to accept. Alternatively, an unsuccessful attempt will bring about incorrigible harm. It is indeed the case that social experiments are seldom acceptable. This is one reason why S may hope to have a resort to the theoretical mode of planning his actions and learning. But it is also known that such theoretical knowledge is seldom available, simply because social experimentation has not been possible. Typically we have theoretical knowledge after we have mastered the skill, not before. The skill and its learning are not based on theoretical knowledge.

It seems, on the basis of the argument above, that in order to learn a skill S should use practical simulations of actions. He can neither act nor utilize theoretical knowledge. He acts as if he were organizing a conference. However, it is important that he acts as much as possible, and not only thinks of the action. The only part which is missing from this program is that which is directly related to the welfare of other people. When S's skills develop he may get closer, so to speak, to other people's interests and life. At the last stage S must take the risk and apply his skill to other people, but then he must be reasonably confident that no harm will ensue. This is the ethical aspect of learning.

Let us now return to the technical side of S's learning task. We already said that S must activate the relevant actions from his list of available actions. These actions serve his intention to solve his problem, that is, how develop a skill of organizing conferences. Now this is a simulated situation which means that S mobilizes only a fragment of the full list, namely those actions which may not bring about unreasonable harm, if they happen to be mistakes. S will make mistakes and he must learn how to cope with them. Once he masters these cases, that is, he learns about risks and their compensation, he proceeds towards more complicated situations by mobilizing more actions from his list. We can say that the degree of simulation diminishes. In this way, S mobilizes a larger segment of his list of action and by so doing he diminishes the degree of simulation, until he is ready actually to organize a conference.

This is not to say that now he masters the skill of organizing conferences. He simply knows how to organize a conference, when "organizing a conference" is understood as a single but very complicated action. But because this action is now an item in his list of available actions, he has made progress towards the corresponding skill.

S has made an effort to develop an skill exactly because his simulations involved a step by step structure in which the key aspect is the gradual mobilization of his action list. Therefore he has been able to learn at every stage about the various consequences which his decisions and actions have. He has also been able to minimize the necessarily ensuing harm. It cannot be avoided because S's practical knowledge is incomplete. If the harm is not first anticipated and later compensated, it will cut the learning process short, especially if the harm is of moral nature.

After S has accomplished his first task he is able to repeat the required sequence of action more effortlessly and he is also able to cope with more complicated situations and unexpected circumstances. He has developed a personal skill.

Skills are useful but also problematic. They are personal abilities and as such difficult to communicate to others. There may be group skills but then the group must be very tight. Of course other members of, say, a team will learn to trust S, because of his established skill, but at the same time they may find it difficult to understand what S does and why he is so successful. They will find co-operation with S difficult, especially if they do not consider him as an authority (see Sennett, 1980: Ch. 5). If they do so the team will develop a hierarchical structure where S is the leader who is trusted by others. This may or may not be desirable. For instance, it may happen that the tasks are so demanding that S, however skillful he is, will be overtaxed. Also if something happens to S, the rest of the team will be in trouble. From the point of view of action learning, it is better to learn a skill than an action; but skills are not enough.

7. Any team needs to learn actions, skills, and methods. To learn a method is different from learning a skill and its consequences are also

dissimilar. A method is an objective and interpersonal rule and therefore by means of it the team can reach the goal independently of any single individual's contribution. Any individual becomes dispensable. At the same time the structure of the team becomes democratic and anti-authoritarian, which seems to be an extra bonus. Of course the required method may be unavailable, but in those cases in which it is available, it should be designed, learned, and used.

We acquire a skill but design a method. We use a method but apply a skill. Such grammatical features reflect the nature of a method as something different from a skill, as something objective, an artifact.

In fact a method is a shortcut between action and its success because it bypasses a skill. This happens as follows. S has acquired the relevant skill but the team needs a method because they cannot share S's skill. By working together with S, for instance by following his example, they become able to act in the way which leads them to a solution and success. However, S cannot offer them theoretical knowledge about the method, or the rules which he follows. According to the axioms of action learning such a knowledge is not available. Instead they are trained to follow a set of rules at the practical level. A method is what allows them to do things together, whether we can express the rules as propositions or not.

It must be kept in mind that not all practical tasks can be handled by means of a method. Those that can are called technical problems, those that require a skill are creative tasks. For instance, one may learn to play piano by using a prescribed method, but such a technical playing cannot compete with musical skill and creativity. But one can learn to solve simple mathematical problems by means of a technical method. One may or may not understand why one is taking a given set of steps, but that does not matter very much. It is exactly this fact, the lack of theoretical knowledge, which makes methods so useful for teams. The theoretical component means an extra risk of confusion and error.

When action learning forces one to accept a method, this may mean the highest achievement or a mere technical capability, depending on the nature of the individual case. If a skill is desirable, for instance because of its creativity, method is a secondary way of achieving the goal. However, in many cases a skill represents just a preliminary stage which must be further developed into something which the whole team, and also future teams, can use in a reliable manner. A method has exactly this advantage, namely, it is an intersubjective and reliable tool whose applicability can be verified and results checked. Along these lines we can also develop a criterion of success which is difficult in the case of a skill. For a team method is more useful than a skill; in the case of individuals we may find the opposite to be true.

A final technical detail must be clarified. This is related to proposition (iii) above. There it was said that "I know a method of killing a cat" can be translated into a theoretical proposition, namely "I know that..." To avoid a contradiction we must say that the practical proposition is something like the following:

(vii) I know how to use the method of killing a cat painlessly.

The same idea can be applied to skills:

(viii) I have a skill which allows me to win.

In these cases any theoretical/practical confusion is avoided. When one compares propositions (iii) and (viii) one can also see a reminder of the fact that just to know a method is useless, compared to knowing how to use it. Sometimes one may know its use but not the method itself.

It may also happen that a skill resurrects after the goal is achieved by means of a method. This happens when one learns how to speak Finnish. One can fine tune one's skill after, but not before, one's competence is sufficiently strong. The same point can be applied to the members of a team.

I hope that I have shown how the logic of action learning functions. It is indeed interesting to study such cases of learning in which we cannot use theoretical premises. We are supposed to work at the level of actions, but as we have seen, much can be achieved nevertheless. To suppose that theoretical premises are permanently unavailable is a realistic presupposition in many cases, especially when we try to solve managerial or, perhaps, military problems.

References

Airaksinen, T. "The Nature and Methods of Practical Philosophy." *Praxiology Yearbook* 4–5 (1990): 35–46.

Hamlyn, D.W. (1978). *Experience and the Growth of Understanding*. London: Routledge and Kegan Paul.

Ryle, G. (1949). *The Concept of Mind*. Harmondsworth: Penguin.

Sennett, R. (1980). *Authority* London: Secker and Warburg.

It's Not Obvious:
How Rational Agents Use Salience

William Kline
Invisible College,
Budapest, Hungary

Instrumental rationality is not enough. A broad range of situations exist where, even though rational, agents will not know how to act. Specifically, rationality does not dictate a clear plan of action in those cases where there are two or more equilibria between which the players are indifferent. This has ramifications both for an account of choice in one-shot games and those accounts of choice in iterated games, especially those attempting to provide an adequate account of convention. In an attempt to solve this problem, a single notion of salience has been advocated that supposedly gives agents a reason to choose a given strategy in both one-shot and iterated games. This conflation can be accounted for most plausibly by an implicit assumption that it is the one-shot game which must be solved first in order to shed light on choice in the iterated game. This procedure, though, is dubious at best since the standard account of salience is wrong on two counts. First, there is not one kind of salience, there are at least two: private and public. Second, these types do not function equally as well in both circumstances. That is, private salience is ill-suited to anonymous iterated games and is hence incapable of supporting an account of convention. Only public salience is capable of providing an acceptable account of convention. Rationality is not enough, and neither is the traditional formulation of salience.

To see why rationality is not always enough let us take an example from Lewis (1969: 5). You and I are talking on the telephone. After a few minutes our call is disconnected. We both wish to continue our conversation. We cannot expect to continue if neither of us calls back. However, if we both attempt to call back the lines will be occupied and our attempt to reconnect unsuccessful. The "trick" to solving this dilemma is for one of us to call back and for one of us to wait. If there are no payoff differences between calling and waiting the dilemma we face can be modelled as the following coordination game.

FIGURE 1.

	You:	
Me:	Call Back	Wait
Call Back	0,0	1,1
Wait	1,1	0,0

Our task is to solve this game. Unfortunately, our task is not that easy,

At the heart of coordination games is the use of conditional strategies and expectations. In a coordination game, I will do my part in a proper coordination equilibrium if I expect you to do your part. The only reason I will expect you to choose a certain strategy is if it will pay you to do so. The only way it can pay you to do so, is if I choose to do my part in that equilibrium. However, you will only expect me to choose a certain strategy if it pays me to play that strategy. The only way it pays me to choose that strategy is if you will do your part in that equilibrium. We come to realize that a choice is rational for a player if and only if she has reason to believe that her opponent will choose the corresponding strategy. Neither player has such a reason, the circle closes, and we are no closer to coordination than when we started.[1]

At this point it is common to invoke notions of salience in order to provide for a solution. The appeal to salience is an attempt to break the deadlock of circular expectations. The lingering question, though, is how salience performs its allotted function. How do rational, albeit imaginative, agents use salience to coordinate? This is the central problem of explaining coordination, and in general choice, based on salience.

What, though, is salience?

Consider the game in Figure 1. Mathematically we should expect agents to coordinate their actions around half of the time. However, a series of informal experiments conducted by Schelling suggested that in many games agents could coordinate significantly better than what the mathematics of the game suggests.[2] According to Schelling (1980), what allows players to perform better in these games is that they are able to read a common message, beyond the mathematical structure of the game, that allows them to coordinate their expectations on a specific course of action (p. 54). A focal point is that which conveys this message. Focal points are usually prominent (p. 57) and unique (p. 58). These characteristics are understandable because both agents must have access to the message and too many messages makes for considerable ambiguity. The focal point itself, though, is not a matter of rationality. Discovering an appropriate focal point

> may depend on imagination more than on logic; it may depend on analogy, precedent, accidental arrangement, symmetry, aesthetic or geometric configuration, casuistic reasoning, and who the parties are and what they know about each other (p. 57).

Lewis (1969) basically follows this lead. Lewis defines the salient as something "... that stands out from the rest by its uniqueness in some conspicuous respect" (p. 35). However, Lewis concentrates his attention on one type of salience: precedent.

"Precedent is merely the source of one important kind of salience: conspicuous uniqueness of an equilibrium because we reached it last time" (p. 36). For Lewis, it does not matter why agents found themselves coordinating (p. 39). The mere fact that they did is a precedent and can be used to facilitate coordination in future cases. In the case of the telephone call, for whatever reason, it may happen that the original caller calls back. This becomes a salient precedent and agents choose accordingly (p. 43).

Interestingly, Lewis makes three slightly different claims concerning how precedence facilitates coordination. First, he claims that regardless of why agents coordinated they *could* still follow the precedent set (p. 39). Later he claims that

> we are entitled to expect that when agents acquainted with the past regularity are confronted by an analogous new coordination problem, they will succeed in achieving coordination by following precedent and continuing to conform to the same regularity" (p. 41).

Finally, Lewis claims that "our experience of general conformity in the past leads us, by force of precedent, to expect a like conformity in the future" (p. 41). Since our concern is on how agents learn to coordinate, we shall focus on the first and third claims. In doing this we are not alone, since it is with these two claims that Margaret Gilbert (1989) takes issue.

Gilbert argues two related points: that rational agents cannot recognize salience and, even if they could, it would not give them a reason to act (p. 332). First, a previous coordination is not necessarily salient for rational agents. By requiring that a coordination problem contain two or more proper equilibria, Lewis specifically builds ambiguity into coordination problems. While Lewis thinks that precedent removes this ambiguity, Gilbert argues that, for rational agents, precedent simply creates a further ambiguity. Whereas Lewis seems to automatically connect precedent with salience, Gilbert does not. In the example of the telephone call, calling back because that is what we did last time is just as unique as not calling back because that is not what we did (Gilbert 1989: 332). Since both are equally unique, something must make the one more conspicuous than the other. Conspicuousness, though, is not a matter of rationality. The differentiation of one equilibrium from another is a matter of an agent's psychology. "Only a specific psychology could make one combination salient in this situation" (p. 332). Gilbert concludes

> that in general it is not the case that salience of a precedented combination of actions is generated by common knowledge of successful precedent, given common knowledge (p. 333).

Rationality alone is not enough to generate salience and the importance of an agent's specific psychology renders game theory useless.

Gilbert, though, fails to note that Lewis and Schelling have already conceded much of her argument. Lewis admits that

> If different coordination equilibria are unique in different conspicuous ways, the subjects will need to be alike in the relative importance they attach to different respects of comparison (Lewis 1969: 35). This comes as no surprise since Schelling clearly states that in the final analysis we are dealing with imagination as much as with logic; and the logic itself is of a fairly casuistic kind (Schelling 1980: 57).

Gilbert, then, misses the point. Schelling, Lewis, and others are not trying to give a strictly game-theoretic account of choice. Instead, they are giving an account that uses game theory among other resources.

Gilbert's second criticism, though, is far more serious: even if rational agents could identify salience they would still be unable to use it to coordinate. Past actions in the context of coordination games, do not give rational agents any reason for choosing a certain strategy in the future.[3]

> Common knowledge of precedent as such will not by itself automatically generate expectations of conformity on the part of rational agents (p. 330). And later, the fact that two agents have in the past done their parts in an equilibrium in itself says nothing about what either one will do in the future (p. 332).

Her point can be stated in more general terms: to say that an option is uniquely obvious does not say anything about what either agent will do in the future. Perhaps she believes the burden of proof rests with those who claim that salience affects rational choice but, surprisingly, Gilbert gives no real argument as to why salience does not perform its reputed task. This is not to say that there is no such argument. In fact, there is. Noticing that an outcome is uniquely obvious does not change the payoffs associated with that outcome (Gauthier 1990: 288). Since it does not change the payoffs, it does not give rational actors any motivating reason to choose the appropriate strategy. In the absence of this motivating reason, agents have no justification for changing the probabilities they attach to their opponent's choices. Salience changes neither payoffs nor expectations and hence does not give rational agents a reason to choose the salient.

Anachronistically it could be said that Lewis recognizes this problem. In an attempt to break the circle of expectations Lewis maintains two similar, though importantly different, propositions concerning choice based on salience (pp. 35–37).

Proposition 1: In those cases where an agent is indifferent between options, an agent arationally chooses the salient option as a tie breaker.

Proposition 2: Agents may or may not have a tendency to arationally choose the salient option when they are indifferent between the relevant options. However, agents believe that people do have such an arational tendency.

The two propositions lead to slightly different accounts of coordination. A proper critique of these accounts, though, requires that we distinguish between two types of salience.

Generalizing from the literature, it is possible to construct a continuum of salience. The continuum is anchored at both ends by a different type of salience. At one end is the realm of private salience. It consists of those things that an individual finds obvious in situations where she is not trying to match her choices with the choices of others. The responses to Mehta et al.'s first ten questions are excellent examples of private salience (1994: 663). Subjects were not asked to match their choices to an opponent and they seemingly answered with whatever came to mind.[4] Close to this point are games played by agents who know each other so well that they are able to use personal idiosyncracies, or little known facts about the other, to facilitate coordination. At the other end consists those aspects of the world that are publicly salient. Here agents are constrained not only with the knowledge that they are trying to match their choices with an opponent, but that they are trying to match their choices with the broadest range of opponents as possible. Perhaps the best example of public salience is the predominant response given to the game "name any number, if you and your opponent name the same number you both win a prize." Since this game is anonymous, the relevant population is all those who know arabic numerals and have some knowledge of mathematics. This is a rather large population, in which a significant portion of students judged that the number "one" was salient (Mehta et al. 1994: 667).

The spectrum depends on two aspects. First it depends on the number of agents one is trying to coordinate with. Second, it depends on how localized the knowledge is that is required to make a certain option salient. The functioning of private salience requires relatively small groups with a rather specific psychology. At this end of the spectrum, Gilbert is correct. At the other end of the spectrum, though, Gilbert's point loses its urgency if still retaining some truth. For example, while it is true that in the number game participants must know arabic numerals, and possibly some mathematics, agents no longer need a "specific psychology" to coordinate. That is, "specific psychology" could mean that all, or most, of an agent's psychological makeup must be stipulated/discovered before we can predict whether she will find a given option salient. On the other hand, it could mean that agents must merely have some, or a few, elements of their makeup in common before they can determine whether they find the same option salient. If agents must possess the first type of specific psychology, then the role of salience in rational deliberation is seriously restricted. The question, though, remains: How does public salience give rational actors a reason to choose the salient?

The major obstacle for such an account is that it seems to require that salience either a) affect the expectations of at least some of the players, or b) change the payoffs in the game. Salience does not change the payoffs, so this leaves the typical account explaining how salience affects expectations. The major objection to the standard account is that the only way for expectations to be affected is if salience gave a reason for anyone to choose the salient. Unfortunately, uniqueness and obviousness, even when combined, do not give rational actors a reason for choosing. Thus, salience does not change expectations. The most promising option fails and with it the possibility of accounting for salience's effectiveness in terms of rationality, that is unless salience functions in a different manner.

According to David Gauthier (1990), it does.

For Gauthier, salience allows players to reconceive of their situation, and in essence change the game being played. Gauthier uses the following example: I live in London and you wish to visit me from Leicester. The time and date of the visit is agreed upon, but on the day of your arrival both of us realize that there are two trains from Leicester, C1 and C2, arriving at the same time, but at different stations, R1 and R2 respectively. If you travel by C1, I should go to station R1. Alternatively, if you travel by C2 then I should go to station R2. (p.274) We face a coordination problem that is formally equivalent to Figure 1.[5]

Gauthier provides three examples as to how one of these outcomes could be salient. First, it could be common knowledge that we both slightly prefer to be at R2 in case we do not meet. This changes the payoff structure of the original game into the following.

FIGURE 2.

	C1	C2
R1	5,5	0,1
R2	1,0	5,5

This would make (R2, C2) the salient outcome (p. 286). Gauthier also notes that if we consult our train schedules more carefully we would notice that C2 trains arrive more frequently. From this information we could conclude that more people travel by C2. This would also make going to station R2 salient for both of us (p. 286). Finally, Gauthier claims that expressly telling someone where to meet them can make a given outcome salient (p. 286). Yet, Gauthier is clear, salience "... does not in itself give either of us a reason for selecting one course of action rather than another" (p. 287). What, then, does the perception of salience give us?

Recall, the hallmark of a coordination problem is that there are at least two proper coordination equilibrium. The typical solution proffered is that agents choose the salient proper coordination equilibrium. However, this solution leaves in tact the other proper coordination equilibria. The presence of another proper coordination equilibrium robs an agent of his reason for choosing one over another, since by definition, she and her opponents are indifferent between these equilibriums. For Gauthier, the solution is for agents to be able to reformulate the game so that there is only one best equilibrium (p. 289). Salience provides the means for agents to make the appropriate reformulation. What agents must notice is that, in the presence of salience, they are actually playing a new game:

FIGURE 3.

	You seek	You ignore
I seek salience	5,5	$(2^1/_2, 2^1/_2)$
I ignore salience	$(2^1/_2, 2^1/_2)$	$(2^1/_2, 2^1/_2)$

In the reformulated game, the salient outcome becomes the best equilibrium. This reformulation simultaneously removes the ambiguity and the indifference. Agents, though, *still* do not have a reason to choose the salient.

The final piece of the argument is provided by Gauthier's contention that it is rational to choose the best equilibrium in those cases where there is only one such best equilibrium (1990: 279). In those cases where the salient outcome is the best equilibrium choosing the salient is a matter of rationality. This is how salience works. At least this is what Gauthier wants to prove. His argument, though, falls short of its goal.

The primary reason Gauthier's argument does not work is contained in his argument of how agents reconceive of the coordination problem in light of salience. Once salience is perceived, Gauthier argues that the agents' actions are restricted to either seeking the salient, or ignoring the salient. Ignoring the salient, though, does not involve simply doing the non-salient. This would return us to square one. Instead, ignoring the salient involves equally randomizing between all possible actions. Unfortunately, this solution is rather *ad hoc*. Why is it that the only two possible strategies are seeking the salient and ignoring the salient? Is there not a third possible strategy, seek the nonsalient? There is, and it makes for the existence of at least two proper coordination equilibrium, restoring the original ambiguity, and once again robbing agents of a reason for action.

Gauthier's original intuition is right. Salience does allow players to reconceive of their situation. Salience does change the nature of a game, but it does so by allowing players to form probability judgements that were, prior to its introduction, not possible. Sugden (1986) provides the best account of how this is accomplished.

Sugden uses two seemingly different concepts to explain coordination: salience and asymmetry. With regards to the definition of salience Sugden conforms to the definition of unique obviousness. On the other hand, an asymmetry is simply a difference either in the payoff structure or in the labelling of the players. For example, in Lewis's game of the interrupted telephone conversation, "original caller" is a labelling asymmetry. The label applies to one player, not the other, and allows players to distinguish between themselves. An asymmetry may be either salient or not. To see the importance of asymmetries, consider a game where there are no asymmetries (p. 35):

FIGURE 4.

Player's strategy	Opponents strategy	
	Slow down	Maintain speed
Slow down	0	2
Maintain speed	3	-10

In the symmetrical crossroads game (figure 4) there is only one equilibrium.

If p is the probability that a randomly selected player in a randomly selected game plays "slow down," equilibrium occurs where p=0.8 (p. 36).

Sugden uses phase diagrams to make his point,[6] but use of these diagrams tends to obscure what is interesting about this analysis. In the symmetrical game I form probability judgements by remembering the percentage with which I encountered certain strategies. The game is anonymous so I can not remember who I played. Furthermore, that the game is symmetrical also means that I must treat agents as if they were homogeneous. All I know is that there is a population of "my opponents." I have no way to distinguish one opponent from another. Since I can make no such distinctions, I must roughly match my strategy to what I have encountered in the past in regards to the population as a whole. Now consider the game where there is a labelling asymmetry (p. 36).

FIGURE 5.

	B's strategy	
A's strategy	Slow down	Maintain speed
Slow down	0,0	2,3
Maintain speed	3,2	-10,-10

The label asymmetric crossroads game simply allows players to distinguish between A and B roles. With a labelling asymmetry I am no longer constrained into treating the population as an homogeneous mass, with a single probability judgement concerning every individual. For example, one of the asymmetries Sugden considers in the crossroads game is whether the driver is on a major or minor road. Once this asymmetry is noticed players can then judge how often major road drivers slowdown as opposed to how often minor road drivers slowdown. There is still a mixed equilibrium point where there is a 0.8 probability of any random individual slowing down. More importantly, there are also two new equilibria points: one where major road drivers always slow down and another where minor road drivers always slow down. In addition to the new pure strategy equilibria, there is no longer any tendency to return to mixed the strategy equilibrium. In fact, there is every tendency to move away from it.

To see this, let us assume that the mixed strategy equilibrium is the current equilibrium. If drivers on the minor roads discover that major road drivers tend to slow down less than 0.8 of the time then it pays those on the minor roads to slow down more than 0.8 of the time. If drivers on the major roads discover that minor road drivers slow down more than 0.8 then it pays the major road drivers to maintain speed more often. The process is self enforcing with each shift in one probability causing a shift in the other. The process continues until almost all major road drivers maintain speed and almost all minor road drivers slow down at the crossroads. The same would happen if the initial shift from the mixed strategy equilibrium would have been minor road drivers slowing down less than 80% of the time.

Sugden (1986) claims that rational players will notice salient asymmetries and tend to coordinate around them. Interestingly, this must be contrasted with a later work which experimentally confirms that agents do use salience (1994), and another which despairs of a satisfactory account of rational choice based on salience (1993). Sugden believes that salience works, but in later years he seems to have backed away from the idea that choosing the salient is a rational strategy. I believe the reason for this later despair is a failure to appreciate the groundwork for a more robust conception of salience that his earlier work provides.

The salient is normally defined as that which is unique and obvious. Privately, anything could be uniquely obvious to me. In order for my opponent to use this type of salience she must know a great deal about me. Furthermore, even if she did know my relevant psychological makeup it is not clear that, from the knowledge that I find something uniquely obvious, she is justified in expecting me to choose the salient. However, in anonymous populations we are not referring to this type of salience. What, then, could make an option salient?

The answer is: how people act. That is, what makes something salient is not simply that I, or even many, find it uniquely obvious. Instead, what makes something salient is that it allows me to refine my probability judgements in such a way as to increase the expected utility of my choices in future interactions. This means that frequency has an extremely important, if often overlooked, role to play in determining both what is salient and why it is rational to choose the salient. Public salience is the result of, first, asymmetries in the environment that allow agents to form probability judgements about subgroups within the relevant population. An asymmetry becomes full fledged salience when the probability judgements it yields allows agents to form strategies that increase their expected utility. That is, an asymmetry becomes salient due to frequency. This simultaneously accounts for how something becomes publicly salient and how rational agents have a reason to choose the publicly salient.

Furthermore, it is not the case that the use of asymmetries relies on a *specific* psychology. Instead, noticing asymmetries relies on the general ability of agents to either find, or impose, order on the world. Finding regularities, though, is not a mere act of fancy. Agents have good reason to attempt to find those asymmetries which best account for the regularity they perceive. The reason is that the process is not merely a passive one. Players are ultimately attempting to bring their behavior into compliance with the regularity they perceive. This process is at the heart of rational-actor accounts of convention. The distinction between private and public salience allows us to note that different types of salience facilitate a different process of coordination in different types of games. In small group interactions, where the parties are not anonymous, private salience combined with a possible tendency to choose the salient facilitates coordination. Solving these types of games depends heavily on me coming to know my partner. It is analogous to how people become good bridge or pinochle partners. In larger groups where the content of private salience may vary widely between agents, or in anonymous games where agents do not have knowledge of what their opponent finds privately salient, public salience serves to give rational agents a reason to act. Here agents focus on those aspects of a population that are widely shared and are known to be e.g. a general knowledge of arabic numerals and simple mathematics. It is in this manner that public salience can account for widespread, anonymous, rational coordination. Rationality is not enough, but rationality combined with public salience is.

Notes

1. Sugden (1993) runs the same argument against both Schelling and Gauthier. See also, Schelling (1980: 70).
2. For a formal examination of Schelling's experiments see Mehta, Starmer, and Sugden (1994). Mehta et al. help confirm Schelling's informal study.
3. Gilbert's main argument is certainly reminiscent of Kripke's arguments about the "rules" of mathematics.
4. For instance, in response to "Name a Day" students answered their birthday, or a holiday that happened to come to mind. It does not seem that students were queried why they made their choices, but it seems likely that there would be close to as many different reasons as there were responses.
5. Gauthier uses formal names for all the strategies, and both equilibrium payoffs are (5,5).
6. For an example of an asymmetric game's phase diagram see Sugden (1986: 37.).

References

Gauthier, D. (1990). "Coordination." In *Moral Dealing: Contract, Ethics and Reason.* Ithaca: Cornell University Press, 274–97. Originally published in *Dialogue* 14 (1975): 195–221.

Gilbert, M. (1989). *On Social Facts.* Princeton: Princeton University Press.

Kripke S. (1982). *Wittgenstein On Rules and Private Language.* Cambridge: Harvard University Press.

Lewis, D. (1969). *Convention: a Philosophical Study.* Cambridge: Harvard University Press.

Mehta J., Starmer C., Sugden R. (1994). "The Nature of Salience: An Experimental Investigation of Pure Coordination Games." *The American Economic Review* 84, No. 3: 658–673.

Schelling, T. (1980). *The Strategy of Conflict.* Cambridge: Harvard University.

Sugden, R. (1986). *The Economics of Rights, Co-operation and Welfare.* Oxford: Basil Blackwell.

Sugden, R. (1993). "Thinking as a Team: Towards an Explanation of Nonselfish Behavior." In *Altruism,* ed. by Ellen Frankel Paul, Fred D. Miller Jr., and Jeffrey Paul. Cambridge: Cambridge University Press.

Ullman-Margalit, E. (1977). *The Emergence of Norms.* Oxford: The Clarendon Press.

Praxiology, Action Research, and Critical Systems Heuristics

Werner Ulrich
Dept. of Philosophy,
University of Fribourg,
Fribourg, Switzerland

1. Introduction

Praxiology, action research, and critical systems heuristics share a basic concern in the problem of rational action: *How can we identify, discuss, and justify rational action rationally?* Dealing "rationally" with the problem of rational action means that we seek to decide upon the merit of a proposed action by means of reason – systematic reflection and discourse – rather than by recourse to mere acts of faith or of power. The difficulty is that we still do not know how to do this. We do not have an operational theory or methodology that would tell us how to secure rational action. Or is the real problem perhaps the assumption that such a theory or methodology exists?

What *is* "rational" action in the first place? Obviously, how successful we are in securing rational action depends on what we mean by rational action. This explains why the three approaches of interest here seem to pursue so entirely different solutions to the problem of rational action:

Praxiologists seek to understand rational actions in terms of a theory (or general methodology) of effective and efficient action. The ideal is a *science* of rational action.

Action researchers approach the problem on the basis that it is the right of stakeholders, i.e., concerned people rather than scientists, to judge the merits of an action that is of concern to them (e.g., because it may affect their daily lifeworld). The ideal is *participatory practice.* To action researchers, a science of rational action is neither possible nor desirable.

Practitioners of critical systems heuristics (critical systems thinkers), finally, take a middle ground between these two positions. We cannot identify relevant effects without listening to people, they say; but how do we know what people we need to listen to, except through an adequate understanding of the actual and potential effects of an action, including unintended side-effects and long-term impacts? The two requirements are interdependent. Neither requirement can be redeemed without the other. Neither science nor "the people" can give us unequivocal answers. The best they can do is to make us aware of how in each case their answers depend on assumptions concerning the other side. Thus for critical systems heuristics there is no such thing as a definitive, unequivocal judgment on the rationality of an action, whether based on science or on people; a better ideal for dealing rationally with the problem of rational action is *critique.*

Despite their different ideals, the three approaches may usefully be considered to pursue complementary methodological goals. Their common denominator is the quest for improving the human condition by means of reason. This shared *quest for improvement* therefore furnishes the fundamental leverage point for this essay. The key to an adequate notion of rational action is seen in a critical mediation between the scientific (theoretical-empirical) and the people (practical-normative) dimensions of the meaning of "improvement."

2. Rational Action and Planning

Rational action has many faces – philosophical, scientific, ethical, emotional, and very often financial, faces. Not surprisingly, a great number of philosophical, sociological, economic, managerial and planning-oriented approaches seek to help us in understanding the meaning of rational action and how we can ensure rational action in practice. I have defined a few concepts and approaches that seem basic for my present purpose in Table 1.

TABLE 1.
Some basic concepts and approaches concerned
with the problem of rational action

Action research: the art of using inquiry for the purpose of participatory → intervention; the art of involving people in inquiry so as to secure both learning and legitimation

Critical Systems Heuristics: a philosophical foundation and practical operationalization of → critical systems thinking

Critical systems thinking: the art of employing the systems concept for (self-) critical purposes; the methodological linkage of → critique and → systems inquiry and design, in the double sense of applying critique to systems thinking, and systems thinking to critique

Critique: a systematic effort of uncovering, through individual reflection and intersubjective discourse, the presuppositions and implications of a proposition or action, especially with regard to their value content but also with regard to their theoretical and empirical content

Intervention: action with a view to changing a given situation toward some kind of improvement; a sociological concept of rational action, meaning an action that is well aware of the ways in which it may change the situation at hand and how these changes may affect concerned people and make them resist or demand participation

Planning: the art of designing and organizing → interventions so as to promote improvement

Practical philosophy: the philosophical discipline concerned with the problem of practical reason, i.e., the problem of how norms and value judgments can be discussed and justified with reason; theory of value justification, ethics

Praxiology: the science (or general methodology) of effective and efficient action

Social planning: the use of → planning for solving social problems, i.e., problems of societal concern

Systems inquiry and design, systems practice: the art of applying systems thinking to → planning and → intervention.

Among these concepts and approaches, I propose to use *planning* (or "social planning") as a basic term that is common to praxiology, action research, and critical systems heuristics. Whenever we want to ensure rational action, we need to plan, in the general sense of thinking and acting ahead. Accordingly, each of the three approaches considered here seeks to secure rational action by some combination of preparatory actions such as inquiry, design, reflection, and debate. Planning in this wide sense is what distinguishes rational action from good luck. Both may lead to a desired outcome, but only systematic preparation can ensure it to some extent. This is why praxiologists typically understand their field in terms of a theory of preparation of actions or of a logic of *preparatory actions* (e.g., Kotarbiński 1965: 72f, 76–80, 171–187; Gasparski 1987); similarly, action researchers see participative or *co-operative inquiry* as the royal way to good practice (e.g., Fals-Borda and Rahman 1991; Whyte 1991; Reason 1994); and systems thinkers conceive of rational practice in terms of *social systems design* (e.g., Churchman 1971, 1979; Ackoff, 1974, 1981; Checkland 1981; Ulrich 1983, 1987).

Now it is of course true that in practice, planning is often the problem rather than the solution. In the name of rational action, planning imposes solutions upon people that are not *their* solutions, as they had no voice in their making. This technocratic kind of planning is common. Planning is usually practiced as a form of purposive-rational action, i.e., a scientifically informed means for accomplishing a given end. In contrast, I suggest to understand planning as *the art of promoting improvement*. This definition has the advantage of avoiding the inherent reduction of practical to merely instrumental reason.

3. Planning or the Art of Promoting Improvement

As soon as we define planning as the art of promoting improvement, a crucial question poses itself imperatively and inescapably: What constitutes an "improvement"? This is probably the central and most difficult issue of planning, for if we do not really understand what "improvement" means in a specific situation, how can we promote it?

It follows that the core business of planning, regardless of whether it is understood in the terms of praxiology, action research, or critical systems heuristics, consists in a systematic effort to unfold the meaning of "improvement" in a specific situation. This raises fundamental issues. They concern both the knowledge and the ethics of "planning." Regarding knowledge, it is obvious that what we may recognize as a possible improvement depends on our knowledge and understanding of the situation of concern. For example, it is quite impossible reasonably to judge an option for improvement without understanding all the available, and ultimately all the conceivable, options. If we do not know what we might achieve with the available resources, how can we judge what is the best use of these resources? But what options are reasonable, and even more fundamentally, what options are conceivable in the first place, depends on our knowledge, which in turn depends on how we define (and delimitate) the situation of concern, i.e., the section of the real world that is to be considered as "improvable."

Regarding the issue of ethics, another question arises immediately: who is/are "we"? Improvement rarely means the same thing for everyone concerned. Promoting it inescapably implies preference; that is to say, it implies choice between the needs and values of different groups of people. Sometimes the choice is not really a choice, of course, but occurs through the mere dominance of certain needs and values of some people over those of others. The basic ethical point is that planning, except perhaps in a world of perfect harmony, invariably implies conflicts of needs and values. Conflicts are the stuff of ethics.

It seems to me that this dimension of rational action is insufficiently conceptualized in Kotarbiński's (1965) account of praxiology as the science of efficient action: What does it mean to be "efficient" in the face of conflict concerning the meaning of improvement, that is, the purposes to be served? While it is clear that the praxiological concept of efficiency presupposes effectiveness, it seems less clear to me whether praxiology's underlying concept of purposive-rationality is apt to deal with conflicts of purposes except in merely tactical or strategic (but not ethical) terms. This becomes apparent, for instance, in Kotarbinski's treatment of conflicts among agents in Chapter XIII of *Praxiology*, where he deals with the efficiency of different "techniques of struggle" and "ruses" such as *divide et impera* and creating *faits accomplis* without considering the more fundamental question of what it means to be "rational" in the face of divergent values (Kotarbiński 1965: 239f, 243, 247). People expect "rational" action to serve many different purposes, for they have different needs and values and hence different notions of improvement; how then can there be a science of efficient action in Kotarbiński's (1965: e.g. 2, 11, 16, 126) sense of a theory from which general standards of efficiency and of "good practice" could be derived?

Likewise, it seems to me that the literature on action research, too, avoids this issue when it locates the conflicts one-sidedly between "the people" and "the powerful." A commitment to the empowerment of people, to the emancipation and liberation of the oppressed and disadvantaged, is always good and hence raises no ethical issues. Or does it? I think it does, and I think action research cannot avoid them simply by referring to its emancipatory commitment, not any more than can critical systems thinking. For the value conflicts are not always simply between the "good guys" and the "bad guys," or between "the people" and those who have the say. Among "the people," too, there exist different needs and hence genuine conflicts of values and interests, for *people are different*. Ethically speaking, the conflict is thus never between a definition of "improvement" which is only good (e.g., because voiced by "the people") and other definitions that are only bad (e.g., because imposed by top-down planning). Top-down-imposed definitions of improvement are ethically and democratically highly questionable, of course, but the point here is that any conceivable definition will have its ethical problems. Planning can never serve all those in need equally; it implies, as we have said, choice, and hence, responsibility. It is thus not sufficient, from an ethical viewpoint, to say that our efforts serve "the people." The inescapable ethical question is: How can we justify the value implications, let alone the "rationality," of any proposal for "improvement" in the face of conflicting needs and interests?

Critical heuristics' answer is simple: we cannot. But this must not lead us into a bottomless ethical relativism and scepticism, for that would be ethically just as questionable as pretending that "we" (whoever that is) "know" what is good and right for the people, i.e., how conflicts are to be decided. Since from an ethical point of view no positive answer is ever available, in the sense that no conceivable definition of improvement can hope to be defended unambiguously and definitively, the only available path, ruling out dogmatism, is a critical one. Critical systems heuristics proposes such a critical path. To this end it uses, perhaps astonishingly, the systems idea – at first glance, yet another hopelessly technocratic concept! It has discovered how the systems idea can help us to tread a critical path in a manner that is not expert-driven but holds an emancipatory potential for ordinary people.

4. A Critical Path

A critical path toward improvement must aim to help ordinary people in dealing critically with both the issues I have mentioned, what counts as "knowledge" and what counts as ethically defendable "improvement." Critical systems heuristics aims to provide a clear, generic, and compelling way to do so. By means of its specific critical understanding of the systems idea, it explains how exactly knowledge depends on value judgments, and how exactly value judgments depend on knowledge. On this basis it can provide ordinary people with a means to challenge knowledge claims, whether by experts or by anyone else, through demonstrating how these claims depend on debatable value judgements, and vice-versa.

The critically-heuristic core concept in this regard is the concept of boundary judgments (Ulrich 1983: 225ff; 1987: 278ff; 1993: 594ff; 1996: 15ff). Boundary judgments determine the real-world context that counts as relevant, whether consciously or unconsciously, when it comes to identifying and evaluating relevant "facts" and "values." All claims to the rationality of a proposed action are conditioned by such boundary judgments; with them, both the facts and the value judgments that we consider change. Just as importantly, our knowledge of facts and our value assumptions condition our boundary judgments. Thus value judgments can make us change boundary judgments, which makes the "facts" look different; conversely, knowledge of new facts can equally make us change boundary judgments, which then makes our previous "values" look different. This interdependence of facts and values is often asserted but rarely if ever explained in precise terms. Critical heuristics provides such an explanation through its specific operationalization of the systems-theoretical concept of boundary judgments. This operationalization provides a useful conceptual framework of cogent critique. Such critical competence is essential for driving the process of unfolding the meaning of "improvement." As mentioned earlier, this process is at the very heart of planning; it is crucial for identifying and discussing what in a specific situation ought to count as "rational" action.

Equally essential are the emancipatory (because non-elitist) implications of this approach. Counter to all existing models of rational discourse, critically-heuristic discourse is not expert-driven, as it does not depend on any special theoretical or methodological knowledge or on argumentation skills beyond the reach of ordinary citizens. Critical heuristics gives a competent role in planning discourses not only to those

who are able to fulfill specified conditions of rational argumentation –
usually experts or philosophers – but also to ordinary people, i.e., to
citizens. It uses the systems idea to show that there are forms of cogent
argumentation – more specifically, *rational critique* – that do not depend on possessing equal knowledge and access to information which is
available to the professionals and decision makers who usually have the
say in planning. (This is not to belittle these resources.)

Critical heuristics does not of course pretend that it can help people to
"prove" what in a specific case might constitute an improvement; it only
aims to protect them against the pretensions of other people to "know,"
or to know better. It can help citizens to question proposed improvements – "plans" – in a systematic way, so as to make it clear to themselves and to others what "improvement" means in each case. In this
way, citizens can become competent participants in planning processes
or, where participation is not possible or does not ensure that their concerns are actually heeded by those who have the say, can learn to argue
their concerns cogently in the public arena.

Furthermore, critical heuristics regards citizens as "witnesses": those
citizens who have the opportunity to participate or voice their concerns
publicly are called upon also to represent the concerns of those who
cannot speak for themselves, whether they be the handicapped, the un-
born (the future generations), or non-human nature.

I cannot explain here in any detail how critical systems heuristics
operationalizes these ideas. I merely wish to convey to praxiologists the
critical spirit of the approach. This critical spirit is essential to the way
how I try to deal with the problem of rational action. It represents
a *"critical turn"* away from our conventional, holistic concept of rationality. I use the systems idea as a critical reminder rather than to buttress
any claims to a "whole-systems" kind of rationality, either on the part of
systems designers and scientists or on the part of "the people." I want to
help people secure a *"critical solution"* to the unavoidable question of
rationality – What is a better, what a less desirable kind of improvement?
– rather than a "total" solution, one that would claim to "know." Any
claim to knowledge (or rationality) in such matters runs a great risk of
implying a technocratic utopia, one that is ultimately bound to design
people and democracy out of the picture; for if it is possible for the right
kind of experts to know what is the right (or "rational") kind of improvement then there is little room for meaningful democratic debate
and decision-making.

If you are interested in the far-reaching implications of this understanding of the systems idea for a non-elitist praxiology, as well as for a different epistemology (theory of knowledge) and practical philosophy (theory of value justification, or ethics) – an understanding that has led me and other systems colleagues to interpret systems thinking in terms of *"critical systems thinking"* – then I invite you to consult the critical systems literature, especially the two early books which I still see as the main sources on critical systems thinking (Ulrich 1983; Flood and Jackson 1991). In addition, my recent *Primer to Critical Systems Heuristics for Action Researchers* (Ulrich, 1996) and a few other recent contributions (Ulrich 1993, 1994, 1995, 1997) may be helpful for understanding how critical heuristics seeks to give ordinary citizens a competent and rational part to play in the process of unfolding the meaning of improvement.

5. Conclusion

What I have said about the purpose of critical heuristics amounts to an effort to introduce "critique" into our notions of planning and rational action and to give it not only a systematic but indeed an *unavoidable* emancipatory part to play – "unavoidable" in the sense that once people have understood its message, there is no way of going back to a pre-critical understanding of planning. This is why I used a famous sentence of Kant (1783) as the keynote to the introductory chapter of *Critical Heuristics*: "This much is certain, that whoever has once tasted critique will be ever after disgusted with all dogmatic twaddle..." (Ulrich 1983: 19). As my reference to Kant may suggest, this effort is philosophically based though practically oriented: it is based on a "dialogical" (or discursive) reconstruction of Kant's Critical Philosophy, a reconstruction that was in part inspired by the *Theory of Communicative Action* by Jurgen Habermas (1984 and 1987) but which in distinction to it pursues neither a "total" theoretical solution to the problem of securing rational action nor a consensus-theoretic approach. It pursues, rather, a discursive theory of practicable critique (see on this Ulrich 1998). I believe that such an approach can provide a useful complement to other theories and methodologies of rational action, and I therefore hope that praxiologists as well as action researchers will be interested to know more about it.

Critical systems heuristics seems as yet little known among praxiologists and action researchers, although it might serve as a useful complement to both approaches. As compared to action research, critical systems heuristics shares with praxiology a stronger methodological orientation. Both praxiology and critical heuristics also emphasise more the cognitive or, if you want, the "intellectual" side of promoting improvement. As compared to praxiology, critical systems heuristics concentrates itself primarily on its mentioned critical core business, the "critical turn." It shares with action research a fundamentally non-elitist, emancipatory and anti-scientistic outlook, though it has its own specific ideas about how to give the people a competent role in matters of concern to them.

Critical systems heuristics has had the good fortune of meeting with sufficient interest among systems scholars to help create the current critical awakening and reorientation of systems thinking; could it perhaps play an equal role for praxiology, action research, and other disciplines concerned with the quest for improvement?

References

Ackoff, R.L. (1974). *Redesigning the Future: A Systems Approach to Societal Problems.* New York: Wiley.

Ackoff, R.L. (1981). *Creating the Corporate Future.* New York: Wiley.

Checkland, P.B. (1981). *Systems Thinking, Systems Practice.* New York: Wiley.

Churchman, C.W. (1971). *The Design of Inquiring Systems: Basic Concepts of Systems and Organization.* New York: Basic Books.

Churchman, C.W. (1979). *The Systems Approach and Its Enemies.* New York: Basic Books.

Fals-Borda, O., and Rahman, M.A. (eds.) (1991). *Action and Knowledge: Breaking the Monopoly with Participatory Action-Research.* New York: The Apex Press, and London: Intermediate Technology Publications.

Flood, R.L., and Jackson, M.C. (1991). *Critical Systems Thinking: Directed Readings.* Chichester: Wiley.

Gasparski, W.W. (1987). "On praxiology of preparatory actions." *Internat. J. of General Systems* 13: 345–353.

Habermas, J. (1984 and 1987). *The Theory of Communicative Action.* 2 vols., Cambridge, UK: Polity Press (Vol. 1 1984; Vol. 2. 1987).

Kant, I. (1783). *Prolegomena to Any Future Metaphysics.* New York: Liberal Arts Press 1951.

Kotarbiński, T. (1965). *Praxiology: An Introduction to the Sciences of Efficient Action.* Oxford, UK: Pergamon Press and Warsaw, Poland: Polish Scientific Publishers. Second English edition by P. Dudley (ed.), *Kotarbiński's Praxiology,* With a foreword by W.W. Gasparski, Hull, UK: Centre for Systems Studies Press, 1995.

Reason, P. (1994). "Three approaches to participative inquiry." In Denzin, N.K., and Lincoln, Y.S. (eds.), *Handbook of Qualitative Research,* London: Sage.

Ulrich, W. (1983). *Critical Heuristics of Social Planning: A New Approach to Practical Philosophy.* Bern, Switzerland: Haupt; paperback edition, New York: Wiley, 1994.

Ulrich, W. (1987)."Critical Heuristics of Social Systems Design." *European Journal of Operational Research* 31: 276–283. Reprinted in Flood, R.L., and Jackson, M.C., eds., *Critical Systems Thinking: Directed Readings*, Chichester: Wiley, 1991, pp. 103–115.

Ulrich, W. (1993). "Some Difficulties of Ecological Thinking, Considered from a Critical Systems Perspective: A Plea for Critical Holism." *Systems Practice* 6: 583–611.

Ulrich, W. (1994). "Can we Secure Future-responsive Management Through Systems Thinking and Design?" *Interfaces* 24 (No. 4): 26–37.

Ulrich, W. (1995). "Critical Systems Thinking for Citizens: A Research Proposal." *Research Memorandum No. 10,* Centre for Systems Studies, University of Hull, Hull, 28 November 1995.

Ulrich, W. (1996). *A Primer to Critical Systems Heuristics for Action Researchers.* Centre for Systems Studies, University of Hull, Hull, U.K., 31 March 1996, 58 pp.

Ulrich, W. (1997). "Critical systems thinking for citizens." In *Critical Systems Thinking: Current Research and Practice*, edited by R.L. Flood and N.R.A. Romm, 165–178, New York: Plenum.

Ulrich, W. (1998). "Critical Systems Discourse, Emancipation, and the Public Sphere." (Paper to be published).

Whyte, W.F., ed. (1992). *Participatory Action Research.* Newbury Park, Calif.: Sage.

PART THREE

Learning by Action: Applications, Techniques, and Case Studies

Applying Action Learning Principles to Academic Seminars: A Study in Praxiological Action

Chris de Winter Hebron
and
Doreen J. de Winter Hebron,
H+E Associates,
Stiffkey, UK

1. Introduction

Praxiology, according to most definitions of the science (e.g. Auspitz, Gasparski et al, 1992) involves the systematic study of the effectiveness of human actions from three basic standpoints
- analysis of concepts
- critique of modes of action and
- normative discussions and recommendations for increasing effectiveness

This paper examines from just such a standpoint the authors' activities over the past fifteen years in applying the principles of action learning, as described in Revans 1971 and 1980, to the conduct of post-doctoral and other high-level academic seminars. In so doing, the paper concentrates on four main areas of our work as case studies:
- the origin and development of the ISSED international academic staff development seminar series (1981 onwards)

- the "Meetings in Scholarly Work" post-doctoral seminars at the University of Kassel, 1987–90
- the training course on Designing and Running International Seminars for Sultan Qaboos University Oman, February 1992 and
- the Warsaw Spring School on Successful Fund Raising, April 1996

2. An Analysis of Revans' Principal Concepts

Reg Revans, for many years the enfant terrible of management training, but now recognised as an international guru, derived his basic concepts of what he came to call Action Learning not from learned theory but from simple – but very acute! – observation of the educational and management processes with which he found himself involved, as an education officer in a London borough during the 1930s and later as a management consultant in Britain's Coal Board and National Health Service from the late 1940s to the 1960s. In essence, his findings may be summed up in the notions that effective learning can be defined as learning that actually gets applied to the solution of real problems in the real workplace, and that this learning is gained only by the combination of formal instruction with the active seeking of answers to open questions, as in his famous learning equation $P+Q = L$. In this equation, Q (open questioning) is very much more crucial than P (programmed instruction), though as the equation indicates, both are necessary for full effective learning to take place.

Revans' prime question thus became, by what process may the ascendancy of Q over P be established in a management learning situation? His answer was, by placing at the heart of the learning process the establishment of groups of learners with shared and similar problems and interests, and the active working of members of these groups on the solution of each others' (not their own!) problems. He described the members of these groups as "comrades in adversity" (Revans 1984). In classical action learning, these groups plus facilitators who provide a process framework and technical expertise (the P of the learning equation) are known as "Action Learning Sets," and meet at regular intervals until the learning has occurred and the problems are solved. It is within them that P and Q are combined. L (the learning effect of P+Q) in Revans' classical scheme takes place at an individual level, in the intervals between Set meetings, when each set member attempts the solution of another member's management problem as a guest within that other member's organisation.

3. Adapting the Concepts to the Academic Situation

The process described above has proved itself to be a highly effective management learning mechanism, both in the two post-war areas in which Revans was working in UK and, perhaps most spectacularly, in the overhaul of the Belgian economic strategy conducted by Revans during the same period. Understandably, therefore, there have been over the years a number of attempts to adapt Revans' ideas to academic learning. Initially, however, these met with only qualified success (and Revans himself was upon occasion more than a little acerbic about their being labeled "action learning" as a result).

There seem to have been two main reasons for this relative lack of success. First, many of these attempts were aimed at rejigging formal undergraduate or taught postgraduate courses, often in the management studies area itself, where the institutional culture firmly valued P above Q – the direct opposite of Revans' theories. (Although the learning equation P+Q=L is basic to all teaching, few academics actually put it into practice.) Second, academic courses almost by definition require a formal assessment of some kind – examination , thesis, or project report – and designing Q-friendly assessment systems is notoriously difficult (Gibbs 1992, Ramsden 1992). The result was, that few of these attempts progressed much beyond the conventional MBA structure with syndicate groups and a project report under another name.

On analyzing this situation further, however, an additional problem in the initial attempts at adapting action learning to an academic environment also becomes apparent. Action learning is intended to promote effective learning as judged by application in the workplace. But what was the "workplace" of the academic learners and their academic teachers? Despite contemporary calls for higher education to produce graduates fitted to take part in the world of work, few academic teachers (including academic professors of management) actually made a living working at anything other than "the professor's profession" until recently. Few students, until now, have had any experience of workplaces other than academe from which to judge the efficacy of their learning solutions [though the number of those few is now beginning to increase as student profiles become more diverse]. And, in terms of management efficiency, it is at least arguable that academe is among the worst managed areas of human enterprise (Denton 1996).

It is therefore certainly possible that attempts to apply action learning principles within the academic environment have in the past been concentrating upon the wrong area of initial application – that they should initially have concentrated not upon the academics' job of teaching others, but upon the learning and development processes of the academics themselves. It is in these areas, if anywhere, that Revans' definition of action learners as "comrades in adversity" can best hold good in academic life; and it is also in these areas that action learning is most likely to change the prevailing P-friendly culture of academic higher education to the Q-friendly culture that would make its wider application possible. It is in these areas, therefore, that we ought logically to look for successful initial applications of action learning to academe.

As the subsequent sections of this paper show, it is in these areas also that the authors have for the past fifteen years mainly concentrated their application activities.

4. Case Study 1: The ISSED Seminar Series

The initials ISSED stand for International Seminar on Staff and Educational Development. Held annually (with one exception) since 1981, it has become down the years the leading interactive seminar for the high-level development of academic staff ("faculty" in US parlance) not as subject specialists but in their capacity as academic teachers and facilitators. It is also, so far as we know, the only totally world-wide seminar of this kind to be based firmly on the principles of action learning described above, to the extent that it can claim Revans' direct blessing through his presence as a keynote speaker at the 1984 meeting.

Initially, however, ISSED (or simply "The 1981 Seminar" as its first meeting was called) was not deliberately constructed *de novo* to embody Revans' ideas. It originated from a dissatisfaction felt both by the first author and a US colleague in the design of the IUT conference series, on the international advisory council of which we both found ourselves during the middle 1970s. In many ways IUT (the International Conference on Improving University and College Teaching, sponsored by the University of Maryland) was – and still is – a ground-breaking event. It was the first international conference series to take academic teaching really seriously: it was the first to replace conventional presentations with an alternative – the panel of pre-issued papers – which enabled the participants to focus primarily upon discussion. Yet we were still dissatisfied with it, because it modeled a lecturing, P-based, teaching style even while it claimed to be promoting an improved form of teaching activity. There had, we felt, to be better ways to run a conference series.

At this point, the first author (again) was invited to join the Maidstone seminar series, a series of advanced seminars for European Union academic staff developers run under the auspices of EARDHE, and embodying all aspects of classical action learning as defined by Revans except the exchange of positions in each others' organisations. The seminars, therefore, had no agenda, until the participants arrived. The first day was spent setting an agenda from participants' own problems, locating facilitators among fellow participants, and dividing into set-like groups. The meeting was completely participant-owned and process-dominated. Speaking personally, it was one of the most exhilarating experiences at which one could conceive being present. It was also very small (maximum 15 persons) and culturally homogeneous (all staff developers from EU higher education institutions, with fluency in at least two of English, French and German), and this created a key problem from our point of view.

The problem was, that such a small meeting would be economically impossible on the fully international scale we had in mind as an alternative to IUT; and also, it would lack sufficient cultural homogeneity to permit the sort of easy understandings of initial problems that had characterized Maidstone. In addition, any larger meeting could not possibly wait to set its agenda until the participants had all assembled: the logistics of a full-scale international meeting doing this meant that so much time would be taken up in on-site planning that no actual Q-type learning would take place at all. What we needed, therefore, was a modified action learning format in which:

- the key features of Q-friendly learning (e.g. self-steering groups of "comrades in adversity") were maintained
- the nature of the problems to be attacked was pre-defined, at least in outline (necessary to ensure a manageable agenda was retained)
- some allowance was made for necessary P-type elements to be combined with Q activity
- some allowance was made for cultural non-homogeneity
- some activity or shape was given to the event to enable participants to relate to it as a whole, rather than just to their group within it and
- some alternative was found for the "exchange of institutions" in which in classical action learning the final learning process took place.

Additionally, since it was already clear that a seminar designed to such a specification would have a very revolutionary and controversial appearance, some way would have to be found to give the event sufficient conventional academic respectability to enable prospective participants to acquire funds to attend – since, even if one assumed six "sets" of around 12 people each (the maximum for easy self-steering), an upper limit of 75 people on a fully international meeting with all the fixed costs that implied would mean that the meeting fee would inevitably be quite expensive.

The seminar design that emerged from consideration of this requirements list had, as we expected, a number of unusual characteristics. To ensure the primacy of the "sets" (we called them Interest Groups, for reasons that will become clear shortly), they occupied at least half the total working time of the seminar . Further, participants opted for a particular group and, once allocated to it, stayed with it throughout the seminar, meeting sometimes several times a day for anything up to two hours at a time. Periodically, participants asked why they could not join several interest groups: the answer we gave was always the same – "It would damage the group dynamics." Strictly, however, this was a blind – what it would really have damaged was the group's commitment to finding solutions to the problems its members had identified themselves as sharing in the first session.

The interest group topics were selected in advance, by a representative seminar committee (at first this was ad hoc, but over the years it has become standardised as the UK and US organisers, plus the local host institution's representative). The host for the year selected the general problem area to be considered that year (we call it the "Seminar Theme"), and the committee, by a version of the Delphi process, then identified leading problems to form the Interest Group titles. At first these were very wide ranging, but this often led to a large number of non-viably small groups: for the last six or seven years, therefore, individual problems have been grouped as "Topics" within a smaller number of overarching Groups, on a tree structure. Wherever possible, we preferred to describe the topics using behavioural verbs (e.g., *"developing* staff developers" or *"creating* access structures") to ensure that the problem being considered was viewed as an active process. Participants selected a first and second choice of group, and were allocated to one or the other depending on group size and cultural balance. The term Interest Groups was coined because we realised that the groups as thus prescribed did not have all the characteristics of action learning sets, and we therefore needed an alternative title – and certainly, participants chose their group out of interest!

Although the groups themselves were prescribed in advance, however, the detailed problems to be discussed in them, and the way of proceeding, were not. Participants were asked to contribute "overview papers" to the seminar – outlines in which they reviewed problems or issues they wanted to share with their group, and on which they wanted their group to work with them during the four days (initially five, until pressures of time and expense forced a shortening) of the seminar. These "overview papers" were printed up in advance, like presentation abstracts in a conventional seminar, and participants were told they could count them as accepted papers for funding purposes. Once sufficient people were enrolled in any one group, an initial chairperson was appointed, and the participants were given each others' addresses and topic choices so that they could correspond with each other and with the chair. (Academic work pressures being what they are, this proved one of the most problematic parts of the whole design.) On arrival at the seminar, groups were instructed to spend their first meeting setting their own agenda and working method, the one restriction being that they must by the end of the seminar produce a "product" – a result of their group work, which could be presented to the whole seminar on the final day, and could subsequently be written up in the Proceedings

The problems of allowing for P-type learning and of shaping the overall event were given a common solution. The Interest Group meetings were "framed" by an opening, middle and closing plenary: the first was a keynote addressing the general theme, the second usually a panel discussion (sometimes also with a keynote element, as in Revans' address in 1984), and the third a report session for the group "products." Individual interactive workshops offered by participants on the seminar theme were also accepted subject to peer review by the organising committee. Initially, no formal paper proposals by group members were permitted, for fear of damaging the preeminence of Q-friendly processes: in more recent years, however, the requirements of funding bodies in particular have forced us to compromise on that initial rule (and some excellent problem-oriented papers have been produced as a result and used as technical material for assorted group discussions). One very important development, initiated at the 1989 meeting, was the requirement that each group produce a poster half way through showing plans and work in progress, to be displayed to all participants at a plenary poster and "educational marketplace" session.

The event was also given a strong social dimension. The seminar was, and is, almost entirely residential: non-resident attendance and single-day attendance are both possible, but are discouraged. There is always an opening reception, a visit event of some kind part way through, and a farewell party. The emphasis on *gemutlichkeit* is not however at the expense of work: on days when no social event is scheduled work can and does continue from 8 a.m. to 10 p.m. where needed.

The problem of cultural non-homogeneity, on reflection, could be reduced to a simpler problem (from our point of view), that of conceptual confusion. An example of this would be, the differing uses as between UK and US speakers of the term "higher education." UK speakers exclude most of technical education from their concept of HE, while US speakers include it, but speakers of each nationality usually assume that the other speakers are using *their* concept when they use the term. At the suggestion of an Austrian participant in the Maidstone meetings, "concept moderators" were initially appointed for each group, charged with looking out for confusions of this sort, and drawing group members' attention to them. As the group structure became more familiar over the years, however, this proved not to be necessary – members became eager to take on the job themselves! Other forms of cultural non-homogeneity (birthtongue or ethnic identity, for example) have, in the generally supportive nature of the group process, tended to become not only not a problem, but in the vast majority of cases a positive enrichment to the seminar process.

Finding a substitute for the exchange of institutions stage in classical action learning has however been one problem that has not so easily been resolved. In some cases a real exchange of institution (for example, by sabbatical leave) or collaboration between institutions has followed from networks created during the group process. A number of international research projects have originated in just such a way over the past fifteen years.. It would however be foolish to claim, no matter how substantial the number of such individual interchanges becomes, that the *majority* of ISSED participants go on to replicate the final stage in Revans' scheme, and without access to substantially more funding than most participants can command at the moment, it is unlikely that they ever will do so. Post-seminar collaboration in group reports and voluntary follow-up through a learning applications exercise are only a poor and partial substitute for the full Revans treatment, but in the present financial and logistic circumstances they will have to do.

In other respects, however, as the above account shows, this attempt to translate action learning into an academic development environment has been remarkably successful. Since 1981, fifteen seminars have taken place to date, and hosts are already known for the next two. A total of over 500 participants have undergone the process described above, involving institutions in 36 countries. Additionally, the structure has been successfully replicated exactly in two specialist meetings on Transformation in Higher Education involving both academics and administrators and in three meetings on Student Well-being and Development involving academics, administrators and student welfare staff, and with only slight modifications in meetings on Entrepreneurship Education and on Ethics in HE. Adapting action learning principles to professional academic staff development activities must therefore so far be deemed a success.

Professional academic staff development is however a very specialised and minority element within the academic environment overall. We – and especially the second author, whose business management background meant that she had independently been using the classical action learning process in her own management development work for many years – were anxious to extend the adaptation process to as many other types of high-level academic learning as might prove possible. We were, of course, aware that in so doing it was probable that additional modifications in the detailed seminar processes would need to be made, and that the ultimate product would therefore be different from ISSED to a substantial degree. The key concern, though, was that it should still retain the Q-friendly climate which had been successfully transferred from Revans' classical Action Learning schemes to ISSED.

The three sections that follow describe, by means of examining three separate case-studies, how this was done.

5. Case Study 2: The University of Kassel "Meetings in Scholarly Work" Seminars

Although, as we have said, the extension of adapting action learning into other areas of academic training beyond professional staff development increasingly involved input from the second author, by a curious irony the initial impetus came via the first author, and as a spin-off from the ISSED series itself. One of the original Maidstone participants, who had also been site host for ISSED in 1986, was Professor Franz-Hermann Riebel of the Faculty of International Agriculture at the University of Kassel. As a result of this connection, we received a commission from the Faculty to design and teach a one-week post-doctoral seminar jointly with Prof Riebel for newly graduated Ph.D.s from developing countries who were about to return to their countries of origin to take up academic or government positions after completing their doctoral studies in Germany. The seminar was to form part of a six-month Reintegration course, coming roughly two thirds of the way through, and was to cover the role of academic communication (especially through conferences and publications) in the conduct of research and the dissemination of research results (*Wissenschaftstransfer*).

The seminar design requirements had a number of interesting characteristics. The major language of instruction was to be both German and English (the language of the Reintegration course as a whole was German). Students' first languages might be any African, Asian or Latin American tongue: their academic "home language" might be English, French, German, Spanish or (in a minority of cases) Arabic. Students were to be required to train specifically for working in teams, which should involve all students irrespective of Ph.D. discipline. Students' Ph.D. disciplines could be from any science, engineering or social science area as well as from agriculture. However, because developing-world agriculture was involved, both research and dissemination were to be regarded from as practical, work-oriented a standpoint as possible in all cases: it was this final design parameter that made action learning so important an aspect of the seminar process.

From an action learning standpoint, the major problem was, what were the "sets" to do? In classical action learning, the set members are "comrades in adversity," sharing problems from the individual places of work: but these post-doctoral students had as yet no "individual places of work." What, then, would bind them together?

The answer, we discovered, lay in the requirement that the students should undergo team training. This training was carried out by Prof Riebel, under licence from the Coverdale Organisation Gmbh, and included a number of exercises aimed at fixing a strong group dynamic within the training teams thus created. We therefore decided to build on this training in the main seminar by requiring these teams, each of which included students from a cross-section of all the Ph.D. disciplines involved, to develop an outline, and then to design the organisation and dissemination, for a multi-disciplinary practical development project located in one of their countries of return, and using the specialist skills of all of them.

This requirement led to there being three major types of problem for the students to define and solve. First, the group had the problem of familiarising itself with the chosen country, which only some of the members would know intimately. Second, there was the intellectual problem of developing a viable and realistic project that would utilise all their specialist skills. And third, there was the substantive management problem of organisation and dissemination. Both defining and solving these problems could only be achieved within the set, since they were unique to that set in every case. Similarly, the formal presentations that formed the P element of the seminar were necessary to providing the students with technical material for a solution to the problems, but not sufficient in themselves to provide that solution, because the material they contained was not group-specific. The group work, in fact, extended beyond the end of the seminar plan, and the learning was completed by the finished proposal being used in another part of the course.

The formal presentations themselves also presented a design problem, because of the linguistic complexity of the audience, and the solution to this problem that we finally adopted in turn became a major design element in our later work. It was, of course, impossible to cover all the students' first languages: we therefore concentrated on their academic "home language." The seminar was to be delivered jointly by the first author and Prof Riebel. The first author was a native English speaker, with competence in French and German: Prof Riebel was a native German speaker, with competence in English, Spanish and Arabic. Between them, the two trainers thus covered all the academic "home languages" used by the students.

The policy adopted was then as follows: the first author delivered formal presentations in English, and took questions in both English and German. Professor Riebel did the exact opposite (lectured in German and took questions also in English). Students were asked to indicate informally who was more and who was less fluent in each language, and a seating plan was devised that placed less fluent students in each language next to a more fluent mentor. The presentations were then structured to allow appropriate pauses for discussion-translation between mentor and mentee. Any students who required additional help in a further "home language" met with the appropriate trainer during the coffee or lunch break that followed each formal session, Both trainers were available as resource persons during all the set meetings: these could be held in any language in which the set felt comfortable, though the posters produced to demonstrate progress and the final reports had to be in either German or English.

As indicated above, this policy became a key design element in subsequent multi-language seminars. The key design points in this respect were: the grouping of set members into linguistic mentor/mentee pairs; the pacing of presentations to allow for discussion-translation pauses; the availability of trainers at coffee and lunch time for informal discussion; and the permission to sets to work in whatever language they felt happiest with.

The Meetings in Scholarly Work seminars were repeated at six-monthly intervals between 1987 and 1990. They proved highly effective in terms of student response and successful re-integration of returning doctoral graduates. They were however somewhat controversial in terms of mainstream German academic culture, in making use of practically oriented team projects, several languages, and trainers from more than one EU member state. Eventually, following changes in the Faculty management structure, the reintegration course as a whole was re-designed on a more individual and theoretical research basis, and the seminar was dropped from the course structure to free up time for such individual research.

6. Case Study 3: The Sultan Qaboos University Course on Designing and Running International Seminars

This course arose from a request from Sultan Qaboos University Oman to the British Council for training in the international conference area for a mixture of academic and administrative staff. H+E Associates was suggested to the Council as trainers by the University, following attendance by the HE the Secretary-General of the University Council at a number of our events, including in particular the Entrepreneurship Education event mentioned in an earlier section, which had used a modified ISSED structure. The Secretary-General had been impressed with that meeting, and had had a range of discussions with both authors, which ultimately resulted in the request being made. We knew, therefore, as soon as the initial approach was made by the Council, that an action learning type of event was implicit in the University's request.

The input material for the course had a substantial amount in common with the Kassel post-doctoral seminar already discussed, and the overall design of that meeting was therefore taken as a starting point. There were however some important differences between the two situations, and in designing the action learning element of the course these had to be taken into account.

The first important difference was that in this case we did have a place of work, and we did have real problems. The University wanted to begin to run international academic conferences, but did not have personnel trained in the expertise necessary to do so. They had actually already run one such event, in the Materials Science area, but had encountered a number of problems in the process of so doing. We thus did not have to engineer a raison d'etre for the sets, or endow them with an artificial group dynamic: experience of the Materials Science conference would do the first, and because the University at the time had only a limited number of faculties, faculty boundaries would provide the structure for the second. The language problem was also much simpler, in that only two languages were involved, Arabic and English. Though neither author was fluent in Arabic, a simple mentor/mentee grouping, discussion-translation pauses, and permission to work in sets in either language provided reports to plenary were in English would suffice.

However, two problems emerged in this particular situation which we had not encountered in the Kassel seminars. The first was, that the technical input for this course, although having much in common with the Kassel material academically, also had a strong management dimension, since successful international conference organisation is a complex managerial and business activity as well as an academic one. The question then became, how was the relationship between the two inputs to be structured? Should we deal with one type of input first in its entirety, and then deal with the other one? Or should the two types of input be dealt with in parallel, and if so, what structural principles should be used? This was not merely a theoretical question: it affected the staffing arrangements for the course as well as the design, since the academic input was primarily the responsibility of the first author and the management input primarily that of the second author.

Eventually, we decided that the general principles of action learning meant that the course structure should parallel the nature of actual conference organisation as closely as possible, so that the course experience modelled the experience of managing an academic conference as far as might be. This meant that the two strands of input, the academic and the managerial, were introduced in parallel – or, to be more precise, in an *intertwined* manner (which is how one comes upon them in organising real conferences).

The second problem was a more complex one, and had to do with the nature of the local culture. We remarked above on the P-dominated nature of much conventional University activity, for example in traditional German higher education. Oman is an Islamic state (though one of the less fundamentalist ones), and at the time of our receiving the commission for the training course its higher education system was very dominated by Egyptian academics, many of whom had a heartfelt commitment to P-type learning as a positive good. In addition, Islam is very much a religion "of the book" (the Book in question being of course the Qu'ran), and traditional Islamic education consists very largely of committing the sacred text to memory.

There was therefore a real danger that the Q-friendliness which the action learning approach sought to foster could be misconstrued in any one of several unwanted ways, of which incitement to intellectual anarchy or dereliction of our duty as trainers were the two most probable. The British Council staff were particularly concerned about this, and their briefing to us suggested that such an approach would almost certainly prove unworkable. Indeed, they were very concerned about sanctioning the course unless we very carefully wrote in any group work strictly as practical exercises.

Naturally, it would have been impolitic not to heed this advice: but we were privately more than a little sceptical about it in practice, partly from both authors' previous experience of Islamic students in our own college classes, and partly from remembering the reactions of the Secretary-General to his experiences of ISSED-style seminars. We therefore determined that one of the early exercises would have a strong action learning flavour, and be a sort of "test run" for problem-solving group work. If that was successful, what appeared on the official programme as "Group Exercises" would in fact become meetings of action learning sets, organised on a faculty basis. However, we did realise that in the given cultural setting group members might need some form of overt "official sanction" to permit them to move into open-ended questioning as a learning mode. We therefore prefaced the first such session with a brief description of what sort of activities we wanted from them and why – essentially, to enable them to consider and report to us how they would expect to apply their learning in a practical setting. We had thus told them, in our capacity as trainers ("keepers of the book") what it was they were to be permitted to do.

The ensuing twenty minutes or so, after the audience had broken up into their groups and were studying the task before them, are remembered by both authors as one of the most nerve-racking periods in our professional career. The formal presentations were being given in a raked lecture theatre, under the full glare of TV cameras (the event was being recorded for the University's staff development TV library). One group was now working on the floor of this theatre, the other in a small room just beyond the main doors. We were waiting, in what can best be described as a "players" tunnel', to be called on as resource persons. As often at the beginning of set work, there was a deadly hush while members took stock of themselves and their situation. Then, suddenly and quite accidentally, the door to the small room outside swung open. Through it came an excited buzz of Arabic conversation and a gust of laughter: it felt like the cork coming out of a champagne bottle.

In fact, the strategy of "permitting" set work succeeded remarkably well. (Curiously, the one person who seemed somewhat disgruntled with it was an expatriate Englishman who was a member of one of the teams). Once the set members had experienced open questioning under conditions of official approval, they developed perhaps even more of a taste for it than many Western academic groups do: so much so, that instead of reforming the two "trial" sets from the first exercise into three mainstream sets for the rest of the course, as we had originally intended to do, we felt the group dynamics would be best served by keeping the momentum of the original trial period. The two "trial" sets therefore became the permanent groupings for the course. Each designed and planned the management stages for a different, self-selected conference on a theme relevant to their particular faculty grouping: each conference design as eventually reported was a true product, perfectly capable of being taken up and used by the University as an actual event, even down to the arrangements for car-park security. There was no doubt that with this group of Omani academics and administrators the action learning approach was a success on the ground.

7. Case Study 4: The Warsaw Spring School
on Successful Fund Raising, April 1996

This was the most recent of our applications of action learning to the academic environment, and perhaps the one which raised the most radical questions of adaptation. It was also the most thoroughly evaluated of this group of case studies. It was designed and facilitated in cooperation with the Science Study Committee of the Polish Academy of Sciences, and held at the Main School of Agriculture Warsaw during April 1996. The school was sponsored financially by, among others, the British Council, the Institute of Praxiology and the Polish Academy of Sciences.

The School was intended to cover fund raising activities both in universities and in research institutes (which in Poland are a largely separate strand of scientific activity). It was intended to concentrate on fund raising for specific projects, but to set this within the more general context of overall funding diversification for higher education and research. Sections were therefore included on longer term fund raising activities, on institutional marketing activities as a source of funds, and on prudent financial management of the funds raised. Some of the cases examined (e.g. Leeds Metropolitan University) were chosen specifically because they displayed a mix of these approaches.

Development of the School Programme Design

The original concept of the School had been for a six-day meeting, making substantial use of a range of real-life case studies of actual fund raising approaches, both successful and unsuccessful. Both we and the sponsors were very anxious that the School's activities should be made as relevant as possible to the Polish situation, and that a common fault of "know-how" importations from Western economies – assuming that the culture and infrastructure of the transitional society does not differ significantly from that of the Western models being discussed – should be avoided. The decision was therefore taken very early on to organise the meeting in an action learning manner involving group discussions of shared problems arising from the case studies wherever possible.

It was however also clear that a substantial amount of practical information-giving would need to take place during the School, as Polish academic society had been very largely insulated from international developments in fund-raising and academic entrepreneurial techniques during the Communist period. The question therefore became, how to organise the sessions to include adequate informational presentations without damaging the action learning nature of the whole event. In the original draft of the programme, as a result, like ISSED, approximately 50% of the School time was devoted to each from of activity, with the first action learning group session placed on the afternoon of the first day in order to set the tone for the remaining sessions.

For logistic and financial reasons, however, it fairly soon transpired that the length of the meeting would have to be reduced to $3^1/_2$ days, and comparatively little use could be made of evening sessions to compensate, because a substantial minority of the participants from the Warsaw region itself were non-resident. The resultant condensed timetable inevitably left little time for set work, since without the information-giving sessions the sets would have no resource material.

This problem was resolved by restricting such formal set timetabling to the first and last sessions of the School. On the first day, as already designed, formal resource-material input on the writing of research funding proposals was followed by work in four groups on accounting for the success of proposals in the set members' own academic areas (or closely related ones). This work was followed by a reporting-back session to the School as a whole, in the course of which issues and problems common to all the sets were laid on the table, and a lively overall discussion followed relating the Western resource material suggestions to these. In this discussion, set members rather than ourselves took the lead.

Having thus established a Q-friendly climate in the group as a whole, the entire group was now treated as a single super-size set for the remainder of the school, until the evening of the third day and the morning of the fourth. This climate was undoubtedly assisted by the selection of the venue (the Rector's Palace of the Main School of Agriculture) and the layout of the main meeting room – light and airy, opening onto a terrace and two adjoining rooms for informal discussion and display of resource materials, and arranged in boardroom style with an excellent individual microphone system. it was also assisted by revision of the timetable to include a regular series of short breaks, and the holding of an initial reception, lunch and coffee (and the evening meal for those not already returned to Warsaw) in a setting involving a number of small "family-sized" tables.

On the third evening and again on the last morning, before the final "wrap-up" session, the group was again broken up into smaller sets, this time on a free choice basis. Individuals were able to request "surgery" meetings, on the action learning principle of "comrades in adversity," on various individual or shared fund raising or research partnership problems, and on the final morning a separate additional group session was run during the announced surgery time, at the request of those participants who wanted to review and cross-compare cases that had been treated separately earlier in the meeting, in order to extract common principles of best practice in funding application.

Development of the Detailed Programme Inputs

A further problem that had to be addressed during the development of the School programme was the question of the balance between fund raising for specific projects and more general funding issues, and between Western inputs from UK, USA, Ireland and Germany and inputs from within Poland itself. This problem could be solved more simply than the problem discussed above, although the process of solution was a fairly lengthy one. An initial draft of the programme was discussed with the Chairman of the Science Study Committee, and the resulting suggestions were fed into a second draft. This was shortened to 3 $^1/_2$ days as described above and the resulting third draft was then reviewed by a panel of Polish experts appointed by the Committee, in much the same way as a funding proposal or scientific paper is itself reviewed. The opinions of this panel were then collated by the Committee, and the resulting suggestions were fed into the final draft of the programme back at H+E Associates' office. Finally, detailed changes were made where needed as a result of local logistics to give the actual final programme. The whole process took about nine months to complete (May 1995 to January 1996).

The School in Operation

As remarked above, the School sessions were held at the Rector's Palace of the Main School of Agriculture, with residential participants staying at the Hotel IKAR nearby. The atmosphere was relaxed and friendly, and subsequent evaluations indicated that the event was very well received by the participants. The modified action learning process described above worked very well, and questioning and participation from among the School members was high, increasing as the event went on. In particular, the participants showed no hostility to, or repudiation of, notions of the need for financial skills to manage funds or the need to raise money for higher education and research, despite the cultural unfamiliarity of these ideas.

This was to a large extent due to the careful structuring of the more formal presentations within the School, which in the revised timetable now formed the larger part of the programme, to be as interactive as possible. Achieving interactivity in such a setting does not take place easily: it depends on the skill of the presenters in building up an atmosphere of cooperation among the participants and between the participants and themselves.

To ensure this atmosphere required careful planning, involving conferences between the presenters before and after sessions in order to capitalise on participant strengths that had begun to emerge, for example a decision to ask participants in the next session to brainstorm the sequence of requirements in applying for a specific kind of grant rather than to list them as resource material, and also to take action to avoid any indication of emerging passivity. It also required "thinking on one's feet" by presenters, so as to turn chance comments or disagreements from the floor into opportunities for genuine dialogue and experiential learning by the group: the first of the cross-cultural problems described below provides a very good example of this. As a result of this activity, the atmosphere became steadily more interactive as the meeting progressed, building mutual support and breaking down barriers, and cooperation between presenters and participants became steadily more spontaneous.

However, as in the events listed in the previous case studies, a number of cross-cultural lessons were learned, which may usefully suggest ways of developing further action learning applications of this type, and three of the main examples of these are now described.

One such lesson involved an important cultural difference between Polish and UK/EU attitudes to making informal approaches to prospective funders in advance of submitting a formal application. There was widespread belief among the participants that in Poland this would always be counter-productive if not actually illegal (though the actual speakers from Polish funding sources were less "hard line" about this). In UK and EU, on the other hand, such approaches are quite normal provided they take the form of requests for information or guidance and not actual lobbying (which is of course improper in both cultures!).

It was here that the strength of the modified action learning approach being used first proved itself. The issue emerged spontaneously from resource-based comments, quite early on in the reporting-back session that followed the set activities on the first day. Although it could not be finally resolved at this stage, this enabled us to ensure that it would be specifically addressed whenever it was likely to emerge in later sessions, including input from the Polish expert speakers, so that satisfactory clarification could eventually be achieved.

A second cross-cultural matter concerned two problems of seeking funding from industry encountered in Poland but not particularly in UK/EU. The first had to do with the lack of spare working capital in most Polish firms to invest in larger-scale research projects. This problem was raised in an informal group activity, during one of the conference breaks, and the group concerned came to the conclusion that a cooperative approach within the local catchment community of the fundseeking institution would probably be the most effective solution. It would thus appear desirable in future events of this type to have resource material available on the US "Community Trust" process, which facilitates just such cooperation.

The second problem had to do with the low salary levels in Polish universities vis-à-vis Polish industry, as a result of which it is often simpler for a firm to hire a scientist away from his/her university than to commission sponsored research. Again this successfully surfaced for discussion through the modified action learning process, but the discussions were not able to provide any clear solution in the time available. Though the problem may still ultimately prove intractable, this would suggest that more time needs to be allocated to it than we were able to give on this occasion.

Results of the School

The results of the School were evaluated in two ways. First, a satisfaction questionnaire was administered by the Polish organisers: the results of this questionnaire indicated a high degree of participant satisfaction, as already noted above.

Second, the potential learning effects of the School were evaluated by means of pre- and post-tests. These tests were designed to elucidate the participants' levels of confidence in their abilities at each stage of the fund raising and funding management process on arrival at the School and again immediately before leaving. 21 items were involved in all, and the items were scored on a 1–5 Likert scale where 1 was "not at all confident" and 5 was "very confident." The overall results are summarised in Table 1.

TABLE 1.
Pre- and Post-Test Results

Item	Pre-Test		Post-Test	
	Mean	Mode	Mean	Mode
	(n=35)		(n=25)	
Knowledge of the range of funding sources that exist	2,4	2	3,6	4
Knowledge of Polish funding sources	2,71	3	3,68	4
Knowledge of funding sources outside Poland	2,29	2	3,44	4
Knowledge of which funding sources are appropriate for my particular project	2,54	2	3,28	3
How to locate an appropriate funder	2,11	3	3,36	3
How to make initial contact with the funder	2,37	2	3,68	4
How to follow up the initial contact with the funder	2,46	2	3,76	4
How to match a funding application to the funder's requirements	2,69	3	3,72	4
How to locate an appropriate research or development partner for a joint funding application	2,23	2	3,08	3
How to design and write a preliminary funding application	2,57	2,5*	3,28	4
How to design and write a detailed funding application	2,57	3	3,32	4
How to organise a funding budget	2,49	2	3,28	4
Knowledge of the stages a funding application goes through	2,17	2	3,64	4
Knowledge of what to do at each stage	2,11	3	3,44	4
Knowledge of what to do if the application is rejected	2,14	2	3,92	3
Ability to solicit funds from or obtain work with industry	2,03	2,5*	2,88	3

How to organise a longer term fund raising campaign	1,6	1	3,48	3
Who to approach for donations to such a campaign	1,66	2	3,16	3
How to make approaches for fund raising donations	1,77	2	3,24	3
How to market the institution's services to clients, students &c	2,29	2	3,24	3
How to manage the funds once they have been acquired	2,54	2	3,48	4

* equal scores on 2 and 3

These results demonstrate clearly that a considerable rise in participant confidence occurred while attending the School. In the pre-test, all
item means were below the mid point of the scale, ranging from 1.6 to
2.9. Modes (the scores checked by the largest number of participants)
ranged from 1 to 3.

In the post-test, by contrast, all means gained substantially: only one
item mean (for confidence about working with industry) now fell below
the mid point, the remainder ranging from 3.08 to 3.92. Modes were
entirely in the range 3 and 4. More importantly still, seven of the modes
showed a score gain of 2, and only one mode (on confidence on how to
locate an appropriate funder) showed no gain at all.

8. Conclusions

One of the persistent problems with the applications of action learning to conventional academic situations, as we have seen, is how to reconcile Revans' preference for Q-friendly situations such as set discussions with the P-dominated modes that are typical of traditional academic
learning. In the original ISSED design we developed a solution to this
problem based on the principle of a 50/50 split between conventional
academic material and set or interest group work, with the set work starting early in the meeting and given "prime time" scheduling. This solution effectively proved itself within the ISSED environment, and could
be applied with equal success to the Kassel and – with a slightly reduced
proportion of set work to presentations – to the Omani meetings. The
latter meetings, however, underlined the need for making sure that the
set groups had real motivation for coming and staying together – real
bonding through group dynamics and a sense of a real or realistic prob-

lem to be solved.. Ways of ensuring this were special to each event, and had to be specially thought out and designed for each occasion.

The Kassel and Omani seminars also highlighted a set of principles to do with linguistic mentorship, cultural permission, and presentation pacing, that seem to be of general application as atmosphere creators in particular in cross cultural or multilingual action learning applications. The Kassel seminars additionally highlighted the extent to which the dominant academic culture has to be favourably disposed to action learning at a high organisational level, as well as at the level of the set participants, if applications of action learning, no matter how successful "on the ground," are to survive in long term institutional practice.

In the case of the Warsaw Spring School this favourable disposition already existed, and this played a large part in the success of the meeting despite the fact that the time and logistical constraints on the school design were considerably more severe than in any of the other events quoted. Thus, given this good will, it is clear that the radical solution of treating the entire group of up to 55 participants as a single set can be a viable response to the problem, provided that an appropriate atmosphere is created initially by preliminary group work (a condition also implied by the Omani event) and maintained by careful selection of setting and facilities. The possibility of such a solution existing despite these constraints is itself a further indication of the robustness of Revans' original Action Learning concept.

References

Auspitz, J.L., Gasparski, W.W., Mlicki, M.K. and Szaniawski, K., eds. (1992). "Praxiologies and the Philosophy of Economics." *Praxiology* Vol. 1.

Denton, D. (1996). *Unpublished Personal Communication*, Glasgow.

Gibbs, G. (1992). *Improving the Quality of Student Learning*. Bristol: Technical & Education Services Ltd.

Ramsden, P. (1992). *Learning to Teach in Higher Education*. London: Routledge.

Revans, R.W. (1971). *Developing Effective Managers*. London: Longmans Green.

Revans, R.W. (1980). *Action Learning*. Wimbledon: Blond & Briggs.

Revans, R.W. (1984). "Address to 3rd ISSED Seminar." Newcastle-upon-Tyne.

Organisational Learning: A Case Study and Model for Intervention and Change

John E. Enderby,
Dean R. Phelan
and
Greg Birchall
Service Industry Advisory Group,
Victoria, Australia

1. Introduction

Organisational learning is a management concept that has been under examination since at least the writings of Burns & Stalker (1961) and Argryris and Schon (1978). Stata (1989) commented,

> organisational learning is the principal process by which management innovation occurs; the rate at which individuals and organisations learn may become the only sustainable competitive advantage, especially in knowledge intensive industries. (p. 64)

It has attracted renewed attention since the publication of *The Fifth Discipline: The Art and Practice of the Learning Organisation* by Senge (1990).

For Senge (1990) the learning organisation is one where,

> ...people continually expand their capacity to create the results they truly desire, where new and expansive patterns of thinking are nurtured, where collec-

tive aspiration is set free, and where people are continually learning how to learn together.(p.3)

There are five "disciplines" that Senge (1990) considers essential to the learning organisation:

1. Personal Mastery: "the discipline of continually clarifying and deepening our personal vision, of focusing our energies, of developing patience and of seeing reality objectively." (p. 7)
2. The surfacing of "Mental Models," described as, "deeply ingrained assumptions, generalisations, or even pictures or images that influence how we understand the world and how we take action." Often these mental models and their effect on behaviour is not apparent to those who hold them. (pp. 8–9)
3. Building Shared Vision. This is a leadership skill that involves the "unearthing of shared pictures of the future that foster genuine commitment and enrolment rather than compliance." Senge warns leaders against "trying to dictate a vision, no matter how heartfelt." (p. 9)
4. The discipline of Team Learning which starts with dialogue, "the capacity of members of a team to suspend assumptions and enter into a genuine "thinking together" and... "learning how to recognise the patterns of interactions in teams that undermine learning."

For Senge (1990) this is where "the rubber meets the road," for unless teams can learn, the organisation cannot learn. (pp. 9–10)

5. The so called "Fifth Discipline" for Senge (1990) is systems thinking, "a discipline for seeing wholes...for seeing patterns of change...the structures that underlie complex situations, and for discerning high from low leverage change." Furthermore systems thinking is the "cornerstone" that underpins all of the learning disciplines and of "how learning organisations think about their world." (pp.68–69)

In essence, for Senge (1990) a learning organisation is one "that is continually expanding its capacity to create its future." (p. 14)

2. This Study

The present study is a report on an extended case study of a large scale organisational change effort undertaken at Epworth Hospital, one of Australia's major private hospitals located in Melbourne, Victoria.

An attempt to create organisational learning was a key component of the reform agenda.

The overall purpose of the substantial re-engineering project was to position the hospital as a leading edge health-care organisation, at the forefront of patient care provision in the Asia Pacific region. The hospital developed a Vision Statement and articulated a number of core values in support of this Vision. These incorporated the following words *"Characterised by the most effective leadership, teamwork and management of resources, we will play a vital role in health-care management, education and research. ...We are continually learning and improving the way we do what we do, and how we present ourselves to the community."*

Two concepts were central in the change effort. First, the redesign of the hospital managerially and physically into four distinct patient care centres located in a purpose – built, $ 73 million building redevelopment designed to facilitate the concept of Focused Care.

The second was to increase the knowledge and skill capital within the hospital through the generation of organisational learning or to, in effect, re-create the hospital as a learning organisation.

The concept of Focused Care had been recommended to the top management of the hospital by external consultants from an international firm. "Focused Care" was a term used to describe a series of interventions designed to focus all activities in the hospital around care of the patient. Each process was mapped and evaluated in terms of how the patient would experience it. Where appropriate, systems, architecture, technology, organisational structures and processes were changed to ensure they were focused on optimum patient care and service delivery. The Chief Executive and members of the management team had visited sites in the USA where forms of Focused Care had been in place, and were sufficiently impressed, at least initially, to support the decision of the Chief Executive of the hospital to install a similar system in Australia.

This extended case study of the attempt to install Focused Care and to generate organisational learning within the hospital had a number of purposes. These were:

> To identify a clear and actionable definition of organisational learning that might help describe similar organisational change efforts in the future. (Garvin 1993).

To identify and describe the interventions that would be most effective and efficient in creating organisational learning.

To develop and refine a model for the identification, creation and management of organisational learning.

To make recommendations concerning best practice in attempts to create a learning organisation.

3. A Study in Praxiology

The study is essentially an illustration of praxiology (Gasparski & Ryan 1996) in its attempt to determine and describe those actions that would be most efficient and effective in the pursuit of organisational learning and the introduction of the Focused Care system into the hospital.

Furthermore it was hypothesised that the practice of action learning and the use action learning teams (Revans 1982), (Enderby & Phelan 1994) would be key interventions in the effort to bring about the required organisational change and to give practical effect to the theory or technique of organisational learning.

The study therefore was a systematic attempt to study the human actions necessary to bring about the change. In doing so, the study adhered to key elements of praxiology. It was concerned first with the identification of effective action. It undertook a close analysis of the key concepts and behaviours. It critically analysed actions taken during the change process to identify those factors and interventions that contributed most profoundly to the change. Finally it arrived at a set of recommendations to increase the efficiency of organisational change and the creation of organisational learning.

Research Methodology

The study is an extended case study of the organisation change effort in a major private hospital as it attempted to confirm itself as market leader in the region through the introduction and installation of Focused Care and the practice of organisational learning.

It addressed the research questions.

What is organisational learning?

How can it be defined in an actionable and readily understandable way?

What interventions are most effective in creating learning organisations?

How might organisational change efforts aimed at creating the learning organisation be understood and managed?

Data were gathered in three main ways.

1. Participant Observer Case Narrative

A case narrative based on the principles of the phenomenology of lived experience as described by Van Manen (1990), was created by the chief researcher who functioned as a participant observer in and of the change process at the hospital. The researcher lived with the project during the 1992–1995 period and constructed the narrative as the "story" of the organisational change process unfolded. This was a reflective process of observation, reflection and writing, as the researcher moved in and out of the action during the change effort. Analysis of the narrative resulted in the identification of recurring themes and recommendations for action.

2. Secondary Analysis of Survey Data gathered by and on behalf of the hospital management

As part of the change effort, systematic surveys were conducted across the hospital. (See Figure 1) .These measured changes in the level of satisfaction, attitudes and views of key stakeholders, e.g. patients, doctors, nursing staff and action learning teams over the course of the project. Data were gathered using surveys, checklist and questionnaire.

3. Tape Recorded Interviews with Hospital Managers

In depth interviews were conducted with twenty senior managers of the hospital to determine their perceptions of the change that was occurring and in particular their perceptions of organisational learning. The transcripts of interviews were analysed using the method of phenomenography developed by Marton (1986: 31) who described phenomenography as:

> a research method adapted for mapping the qualitatively different ways in which people experience, conceptualise, perceive, and understand various aspects of, and phenomena in, the world around them.

The conceptions of the phenomenon, in this case organisational learning, were then presented as categories of description. These categories were drawn from the data and no attempt was made to fit the data into pre-

FIGURE 1.
Patient Satisfaction surveys 1992–1994

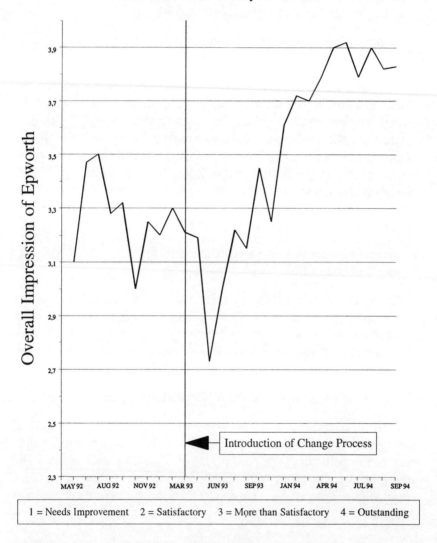

1 = Needs Improvement   2 = Satisfactory   3 = More than Satisfactory   4 = Outstanding

determined categories. The logically structured complex of the different ways of experiencing the phenomenon constitutes the "outcome space" of the object of research: i.e the essence of organisational learning.

Findings

An extensive literature search revealed the centrality of learning as an organisational imperative in the increasingly competitive business world and a vast array of definitions and perceptions of organisational learning.

Limerick and Cunnington (1993:202), for example, in their discussion of the use of the "Fourth Blueprint" in the management of "the new organisation" argued for the creation of a learning organisation and the management of the organisation "as an action learning community." This involves an organisational learning paradigm that is:

> Self reflective and can transcend and critique its own identity, values, assumptions and mission...one that is initiated and controlled by line managers themselves.

Further, in their view "action learning has the capacity to turn the reactive organisation into a learning organisation" (Limerick and Cunnington 1993:220) .This view parallels closely the findings of the present study.

Defining and Describing a Learning Organisation

As an outcome of the study the authors now define a learning organisation as :

> one which continuously monitors its performance and health, reflects on that data and then modifies its behaviour in the light of the knowledge gained, so as to ensure its long term survival and growth. A learning organisation is one that is continuously improving.

4. Categories of Description of Organisational Learning

The phenomenographic analysis of the transcripts of interview revealed a "wide meaning space" across the "categories of description" (Marton 1986). Initially six categories were identified and defined.

Organisational learning is :

– A process which occurs when the right levers are pulled (a mechanistic-instrumental view).

This emerged as the most basic view. It states that the end-result variable of organisational learning can be produced by manipulating other causal variables such as communication and leadership. This view is essentially a practical, linear perspective of what is required to produce results.

– A process of remembering and learning from what has happened in the past (an historical view).

This view states that organisational learning is determined by history, by remembered events that have been somehow codified and chronicled in a way that influence current thoughts, beliefs, and practices. Past events become significant when put in context. Experiences, stories, myths, legends and traditions are kept alive and shared. What has been learnt from past mistakes and successes determines the organisation's capacity to survive and flourish in its environment.

– A process of keeping focused on the vision even when faced with apparent chaos, dissonance and resistance (a no pain no gain view).

This view suggests that any planned change effort will be accompanied by instances of upheaval, chaos, resistance and dissonance. It acknowledges how difficult it is to foresee accurately all the problems involved in the change effort, the time needed (six months to two years) to iron out all the kinks, and for people to fully accept the new way. A resilience to disappointment, setbacks, conflict and attack is required, whilst at the same time maintaining an unswerving focus on the vision and a willingness to keep solving the issues that come up.

– The creation of a certain culture which emphasises learning and continuous improvement (a transformative-cultural view).

This view states that the most important avenue of change is culture or paradigm – a wide belief that organisational learning occurs through the adherence to a common set of beliefs and core values. It is a mindset which says that if culture is "the way we do things around here" a learning culture means "what we do around here is learn; we learn continuously and use our learning to improve everything we do." The values and beliefs of people, described by Dixon (1994:37–39) as "accessible meaning structures" enable the collective culture to form (see also Dixon 1995). These beliefs and values, including those flowing from the edges of the organisation, are valued and directly influence the behaviour of the organisation.

– A process of questioning of assumptions, mission, values and norms (a critically-reflective view).

This view is radical in the sense that it involves the questioning of the prevailing operating norms and values of the organisation. It is a more fundamental view than the other categories because it challenges deep set beliefs and assumptions. The consequences are the modification or reframing of beliefs and norms via a regular process of intensive scrutiny. It involves a constant "why?" aspect in reflection and discussion. This process is accelerated when the leadership group develops and practises a climate of candour, openness and freedom to "tell it like it is."

– A process of creating, capturing and "hardwiring" new knowledge and skills into the systems and process of the organisation. (a hardwiring – circuitry view)

This view states that learning is best achieved by a process of physically changing things to incorporate what has been learned, e.g. systems, technology, policies, procedures, job redesign etc. Actions that remain isolated seldom take hold. Hardwiring of learning most often occurs when structures (the "circuitry") are adjusted to support action. Then the action becomes part of legitimate and ongoing practice. Organisational action flows according to the rewired circuitry. Hardwiring enables recruits to learn more quickly as they can operate with more effective processes and can more effectively access the knowledge of the organisation.

5. Two Dimensions of Organisational Learning

Further analysis of the interview transcripts and categories of description outlined above, revealed two critical dimensions that are at once both essential and reciprocal if sustained organisational learning is to occur.

1. The Personal-collective Dimension of Organisational Learning

Viewed from this perspective organisational learning consists of something individuals or groups within the organisation do, or have done to them, in order to improve the knowledge and skill capital of the organisation, and in doing so create sustainable competitive advantage.

This is largely a management education and training function aimed at increasing individual and collective learning within the organisation. It is a view similar to that put by Senge (1990) and Kim (1993). As individuals or groups within the organisation get better at reviewing mental models, systems thinking, or whatever, as a result of training or experience, the incremental efforts of these individuals and groups transforms the organisation into a learning organisation.

There were several "Executive retreats" for management staff held during the period of the study where attempts were made to educate and train them in the necessary leadership skills. This form of organisational learning is a result of, and dependent upon, the knowledge and skill capital gains of groups and individuals within the organisation.

However, these may not be sustained unless deliberate and systematic measures are taken to capture and hold the learning within the organisation. Such measures are described in dimension two.

2. The Structural-cultural Dimension of Organisational Learning

Viewed from this second perspective, organisational learning consists of ways of recasting the structures (physical and organisational), values, and culture in order to increase, capture and retain the knowledge and skill capital of the organisation.

This is largely a re-engineering function which may be achieved by such strategies as flattening the structure, the creation of management and self directed working teams, opening the information flows, the appointment of trainers and knowledge managers, installation of up to date management information and data processing networks such as Lotus Notes and valuing and rewarding learning within the organisation. In the present study, some of the interventions designed to bring about and capture organisational learning were:

– the construction of a specially designed building,
– the introduction of computers at the patient bedside,
– the creation of critical care paths to guide patient treatment and care,
– an organisational restructure, resulting in four operational care centres rather than the traditional functional divisions such as nursing,
– the use of pilot studies,
– the introduction of new roles such as a multi-skilled Patient service associate, rather than the traditional separate cleaner, food service assistant, orderly, and lifter roles,
– the formation of action learning teams,
– in -house journals to disseminate ideas and learning.

However, both the dimensions of personal-collective and structural-cultural are essential for the creation of a learning organisation. The relationship between the two dimensions is both reciprocal and symbiotic. To emphasise one without the other will be unbalanced and ineffective, leading to what Senge (1990:17) termed an organisational "learning disability."

6. Hardwiring the Learning

It has been argued that both of the above dimensions are essential to the creation and retention of organisational learning within an organisation. Analysis of the case narrative in particular, however, highlighted the clear need to capture and retain learning outcomes within the organisation as they occur so that, over time, knowledge and skill-capital is increased and competitive advantage is built and sustained. In the organisation under study several "learning deficits" resulted when knowledge and skill was lost to the organisation as a result of key figures resigning or, in one tragic instance, one person died. To describe the essential process of capturing and retaining organisational learning outcomes within the organisation we have used the term or metaphor "hardwiring."

Hardwiring is defined as any means of inculcating or ingraining any organisational change or learning outcome into the structure, systems and processes of the organisation so that it becomes a regular and invariable element of the operations of that organisation.

Hardwiring may be achieved by adding documentation or computer programming into management information systems. It may also be achieved by creating new positions, new roles, divisions or departments to ensure that the process occurs. It may involve redesigning jobs, forms, policies, procedures, suppliers, buildings, outsourcing and so forth. In the case of Epworth hospital the most dramatic form of "hardwiring" was the creation of a specially designed $ 73million building to ensure that Focused Care became an invariant part of the hospital's patient management system.

Seen in this way knowledge and learning become the greatest assets of the organisation, rather than, as is often claimed,"our people are our greatest asset." The experience of this study has shown that people leave organisations and often take their skills, knowledge and the value they add to the organisation with them. When this happens temporary or even permanent learning deficits are likely to occur which delay the organisational learning process. Hardwiring then is the capturing of new knowledge, skills and learning and ingraining them into the very fabric and processes of the organisation before the learning is lost.

7. The Enderphel Model
and the Key Role of Action Learning Teams

Organisational change in a rapidly changing environment is a complex and at times confusing phenomenon. Because humans are involved it is also at times highly emotionally charged. Under these conditions it is often difficult for participants and change managers to maintain a grasp of just where the project is and to where it is headed.

To this end, the Enderphel Model for Organisational learning was created and refined in the study to provide a framework and road map for charting and planning the charge. It is to be noted that Action Learning teams are a central feature of the model and these proved to be a key intervention in the change effort in the hospital.

8. Components of the Enderphel Model
for Organisational Learning

The model is anchored by a shared vision for the organisation, together with a shared view of the current reality, both defined by customers' / stakeholders" expectations.

Leadership is the driving force, together with action learning teams, leading to innovation and systems reengineering. The leadership and action learning teams pick up the personal – collective dimension of organisational learning, and the hardwiring and systems reengineering are the structural – cultural dimension of organisational learning.

Each component of the model is outlined below. With this approach to learning, organisations will be better able to adapt to changing environments and sustain competitive advantage through acquiring and building on new knowledge, ideas and innovation.

Leadership

Leadership is the driving force that coalesces the vision, models the values and creates the energy and momentum for transition to occur. Leadership defines where we are, where we need to be, and creates a positive tension between the two. Leadership comes not only from those in formal positions but more importantly from those who feel passionate about what the organisation is trying to achieve and are prepared to do something.

FIGURE 2.
The Enderphel Model of Organisational Learning

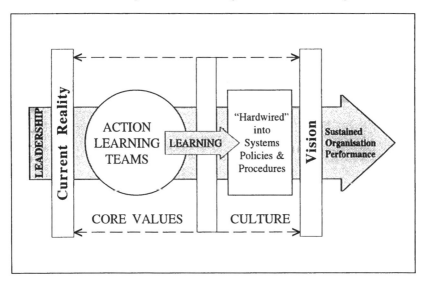

Mission and Vision

The study highlighted the importance of the guiding mission and vision in the learning process. The mission defines why we exist and the vision defines what we want to be like.

Without a dream there is no point in learning. They become the motivation and anchor points for learning. A shared vision is a

> force in peoples' hearts, one of impressive power. It is not an idea ... it is palpable. People begin to see it as if it exists. Few, if any, forces in human affairs are as powerful as a shared vision (Senge 1992: 206).

Current Reality

As the organisation starts to take hold of the vision, it simultaneously needs to gain a clear, unambiguous and shared understanding of where it is in relation to the vision. Both internal and external data are required eg financial position, human resources position, marketplace position, quality position and so forth. Comparisons with competitors, key performance indicator trends, and best practice processes, are examples of how an honest appraisal of the organisation's current reality can be gained.

Action Learning Teams

In this study Action Learning Teams were the mechanism for the organisation to learn and for the knowledge to translate into improved systems and processes. The teams became the vehicle for problems to be solved and for the individuals to collectively learn.

Revans (1979) describes action learning as a process where people come together to "learn from and with each other." They try out new ways of doing things relevant to a specific issue or project. They observe and reflect upon what happens, learn from it and make appropriate changes. It is an intentional process of learning from actions taken. It is a way of moving forward when the answers are not known – a situation that people and organisations commonly find themselves in.

The major resources that any manager has are his/her experience and knowledge of the work situation. Learning consists mainly in new perceptions of what they are doing and in their changed interpretations of their past experiences. It is not any fresh program of factual data, of which they were previously ignorant but now have at their command, that enables them to surge forward. Rather, it is through insight gained through sharing of experience and experimentation.

In this study it was found that those action learning teams who were deliberate and conscientious in trying to put the Learning Wheel into practice, worked best.

Some of the behaviours which the study identified as helpful to teams in accelerating their learning are:
- Establishing trust between team members
- Sharing and comparing insights
- Free flow of valid information
- Exposing and defusing defensive routines (Argyris 1991)
- Balancing enquiry with advocacy
- Distinguishing espoused theory from theory in use (practice)
- Distinguishing assumptions from facts
- Asking why
- Balancing divergent thinking (brainstorming) with convergent thinking (decision- making)
- Writing up of critical events and discussing them

FIGURE 3.
Action Learning Wheel

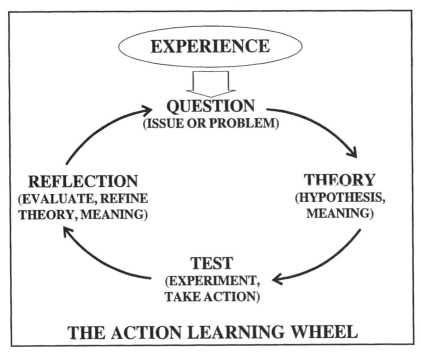

THE ACTION LEARNING WHEEL

Customer Focus

Every organisation was created, and continues to exist, to serve some sort of need. The assessment of current reality and formulation of vision both pivot of an understanding of current and future customer needs. Sustained organisational performance and learning are dependant upon having meaningful data to show how well the organisation is servicing its customers' needs. This focus also applies to internal customers. Albrecht (1990) emphasised this point when he said that you are either directly serving a customer, or serving somebody who is. Otherwise the purpose and value of your role should be seriously examined.

The organisational change effort documented in this study resulted in a strong positive effect on patient perceptions of care and service.

9. Conclusions and Recommendations

Survey data clearly reveal increased levels of patient satisfaction at the hospital. As this was a major goal the charge effort can be judged positively.

Time will tell as to whether this will leverage and maintain the hospital into a position of market leadership and recognition in the Asia Pacific region. This will be revealed in occupancy levels and bottom line results into the future. To date, some four years since the change effort first began, the results have been encouraging – occupancy has been strong and the hospital is regarded as one of the finest in the South Pacific area.

A range of perceptions of organisational learning were identified among the participants in the change process. However despite the claim to be "continually learning and improving the way that we do what we do" enshrined in the hospital vision statement and an apparent desire on the part of top management for the institution to be recognised as a learning organisation, there was little evidence of a highly developed conceptual grasp among the participants in the process. Certainly there was little or no evidence in any close way of Senge's Fifth Discipline, of systems thinking (Senge 1990).

Perceptions ranged from an instrumental – "pull the right levers view" to a more radical questioning of assumptions, values and mission. If anything these extremes parallel what Argyris called single and double loop learning (Argyris & Schon 1978).

The study indicated however that change managers and management educators need to consider both the individual-collective and the structural-cultural dimemsions in order to achieve enduring organisational learning outcomes.

Such outcomes should be hardwired into the structures and process of the organisation before the learning is lost. This makes the organisation less dependent on the continuing presence of key figures within the organisation.

Change managers should employ a wide repertoire of interventions in pursuit of organisational learning. Among these the introduction action learning teams is likely to result in positive learning outcomes.

Change efforts are best managed with reference to an organisational change model. In this study the ENDERPHEL Model for Organisation Learning proved to be a valuable guide to action. It is important also to create time and space for reflection on action within the change process in order to maximise the organisational learning outcomes. Unfortunately, however creating time for reflection and even reverie appears to run counter to the "can do" ethos of many organisations. The experience of this case study also showed that creating experiments and pilot studies before embarking on the main change will save time and effort in the long term. Finally it is important to gather data on the change, share this across the organisation and use it to periodically check on the current reality in relation to desired outcomes.

References

Albrecht, K. R. (1990). *Service Within: Solving the Middle Management Leadership Crisis.* Illlnois: Homewood.

Argyris, C., & Schon, D. (1978). *Organisational Learning: A Theory of Action Perspective.* Reading, Massuchusetts: Addison-Wesley.

Burns, T., & Stalker, G.M. (1961). *The Management of Innovation.* London: Tavistock.

Dixon, N. (1994). *The Organisational learning Cycle: How can We Learn Collectively.* London: McGraw Hill.

Dixon, N. (1995). "Reflections on the Relationship between Organisational Learning and the Democratic Organisation." In *Australian Systems Thinking and Organisational Learning Group (ASTOLg)* Volume 2 Issue 3 (September 1995).

Enderby, J.E., & Phelan, D.R. (1994). "Action Learning Groups as the Foundation for Cultural Change." *Asia Pacific Journal Of Human Resources* 32(1).

Garvin, D., (1993). "Building a Learning Organisation." In *Harvard Business Review* (July/August 1993).

Gasparski, W. & Ryan, L. (1996). *Praxiology : International Annual of Practical Philosophy and Methodology, Volume 5.* New Brunswick, NJ : Rutgers – The State University of New Jersey.

Kim, D. A. (1993). "The Link between Individual and Organisational Learning." In *Sloan Management Review* (Fall 1993).

Limerick, D., and Cunnington B. (1993). *Managing The New Organisation,* Business and Professional Publishing Sydney.

Marton, F. (1986). "Phenomenography: A Research Approach to Investigating Different Understandings of Reality". *Journal of Thought* 21(3):28–49.

Revans, R. W. (1979). *Action Learning.* London : Blond and Briggs.

Revans, R. W. (1982). "The Enterprise as a Learning System." In Revans, R.W. *The Origins of Action Learning.* London: Chartwell Bratt.

Senge, P. M. (1990). *The Fifth Discipline: The Art and Practice of the Learning Organisation.* New York: Doubleday Currency.

Senge, P. M. (1992). *You Can't Get There From Here: Why Systems Thinking is Inseparable from Learning Organisations.* Michigan Institute of Technology.

Van Manen, M. (1990). *Researching Lived Experience: Human Science for an Action sensitive Pedagogy.* State University of New York Press.

The Relevance of Action Learning for Business Ethics: Learning by Solving Ethical and Praxiological Dilemmas in Business

Wojciech W. Gasparski
Research Group for Ethics
in the Economy and Business,
Institute of Philosophy and Sociology,
Polish Academy of Sciences,
Warsaw, Poland

1. Introduction

Among the numerous dilemmas connected with business activity, businessmen encounter praxiological and ethical ones. The praxiological dilemmas concern the relationship between the means and ends of economic actions and the effectiveness and efficiency of these actions. The ethical dilemmas are connected with the moral dimension of behaviors in the economy and business. The principal praxiological and ethical dilemmas are grouped in types depending on the causing underlying these dilemmas. This paper[1] describes some kinds of dilemmas encountered in economic life, namely: dilemmas of the patent and latent system of values, dilemmas of attitudes, role, the goal and the means, dilemmas of the time horizon, and dilemmas of auto- and heteronomy. Solving the dilemmas in practice is the way to learn how to overcome them and this is why the inclusion of the paper to the volume on Action Learning is fully justified.

> The essence of action learning is to extract from the *new* task itself a sustainable desire to know what one is trying to do, what is stopping one from doing it, and what resources can be found to get it done by surmounting what seems to stand in the way. (Revans 1980: 287).

Since the subject-matter of this paper are problems connected with ethical and praxiological dilemmas in business, at the outset we should define what we mean by the word *dilemma*. We have to do with a dilemma in a situation when it becomes necessary to make a difficult choice between two different alternatives. Consequently, we are not going to examine all aspects of business ethics but only some problems which cause difficulties because they require making a difficult choice. Moreover, we are not interested in choosing between good and bad, because as a rule there are no problems in choosing the good; the problem arises when we have to choose between two possibilities (alternatives), each of which is both good and bad in its own way. Then the question is: "Which of these possibilities should be chosen?"; and we know that we have to make a choice. This is a *compulsory situation*, one in which refraining from making a choice would make matters worse. The complexity and compulsory nature of the situation creates difficulties. This question is the main topic of this conversation.

Why a conversation and not a paper? Well, because I would like to invite you to participate in the attempt to identify the reasons for ethical and praxiological dilemmas in business. Participation is the very method of Action Learning. I thereby want to call your attention to the fact that the reasons inhere in us, not as a collectively but in each of us as an individual, for each of us has something else in mind when referring to ethical behavior in the positive sense. Let us show this on the following example.

I'm going to ask you to choose one of the possible answers listed to the question "What do you regard as ethical?" Let us note that *what* somebody says isn't important; what is important is *the point of view of each of us* for recognizing something as deserving the adjective "ethical."

What do you regard as ethical?
1. What is legal;
2. What is consistent with your religion;
3. What is consistent with the principle "do unto others as you would have them do unto you";
4. What brings the greatest good to the greatest number of people;
5. What is consistent with the normal behavior of people in our country;

6. What is in your interest;

7. What you feel is right.

Now, dear reader, I'm going to ask you to stop reading this text and note your answer on the margin of the page.

We will examine the answers to the question a little later.

Before doing so, let us take up the answer to another question, namely: "Is business morally neutral or morally suspect? Or perhaps it is neither?

2. Business and Morality

Let's start by recalling that business people in Poland express two different views on the sense of practicing business ethics *hic et nunc*. Some say that perhaps business ethics is worth practicing, although not everybody who holds such a view utters it with strong conviction. Other people believe that business ethics is not worth pursuing, at least as long as Polish business is still unseasoned. We should wait – they say – until it grows wings and not hamper its development with moralizing in the style of Mrs. Grundy.

Views on the interrelationships between business and morality – not only in Poland – may be reduced to three lines of argumentation:

According to the first one, business is amoral, that is, it is independent of morality, and no relationships between economic life and morality occur. Amoral means "free from," "morally indifferent." This view reduces business in particular and economic activity in general to technical skills, more precisely to the praxiological (technical in the sense of efficacy of actions) skills of achieving success.

The view on the "zero morality" of business is professed despite the fact that we all know that every transaction, even the most trivial one, requires a minimum of honesty and trust. What is more, even the most advanced technology, including praxiological technology, is not guarantee in itself of high quality of products and services. An additional condition of high quality is solid workmanship and satisfaction from work well done. This has even been given the special name of "total quality management."

To express this thought to the end, there is no possibility of carrying out any organized action without "social chemistry" in the form of ethical ties between members of an organization. This hold true irrespective of whether the actions of the organization are assessed positively or negatively by the community at large. To be more clear let me use a negative example: It would be impossible to commit even a reprehensible act, e.g., a tax offense on the part of some firms, if the heads of these firms and their accountants did not act in collusion. This means that they are guided by their own local "morality." If you have read Dickens, you will remember his descriptions of thieves' morality. They, too, have their morality, which – of course – is not recognized by society that sets taxes. Here is a positive example: The discovery of an offense requires honest behavior on the part of tax inspectors, their loyalty to the Tax Office and not to the accountant of the audited firm, who may be a good neighbor from the same stairwell.

Consequently, it is a practical mistake to leave out the ethical dimensions of actions connected with economic life for supposedly praxiological reasons.

Why? For on the one hand society says: The local morality of those pursuing their interests in the gray zone of the economy is not a valid morality, because we the society do not approve of it. On the other hand, some members of the same society are guided by a local morality. But in order to speak of this explicitly, in order to identify various local moralities, we must turn to business ethics. Without this, knowledge about the norms governing economic activity would be based on fallacious mudslinging, suppositions or tales people like to tell in trams, buses or when visiting relatives (the aunt who acts like Mrs. Grundy) on birthday parties: "They're stealing!!" There are always some "they" about whom there is such talk.

Another view concerning the relationship between business and morality is unequivocally hostile towards business, even though it is sometimes uttered by some businessmen (or perhaps for that reason?). This view says that business is fundamentally immoral, at least in the initial phase of pursuing it (making one's first million), and that this is its characteristic feature. It is argued that on account of its ruthlessness the market is immoral; the market favors the stronger players, who are not necessarily the better ones. In other words, business is a jungle in which the stronger prevail over the weaker. We have to do here with a forbidden anthropomorphism of the market, assigning human attributes to it, namely, the capacity for good or bad behaviors, in this case – bad ones. What is more, attributing the value "better" to other criteria than market ones and then blaming the market as such ("the carpenter goofed, but they hung the blacksmith").

Let us note here that even those who say that it is too early to cultivate business ethics believe that on holidays one should get dressed in one's Sunday clothes. For them business ethics is something for holidays; it is something like an elegant business suit. However, today – they say – when we are working hard to build the foundations of business, we put on our overalls (even if they are in the form of a Pierre Cardin suit) because we might get dirty (*see* "dirty money"), and we don't intend to dirty our ethical suit. We pack it in moth-balls and store it away for better times.

Now, it isn't true that ethics is a suit of Sunday clothes. Ethics is a garment thrown over the realities of human activity. Ethics is reflection on people behaviors; and people's behaviors are either moral or immoral or in some degree moral or in some degree immoral. From the praxiological point of view these behaviors are obviously either efficient or inefficient, but in addition to this they are moral or immoral irrespective of whether anyone views them in this way – for they are such by their very nature! Ethics, on the other hand, enables us to speak about them in moral categories, it enables us to call a spade a spade, to take up a discussion on the matter in question, *to recognize* whether given actions are moral or immoral in respect of the accepted norms. Moreover, it enables us to perceive the richness of norms and thus the multiplicity of value judgments.

Now we can describe the third position, one held by those who believe that *honesty is the best policy,* a principle attributed to Benjamin Franklin (Ossowska 1985). According to this view, all human actions, economic ones in particular, are governed by values recognized by the actors. Ludwig von Mises, the founder of the Austrian-American praxiological school, wrote about this. No one can impose his own standards of behavior on others, at least not over the longer run, because, being dependent on others, he must respect *their* norms or at least know them. It was not without reason that I asked you the question: "What do you regard as ethical?," because what each of us regards as ethical is connected with what we as people regard as ethical in our actions.

It would be highly desirable for this third point of view to become widespread in Poland (and any other country alike) for both ethical and praxiological reasons: virtue pays! In Poland at large, not only in Polish business or Polish economic life. For the business community is not the community of businessmen, but is a community in which institutions of exchange play an organizing role (Boulding 1985).

Now that we have agreed on the usefulness of business ethics and the need to cultivate it, let us examine the ethical and praxiological dilemmas with which economic life is fraught.

3. Dilemmas

3.1. It's neither white nor black. We will say – if we all have agreed that ethics is reflection on people's behaviors – that all behaviors are subject to valuation, that from the praxiological point of view we assess these behaviors as efficient or inefficient, effective or ineffective, while from the moral point of view we speak of moral or immoral behaviors. A praxiological as well as ethical dilemma arises not when we have to do with a bipolar division: "white – black," "cold – hot," "efficient – inefficient," "moral – immoral." The dilemma appears when we have to do with actions which are "more or less efficient," "efficient but immoral"; "to a certain degree efficient – to a certain degree moral," "from a certain point of view moral – from another point of view immoral." In other words, when we have to do with actions which have their pluses and minuses, actions which are hard to put into white or black, positive or negative pigeonholes. Among such situations we will discuss the most important ones, namely, dilemmas of the manifest and latent system of values, dilemmas of attitude, dilemmas of the goal and means, dilemmas of the time horizon, dilemmas of auto- and heteronomy.

3.2. The dilemma of the manifest and latent system of values. The manifest system of values is a system which is publicly professed. It is a public declaration that "these and these" values, "such and such" a manner of behavior is good. Latent systems of values are the ones which direct our real behaviors. If a manifest ethical system contains elements which are not adapted to the social system in which it appears, people will act in conformity with the latent ethical system.

The manifest ethical system in the political order which previously existed in Poland was the system of so-called "socialist morality," which had little in common with the latent system according to which most Poles acted. This previous manifest system lost because it had no support in the values of the latent, real ethical system. One of the reasons for the decline of political systems and organizations is that the latent systems of values, behaviors, organization of social structures take precedence over what is manifest, what is officially declared but which is incongruous with people's real actions. Social dynamics depend largely on the degree of tension between the manifest and latent ethical system. The greater the tension, the more irresistible the ideals, the greater the dynamism. On the other hand, a "society with ideals that match its possibilities remains in stagnation" (Boulding 1985).

The institutions of such exchange as take place in the market by themselves do not generate control, nor do they cause the assimilation (internalization) of moral values thanks to which they values could be preserved. The fact that I exchange something with someone hardly makes me better. The exchange itself does not have such an effect, though it unquestionably organizes society more efficiently than other factors.

It might seem that there is nothing more noble than sports. Sports should release nothing but positive qualities! But what happened at one of the stadiums in Warsaw in 1997? Was there anything positive about that? What happened in Heysell several years ago? Where are the positive outcomes? There are none. And yet athletics are a kind of activity based on rivalry between people, which is a certain kind of exchange. It turns out that the "sports attitude" as a model of the manifest ethical system by itself does not evoke such an attitude in the fans sitting in the stands.

Kenneth E. Boulding notes that a society which devotes a disproportionally large part of its life and energy to a system of exchange may eventually undermine this system. On the other hand, an overly large system of compulsion, that is, the law, its guardians, police of various kinds, the excessive interference of this compulsion in the system of exchange may bring about the disintegration of moral life, even the disintegration of society. For one does what one must and not what one wants to, or one does what one wants to but not what one ought to do. This gives rise to a conflict between what the manifest system tells us to do and what we ourselves in fact avow and what enters into the domain of the latent system. How should one behave in such situations? "The manifest or latent system of values: the choice is up to you" the ministry of spiritual health might say (imitating warnings on cigarette boxes), if such an institution existed. But this would have an Orwellian flavor. That is the background of the dilemma of the manifest and latent system of values.

3.3. The dilemma of attitude. The matter here concerns our attitude, the attitude of people, of each and every one of us, not some abstract attitude. In this connection, two thesis may be put forward after Kenneth E. Boulding:

- In a person whose life is spent exclusively among accounting books and who concentrates all of his attention on the details of economic life and an organization, the internalization of the basic virtues of honesty and dependability are gradually weakened.
- A system of exchange almost always afford individuals the opportunity of gaining individual benefits by sacrificing moral principles.

This is so for as long as the concentration on a book draws attention away from the whole picture, just as concentrating attention on minerals may blind one to the beauty of the Tatra mountains. By limiting ourselves to a "book" we become accountants of virtues.

As regards the second thesis, it suffices that I like some spoons lying on this table, why they are so pretty! Oh, how I could use such a spoon. I hide it in my pocket, no one will notice. Besides, what harm will there be to anyone if one spoon is missing? How many spoons every day disappear from so many restaurants?

But a spoon is only a symbol. The matter does not concern a spoon! Things disappear! This is so simply because we think like this: "Since I'm paying the bill in the restaurant and giving the waiter a tip, then something is also coming to me, if only a spoon." Someone else will not collect spoons but something else ("he that will steal a pin will steal an ox"). And so – let's be candid, at least with ourselves – that is how we behave. This is the dilemma of attitude.

The source of the dilemma of attitude is that moral principles are often too abstract and difficult to apply in specific situations. Whom do we value more – the dishonest industrialist who knows that he is doing, or the honest industrialist who doesn't know what he is doing? Or to bring the situation closer to the experience of life: To whom do we go when the need arises, to the crackerjack surgeon who carries out successful operations or to the bungler who does not take bribes? This is the dilemma of attitude.

3.4. The dilemma of role. Each of us appears on the stage of life as an actor of sorts who plays a role. Suppose I am delivering this paper to the audience gathered in the auditory of a Chamber of Commerce. At that moment, for example, in that auditory I was appearing in the role of a lecturer. They, the audience, were playing the role of listener, you, Madame, as playing the role of chairperson, and you, sir, the role of technical supervisor of our undertaking. But, at the same time, in our families we played, and still play, the role of father or mother, son, daughter, sister, brother; we also perform of the role of citizen of our country and many other roles simultaneously. We perform different roles in different periods of time. Different relationships, various roles occur between the roles we play.

Mr. (Mrs.) A and Mr. (Mrs.) B are performing some role and one says to the other: "Do what I ask of you, and if you don't you must expect serious consequences." The second man or woman replies: "If you carry out your threat and do something bad to me, I will give you back as good as I get."

Mr. (Mrs.) C and Mr. (Mrs.) D are performing different roles. Unlike the previous pair, they say to each other: "If you do what I ask of you, then I'll also do something nice for you." Here we have to do not with a threat, as in the first case, but with an exchange.

And finally, the third relationship, an integrative one, between roles, one persons says to the other: "If you want this, then I want it also."

A threat is not only a threat between roles in private life, a threat may also be institutionalized. For the legal system is based on a threat, and the policeman says: "Behave yourself, don't go through a red light at a crossing; in other words, do something nice for me, and if you don't, I'll give you a ticket, I'll do something bad to you." A similar exchange: "If you do what I want (if you do something nice for me)" – says a director to a subordinate – "then I'll give you a bonus (do something nice for you)." The integration is also institutionalized. In saying "I want what you want" we strike up friendships, we establish families, we create national, cultural and religious communities. These three types of relationships intervene in our lives. The dilemmas of role arise in this context.

Examples: (a) employees versus private person – on the one hand, "I" as an employee, on the other – "I" as a private person; (b) "I" in the role of employee, someone else in the role of manager; (c) "I" in two roles: I am both an employee and a manager; (d) sometimes I appear in the role of entrepreneur, sometimes as a client. These are all roles: entrepreneur – competitor, supplier – customer, petitioner – official, politician – citizen, partner – partner. The same person may appear in different roles, and different persons may also appear here.

I encourage you to think about this, even to write brief scenarios in which these roles appear. You will find that when you think about these roles, you will immediately see these three types of connections in various proportions – threat, exchange, integration – and the dilemmas arising from the conflict of roles.

3.5. The dilemma of goal and means. Here are two positions: According to the first position, "the goal justifies the means." It is argued: This goal is noble, I must do everything to achieve this goal, I must be effective, I must accomplish this goal. The goal justifies the means, for I am so convinced of the value of this goal that I am going to accomplish it. The justification for this position is the following: "After all, everybody behaves this way"; this is the so-called argument from common practice. What is the paradox involved here? Most people agree that the behavior of others is not the best criterion for individual decisions, but despite this people maintain that the behavior of their boss is the main reason for their unethical behavior. ("For I am an employee of this firm, and since my boss acts this way, then I too must act this way, for where will I find another job? Am I supposed to be unemployed?!").

The second position, according to formulation of Tadeusz Kotarbiński, a Polish philosopher and praxiologist, states that the "goal does not justify the means, but only befouls them." In other words: If the goal is bad, then no means, even the most noble ones, will not improve the goal. If the goal is good, no means, even the worst ones, are worthy of being applied to attain this goal. There can be no conflict between the goal and the means. For while the means are instrumental, the means are also an intermediate goal. By bringing about a certain state of affairs, which is the means to accomplish another state of affairs, we are initiating a certain sequence of actions, and that is why the means applied (like the spoonful of birch tar in barrel of honey) destroys the goal.

What should become the norm is resourcefulness, effectiveness of actions towards a worthy goal. And both of these criteria must be taken into consideration: The goal must be worthy, and the means leading to its accomplishment must be both effective and not destructive.

The source of the dilemma of goal and means is what one may call the "illusion of single goals." In working for some firm we act so that our firm will make a profit. And this is our goal, but we should remember that, whatever we do, at the same time we are not 100-percent only actors on the stage of this firm. In addition to this (as we saw from the previous characterization of dilemma of role), we are also actors playing other roles, roles which also have other goals to accomplish. If we have other goals to accomplish, for example, if we want to bring up our children to be decent people, then in our behaviors in our jobs, in our business, in our economic life we should not give a negative example which would be counterproductive to fulfilling the role of parent. And if a situation occurs in which this conflict appears, we have to do with a joint dilemma of role and goal and means.

3.6. Dilemma of the time horizon. Many business people believe that the more precisely ethical behavior is defined, the more profit suffers. On the other hand, it is held that ethical behavior is consistent with maximizing profit over the long-term, even though in short periods profit may be gained by not observing moral principles. This is another dilemma encountered in doing business (Hartley 1993).

3.7. The dilemma of auto- and heteronomy. This is the dilemma between what is mine or individual (autonomy) and what is theirs or ours, that is, society's (heteronomy) .

Collectivist (heteronomic) ethics is based on the following assumptions:

- people are dependent on others,
- social values, for example, the durability of social structures, are more important than individual values,
- obligations to social organizations, firms, local communities, the nation, sate should take precedence over the obligation to the individual, and both of them over rights of the individual,
- the individual is only an instrument for the society and is supposed to serve society,
- the conflict of individual and social values is resolved in favor of social values.

The assumptions of individualistic ethics are the following convictions:

- people are autonomous, that is, they are dependent only on their own will,
- individual values, for example, freedom, hold a higher place than social values, for example, social justice,
- rights of individuals should take precedence over social obligations,
- society is only a means, an instrument for protection of the individual's rights,
- morality and law are created for individuals,
- the conflict of individual and social values is resolved in favor of individual values.

Mario Bunge, to whom we are indebted for a systematic exposition of the problem, proposed a so-called *systemic ethics* as an attempt to reconcile auto- and heteronomy (Bunge 1989). According to this philosophy, individuals are partially autonomous and partially heteronomous; individual and social values determine each other – for example, equality and mutual assistance (brotherhood); rights imply duties, and duties imply rights; the individual can exist only in society, whose organization should be designed in such a way that each person can satisfy his or her basic needs and justified aspirations; morality and laws and created for individuals living in society and not for an individual on an uninhabited island; although the conflict of individual and social values is resolved in favor of social values, social organizations ought to be designed in such a way as to minimize the frequency and intensity of conflicts of this kind (which belongs to the duties of those who pay the role of specialists).

4. Our Understanding of What Is "Ethical"

It is time to return to the question asked at the beginning: "What do you regard as ethical?" and compare the answers given by Polish participants of two seminars with answers of American respondents in studies conducted by R. Baumhart (Weber 1990):

No.	What do you regard as "ethical"?	Answers of Polish %		Answers from respondents American studies (Weber 1990) %
1	What is legal	7	0	0
2	What is consistent with your religion	7	3	25
3	What is consistent with the principle "do unto others as you would have them do unto you"	29	24	18
4	What brings the greatest good to the greatest number of people	36	9	3
5	What is consistent with the normal behavior of people in our country	7	0	3
6	What is in your interest	0	3	1
7	What you feel is right	14	61	50

Only 7% of the Polish respondents at one seminar and 0% at the second chose the first answer, which is similar to the position taken by Americans, namely, "what is legal" is not generally regarded as tantamount to "ethical." Surprisingly, 25% of the American respondents chose the second answer, "what is consistent with our religion," whereas at our Seminar, in a *par excellence* Catholic country, only 7 and 3 percent of the respondents did so. In America 18% of the respondents picked the third choice, "do unto others as you would them do unto you," but this answer was chosen by as many as 29–24% of the persons at our seminars. The fourth choice was the most popular among the seminars participants – "what brings the greatest good to the greatest number of people"; this view on what is "ethical" was expressed by more than one-third of the Polish respondents at the first seminar, but only by 3% of the American ones and 9 of the Polish respondents at the second seminar.

The fifth statement – "what is consistent with the normal behavior of people in our country" – is shared by a surprisingly small number of people in both countries – in the USA 3%, in Poland 7.0%. Even greater agreement appears in not accepting, or rejecting, the statement that "ethical" is "what is in your interest" – at our seminars 0.3%, in the USA 1%. On the other hand, only 14% of the participants of our first seminar in contrast to half of the Americans and 61% at Polish second seminar recognize "what you feel is right" as "ethical."

Thus at our seminars the predominant view that the "ethical" is synonymous with "what brings the greatest good to the greatest number of people" for older people who attend the first meeting and "what you feel is right" for young people who attend the second meeting and whose belief is similar to the Americans' one. Does this suggest the dominance of heteronomy among older members of the Polish society and the dominance of autonomous ethics in American society and among young members of the Polish society? In order to answer this question, a study would have to be conducted in Poland at a representative sample of the population and not among a small number of seminar participants.

After conducting such a study we will know what we regard privately, and not from books, as ethical behavior, as – to state it more correctly – "morally positive" behavior. Please observe that when we have to act, before we act we do not ask "what do I regard as ethical?," but we simply act. We act guided by the internal conviction of each of us, which has been shaped by the life history – biography – of each of us, by our knowledge, experiences, etc. Each of us behaves in conformity with what he or she regards as ethical and what (in the answer to the question) was indicated here.

The differences in views on what each of us regards as "ethical" are the reasons for the ethical dilemmas we encounter in economic life, in business, management and not only in professional activities. In private life as well, which the following event described by Moshe F. Rubinstein in his book *Patterns of Problem Solving* (1975) irrefutably illustrates.

> One summer my wife and I became acquainted with an educated well-to-do Arab named Ahmed [...]. Following a traditional Arabic dinner one evening, Ahmed decided to test my wisdom with his fables. One of them caught me in a rather awkward setting. "Moshe," he said as he put his fable in the form of a question, "imagine that you, your mother, your wife, and your child are in a boat, and it capsizes. You can save yourself and only one of remaining three. Whom will you save?" For a moment I froze, thoughts raced through my mind. Did he have to ask this of all questions? And in the presence of my wife yet? No matter what I might say, it would not be right from someone's point of view, and if I refused to answer I might be even worse off. I was struck. (p. 1)

Before I tell you what the American professor answered and how his Arabic colleague reacted to this, I want you to answer how *you* would behave in a similar situation. This is yet another opportunity to apply action learning approach.

If you have made a decision you may read continuation of the Rubinstein's story:

> ...So I tried to answer by thinking aloud as I progressed to a conclusion, hoping for salvation before I said what came to my mind as soon as he posed the question, namely, save the child.

> Ahmed was very surprised. I flunked the test. As he saw it, there was one correct answer and corresponding rational argument to support it. "You see," he said, "you can have more than one wife in a lifetime, you can have more than one child, but you have only one mother. You must save your mother!" (p. 1).

Here are the answers given by participants of the seminar I had in Poland: the mother – 14%, the wife – 28%, the husband – 6%, the child – 40%, we'll die together – 6%, "one doesn't ask such questions" – 6%. The vast majority chose the child. Whenever I ask this question, and I have done so many times – in Poland and in countries with a Judeo-Christian tradition – the answer is always the same – the child.

Whenever there were students from Arabian countries in my group, they always said "the mother" in response to the question whom they would save.

This anecdote is not an example that Arabs behave better and we behave worse or vice versa, but of the fact that in different cultures we are guided by different values. We believe that it is the weakest who must be helped, i.e., in this case the child, whereas in the Arabian countries it is believed that help must be extended to the one and only person, and the one and only person in our lives is our mother. In the Arabian countries the woman appears in two roles: in the role of a woman as a wife, concubine, member of a harem and in the role of a woman as mother, who is the matron and is above everyone else in the family. This is the difference in values to which I wanted to call your attention.

I respect the answer that "one doesn't ask such questions," and share the view that it is very hard to answer such questions, because it puts the respondent in a dramatic situation by facing him or her with a moral mirror in which the other members of the family are condemned to be drowned. But please note that in practice we have to do not with storms in the sense of sailing the oceans, but almost every day we encounter situations in which we have to save or not save other people, in which we have to help other people. Whom are we more willing to help, how do we behave in life in general and in economic life in particular? That is it why we should reflect on this and be honest with ourselves; we should answer the question and get to know what others think about this matter – that's the first thing.

Secondly, we should remember that the Austrian praxiologist Ludwig von Miscs (Ossowska 1986) clearly stated that praxiological rules are the foundation of people's economic behaviors. Economic behaviors are behaviors consisting in exchange. For each person, for each of us, actions performed by people in their microworlds are what has the highest value. We answered differently than the Americans to the question "what do you regard as ethical?" and differently than the Arabs to the question "whom will you save?" If we asked ourselves similar questions, we would see how greatly we also differ among ourselves. Let us remember that in everyday, practical situations in which we have to act, in which we very often are incapable of reflecting on how we ought to behave, but behave impulsively, quickly, on the spur of the moment (sometimes blurt out something for which we are later sorry), we act as we do on account of these differences, because these are our systems of values. Our behaviors are dictated by the system of values which we have internalized during our entire lifetime.

5. Business Ethics: Ethics of a Profession or Society?

In conclusion I would like to call your attention to one more dilemma that appears in connection with business ethics. This is the fundamental question which we must answer for ourselves. The answer may be important for those who are wondering "should we take up business ethics or not?" For the question is the following: is business ethics the ethics of a profession or the ethics of society? Is business ethics the ethics of a profession in the same sense as we speak of the ethics of a doctor, teacher, the ethics of a military man, or is it the ethics of society?

5.1. Business ethics is the ethics of a profession. The first position that "business ethics is the ethics of a profession" is expressed in the following three theses:

– Every firm must observe the code of elementary moral norms if it wants to win the confidence of partners and clients,

– Many firms are guided by the so-called code of professional behavior. In Anglo-Saxon terminology these are not ethical codes but only *codes of practice,* codes of practice are understood as rules of behavior set by professional associations and which are binding on members of a corporation in their business activities,

– The growing awareness that business ethics is a necessary condition for success in business has resulted in tying it with the efficacy and work organization of a firm (quality of its products and its profitability).

Given more or less equal, highly advanced manufacturing technologies, the quality of products offered by firms competing in the marketplace is comparable, is almost the same. How then can clients be won over? The clients should be won over by what is offered to them *above and beyond* this product – for which he comes and whose high quality he takes for granted – "something" which he does not expect. The *surprise* is the form. And the form is connected with business ethics, with the fulfillment of roles: salesperson – client, except that "as a salesperson I offer something more, I offer something extra, I offer a special service – such that You, dear customers, will never have to come to us with complaints, we will continue to be interested in how this equipment works, we will come to find out, we will ask."

Business ethics understood as the ethics of a profession receives its praxiological, financial dimension. It sells itself. The firm sells itself. "I like to go to this merchant. The service there is friendly." This is not, ladies and gentlemen, that traditional English "cheese" smile, where girls behind counters or shop assistants are taught to say "cheese" so that they would have a smiling face. It is not treating the customer deceitfully but treating him or her seriously. While it is not treating the customer like a lover treats his beloved, it is surely treating the customer like a good suitor treats the object of his affections. In other words, it is conducting business professionally.

5.2. Business ethics is the ethics of society. The second position takes a different approach and was expressed by Kenneth E. Boulding in the words: "Business ethics is the ethics of society."

The *society* in which business is conducted, in which the free market economy is pursued – is the business society. Consequently, business ethics is its ethics. Business ethics, according to this position, should not be reduced to the ethics of a profession, because business ethics encompasses all parties participating in the processes of exchange. Business is pursued for the sake of the client, but this client may be another businessman as well as someone from the street who is not a businessman.

Business ethics is the ethics of the business society, and the society of business is a social system which is organized in a certain way by the institutions of exchange, where the commodity, no longer with negative connotations, is everything. Education is even or first and foremost a commodity, because it offers knowledge as a commodity. Knowledge today is becoming the number one resource. Peter F. Drucker, an American author of numerous books on management, calls society in the developed countries a post-capitalist society or a society of information capitalism and not of financial capitalism (Drucker 1993). The reason is that knowledge is the primary resource, and those who have it are able to acquire the other three basic resources, i.e., money, natural resources and human resources. However, no society is a pure business society.

The condition for the duration of a society of business is the development of a system and integrative institutions, those which are connected with integration (for exchange itself will not ensure this integration).

Whatever undermines the institutions of exchange and its organizing force also undermines the business system. In other words, if someone says that we must "tinker" with the mechanisms of exchange, such a person undermines the business system. For here the principles must be clear and simple, measurable, as – one would like to say – in sports conducted according to the rules of fair play.

Second, there are certain individual systems of value which may undermine the institutions of exchange and are consequently a threat to the business system. For this reason it depends on individual systems of values (mine, yours, hers, his; and what they are) whether the institutions of exchange in Poland will be undermined or not. Boulding argues that capitalist institutions cannot function properly where "Puritan values" are completely absent. I would put this in the following words: In business – just as in the olden times one spoke of camp-followers and knights – here we have to do with *camp-followers and knights of business.*

What is dangerous is what could undermine the working of the system of the society of business, and this is the persuasion that business is controlled by the camp-followers. Those who say that this is not the time to take up business ethics are the camp-followers of business. The knight of business will not make such a statement. The ethics of the knight of business should give the tone in the society of business. The knightly ethos is the ethos to which Maria Ossowska (a Polish late professor of ethics) referred as a model, as a norm of behavior (Ossowska 1986). That is why for capitalism to work well what is important is not its ideology, which was used in Poland in the previous system to frighten us. Capitalism should be treated in the praxiological sense, i.e., as a system based on the use of a monetary measure. A system of exchange in which the measure is money, just as length is measured in meters, like time is measured in seconds, so the process of exchange is measured in monetary units. That is why our currency i.e. *złoty* cannot be made of elastic. (Let the ladies who go to dressmakers just imagine that the seamstress has an elastic measuring-tape, and stretches it to get one measure here and another measure there.) That is why inflation must be combated, for money must be the measure par excellence. There cannot be any tinkering with measures. Measures must be dependable, for otherwise we are going to mislead one another. Tinkering with measures is both anti-praxiological and unethical.

If capitalism is to work properly, society must have a defense mechanism against dishonesty such as "The Bureau for Legalization of Monetary Measures and Weights" – as I would call it. The independent national bank should play this role.

Finally, a minimum government and administrative structure is indispensable, for exchange by itself is not an adequate organizing factor. On the other hand, this structure should be confined to a minimum.

Here we must mention James McGill Buchanan, an American economist and winner of the Nobel prize for economics, author of a work on political decisions and the consequences of economic choices in the public domain. To simplify, the idea of this Noble prize winner can be summed up as follows: Politicians treat their functions as their businesses by running constant budget deficits. Consequently, their prerogatives must be restricted by constitutional regulations. For as long as a politician realizes his own goals in conformity with the social interest, everything is fine. But it is bad when there is a conflict, a conflict of roles, once again a conflict of roles!

For the above reasons it is important to reduce administrative structures to a minimum. On the other hand, as Boulding observes (Boulding, 1985): "Political conceptions and systems of values which are hostile to the indispensable governmental framework, even if they stem from the moral commitment to an economy based on exchange, in fact are harmful to such an economy."

The above authors adds that institutions of exchange by themselves do not adequately develop a system of integration, of friendship, of love and of all those various interpersonal relations based on emotions. If society and its activities are to have some sense for individuals, for every one of us, they must contain personal relationships which in their richness surpass relations of exchange. And only a whole composed in such a way may make up the society of business, that is, a society in which exchange is pursued on the basis of a scientific mechanism and which at the same time is guided by the ethical norms indispensable for being a society of business.

6. Instead of a Conclusion

You may ask me the following question: How can we the Polish people resolve the dilemma between the values of each of us as an individual and the norms which would enhance the society of business? Polish society may only be enhanced by a dialogue among all of us as carriers of different values, so that we may agree among ourselves on how the economy should work in Polish society so that this society has the chance of becoming a society of business in Boulding's understanding. This would be a contribution by each of us in creating a business society.

Without mechanisms of democracy for the articulation of the different values which each of us professes individually and without respect for the values of others or even an open criticism of these other values but with respect for the one who professes them as a person, there is no possibility of resolving this dilemma. On the other hand, this dilemma will never be resolved once and for all, because this is a process. And for this reason business ethics is worth taking up, because it provides us with a forum on which such and many other discussions may be conducted. And this is why action learning approach is needed. This stands not only for the Polish society but for other societies too.[2]

Notes

1. This paper is a revised version of the contribution to 9th European Business Ethics Network (EBEN) Annual Conference "Working Across Cultures," September 18–20, 1996, Frankfurt, Germany.
2. What really happened in Warsaw some time ago.
3. See Gasparski and Ryan 1996.

References

Collin P.H. et al., ed. (1991). *American Business Dictionary.* Teddington: Peter Collin Publishing.

Boulding, K.E. (1985). "Ethics in Business." In *Beyond Economy (Polish edition),* 59–69. Warsaw: PIW.

Bunge, M. (1989). "Treatise on Basic Philosophy." *Ethics* vol. 8. Dordrecht: Reidel.

Drucker, P.F. (1993). *Post-capitalist Society.* Oxford: Butterworth-Heinemann.

Gasparski, W.W. (1995). "Between Auto- heteronomy." In *A Man As a Citizen* (in Polish), edited by M. Szyszkowska, 47–57. Warsaw: ISP PAN.

Gasparski, W.W. & Ryan, L.V., eds. (1996). *Human Action in Business: Praxiological and Ethical Dimensions.* New Brunswick (USA) – London (UK): Transaction Publishers.

Hartley, R.F. (1993). *Business Ethics: Violations of Public Trust.* New York: Wiley.

Hitt, W.D. (1990). *Ethics and Leadership: Putting Theory into Practice.* Columbus: Battele Press.

Mises von, L. (1966). *Human Action: A Treatise on Economics.* Chicago: Contemporary Books.

Rubinstein, M.F. (1975). *Patterns of Problem Solving.* Englewood Cliffs: Prentice-Hall.

Ossowska, M. (1985). *Moralność mieszczańska (Middle-class morality,* in Polish). Wrocław: Ossolineum.

Ossowska, M. (1986). *Knight's Ethos and Its Types* (in Polish). Warsaw: PWN.

Revans, R.W. (1980). *Action Learning: New Techniques for Management.* London: Blond & Briggs.

Weber, R.A. (1990). *Management: Basic Elements of Managing Organizations* (cited after Polish edition, Warsaw: PWE).

Modifying Group Architecture to Manage Conflict – the Dance Card Technique, a Novel Methodology for Managing Group Dynamics

Gerald M. Levy
Liverpool John Moores University,
Liverpool, England

Any statement which holds that humans necessarily act
or believe in particular ways under particular circumstances
refers as much to the social scientist as anyone else.
Gruenberg

1. Introduction

This paper introduces a novel group architecture called Dance Card. Dance Card offers group facilitators an alternative technique for managing groups and avoiding or minimising a range of common problems including:
 – inappropriate leadership styles (for example bullying);
 – groupthink (where individual ideas converge due to the dynamics of the group) and
 – social loafing (individuals taking little or no part in the activity of the group).
The technique is discussed and placed within the context of the problems that are common in groups and teams.
The protocol of a Dance Card meeting is fully described and its application illustrated by a case study.

Most managers will be familiar with participating in groups and teams. Indeed, it seems that within management, the ability to be a "good team player" is as much a pre-requisite of the "good" manager as any of the more "hard" skills that dominate the hiaerarchy of management competencies, and that are taught with enthusiasm on MBA's world-wide. Unlike the 19th and early 20th Centuries when management was characterised by the "Great Man" (Buchmann and Huczynski 1986: 396–99) theory, since the second world war the predominance and dependence of groups and teams has become all persuasive. This western management style has been reinforced by the influence and perceived excellence of Deeming (Deeming 1986) and our understanding of Japanese management styles, for example, quality circles.

It would be foolhardy to suggest that team work is inappropiate to management, or that many problems are not best addressed by teams. The very complexity of business life dictates that many tasks can only be addressed by individuals working as a group. However, the idea that a number of people who meet together, even though they may have apparently common goals, will automatically (or even probably) produce a synergy, or even be able to work effectively together, is patently false to many of us who have been placed in such groups over the years.

Given this orientation away from individual towards group competencies, considerable effort has gone into improving manager's abilities to work in groups. Attempts to produce the "good" teams range from engineering groups within leadership training programmes to encompass the "appropriate" roles, using for example the Belbin model (Belbin 1981), to extensive training programmes addressing issues of awareness and sensitivity training. The debate as to whether individuals can have their behaviour modified to meet the needs of this management style continues apace. There is, however, another growing debate as to the validity of the former or effectiveness of the latter. In addition to this debate continuing, concern as to the morality of attempting to modify behaviour and attitudes raises important ethical questions.

This paper offers an alternative approach to the management of groups called Dance Card, which is radically different both in practice and philosophy. The Dance Card technique is in effect a protocol that modifies the very architecture of groups. It does not suggest ways of managing or modifying for example poor leadership, social loafing or group think, but rather seeks to eliminate or minimise these problems altogether. The question posed is: "Why modify behaviour to fit into a group structure, why not modify the group structure itself?" Dance Card has been influenced to no small degree by the work of Professor. Reg Revans (Revans 1980) on Action Learning. Perhaps given the influence Revans has had on management education in the U.K. in general and the author in particular this is not surprising. Like Action Learning, Dance Card encourages the development of people through the Revans concept of "Comrades in Adversity" and like Action Learning, Dance Card works best when people address real problems that impact upon their lives. Action Learning differs from many conventional forms of management development by not ascribing all wisdom to the "expert." In a similar vein Dance Card also does not place reliance on great expertise from a group facilitator, but, rather the very architecture of Dance Card is such that power and influence rests with the participant.

The Dance Card was first used in 1989 by the author as a desperate attempt to facilitate a somewhat difficult group situation (it is this case that is studied in some depth later in the text), since when it has been applied in over 30 group situations. This paper is its first exposure to the academic community.

It is not the author's intent to challenge perceived wisdom but rather to share with the reader the opportunity to consider an alternative.

2. Why Dance Card?

But let there be spaces in your togetherness.
And let the winds of the heaven dance between you
Kahlil Gibran

In the 18th, 19th and early 20th centuries society dances and social balls were conducted and controlled with considerable formality. This perhaps reflected the importance of order and protocol within society generally, and was to ensure order and propriety were maintained at all times. Such events were the subject of many protocols, an example would be the extensive use of Dance Cards. Ladies would possess a Dance Card which would list every dance scheduled for the Ball with blank spaces against each dance. Gentlemen would formally request their name be placed along one or more vacant slots, thus ensuring the presence and attention of their desired partner for at least some of part of the evening. Protocol, social pressures and norms prevented any other would be suitor from "cutting in" and, as a result, inclusion on a dance card would offer

partners an uninterrupted period within the evening. The process elimi-
nated much uncertainty for the ladies while at the same time allowing
them to control who interacted with them at a given time. It must be said
that although getting on a desired Dance Card offered opportunities to
the dancers, these were also subject to constraints also. It was accepted
that dancers would dance to the tune of the orchestra and would not
therefore dance a two step when the everyone else was dancing a waltz.

The Dance Card methodology offered in this paper exploits some of
the features of its historical namesake. It is, in effect, a protocol for de-
constructing groups into dyads, for each of these dyads to meet in
a controlled environment and, for the outcomes to be reported and reflected upon. In addition, it offers some freedoms for individuals from
the group as a total organism as well as freedom from individual members within the group. The Dance Card methodology does not depend
on a high level of "group work" skills from its members, as it structures
group activity in such a way as to allow group members to participate in
the task of the group while reducing the stress of managing the dynamics of the group.

It is, perhaps, important to define the term "group" in the context of
this paper .

3. What Is a Group?

I would not wish to join any club
that would have my sort of person as a member
Marx (Groucho)

Social science phenomena often seems to resist a common or even simple definition. For some researchers engaged in the study of groups, it is
enough for members to share a common fate to define them as a group.
This definition from Lewin in 1947 (Levin 1947), and supported by
Campbell (1958), has an appeal because it is in many ways all encompassing and simple, and thus does not put up barriers or constraints that
may otherwise inhibit. This definition suits the needs of large groups well
i.e. ethnic groups. Such a definition is not however very helpful to those of
us who are both engaged in the study AND practice of small groups (Lewin
[1948] was in fact both a active group worker and theorist and originator
of the phrase "action research"). Perhaps a more pragmatic definition would

include the concepts of common goals, behaviour and awareness. Including these constructs one can define a group as :

> Any number of people who are psychologically aware of each other, share common aims, and perceive themselves to be a group (Schein 1988).

Added to this is an awareness that a group has a structure which defines acceptable norms and behaviours. It is at this point that the question of synergy may be addressed. An early researcher in this field, Allport (1924), believed that there was in essence no difference between the total of the individuals and the sum of the group. This contradicted even earlier thinkers such as Le Bon who reported observing a crowd possessing a "group mind" which made them act beyond what would be expected of individual members on their own. This idea of synergy is now widely accepted and often expressed as 1+1= 3.

Returning to the context of small groups, it is often accepted that a limiting factor is span of control, i.e. that number of people one can be aware of, and both influence and be influenced by, at any given moment in time. Adding this size constraint provides a "normal" small group of having at least two members and not more than twenty (Brown 1988). Such a definition may allow us to define a team as having all the above attributes and elements, plus an ability or will to in some way collaborate to achieve a shared goal.

The study of groups and, in particular, group dynamics is complex. It is reasonable to suggest that groups exist in the bi-dimensional environment of both space and time. Therefore, a group can never be fully replicated. At best one can place the same people in the same environment, for the same goals. This can produce a similar but not identical group as such researchers look for consistent rather than replicable phenomena. It is from looking at the way group members communicate and act that we infer the abstractions of dynamics and processes that occur within groups. Like Bales (1970), we can observe and to an extent measure behaviours inside small groups. We can with some degree of accuracy place on a matrix who said or did what. We can also observe the myriad of non-verbal communications that occur. However, in order to analyse what these behaviours are telling us about the group requires interpretation. Such interpretation, while being worthwhile, is nevertheless subjective. This creates problems in assessment when comparing two differing methods of group facilitation. It is within this complex and ambiguous environment that the group worker must live. However, even given this constraint, it seems (perhaps!) that there is room for offering an alternative technique. This is supported by looking at some of the issues that can be addressed by Dance Card.

Dance Card addresses the following:

1) Reduction of any individual dominance within the group.

Often even "democratic" groups encompass an individual member who can dominate or even dictate to the rest of group. The use of such power, often of a coercive nature, can have influence well beyond what would reasonably be expected. Where this power base is external from the immediate group, i.e. where a "boss" is working with a group of subordinates, this influence can be considerable. Although it is often argued that groups need "strong leadership" in order to achieve the task, such leadership, formal or informal, can corrupt the process.

2) Reduction of groupthink.

The effects of so called groupthink were identified by amongst others Janis and Mann (1977). Groupthink refers to the situation where the strength of the force for consensus minimises the critical analysis of group decision making. Janis suggests a number of possible causes of this phenomena, including, highly (or overly) cohesive groups. Strong leadership, strong pressure to achieve a solution and perception that the range of options open to the group is narrow. The effects of groupthink are considerable. They can include perceived invulnerability and side lining of moral and ethical questions ("I was only following orders like everyone else"). In addition, groupthink can affect the quality of activity within the group as there is both a perception that the group is unanimous in its opinion and, at the same time, censoring any deviant thinkers in the group.

3) Positively encourages open expression and freedom of speech.

Open expression and free speech within small groups can often be inhibited due to a number of factors including social bullying, and the so called Ringelmann effect (social loafing). Social loafing can be caused by individual members of the group not sharing a common purpose. In effect, group members either cease to take an active part in the group or take only a minimal part in interactions. Social loafing is of considerable concern as it not only inhibits the quality of the group activity but also can support groupthink, as it is often considered, at least in a western culture, that silence constitutes consensus. In the workplace, social loafing can make meetings very costly as often every member of the group will be paid to be in attendance. Given that the Institute of Management estimates that managers can spend anything up to 70% of their time in meetings, the cost of them not contributing to these meetings can therefore be seen to be considerable.

4) Ensuring that meetings fulfil the needs of all members.

Human beings join groups for a wide range of reasons. These range from fulfilling social and psychological needs to achieving more tangible goals and outcomes. Where people are placed into groups rather than electing to join them, this range of needs are often not met. Although many popular "how to do it" books for managers extol the virtue of ensuring that group members are fulfilled, this seems, in practice, often to be subsumed by the pressing demands of the group task. If, as Maslow suggests, the need for "belonging" is a higher order need, then in order for this to be satisfied, the dynamics and environment of the group become critical.

5) Eliminates role requirements.

I have previously referred to the work of Meredith Belbin (1981). His model of an effective group encompasses 12 different roles that need to be present to form an "ideal" group. It is self evident that in the main individuals are formed into a group not because they will fulfil a particular role, but rather due to their status or perceived technical expertise.

However, Dance Card can also
- reduce the influence of the group facilitator / moderator
- require commitment from group members
- highlight isolates within the group
- manage overt hostility

Dance Cards have been applied in a range of situations and have been shown to be useful in developing groups and group members; in particular, where there is considerable conflict existing between group members, where creativity is important, where there is a wide perceived range of status amongst members, and lastly, where problems are complex or diverse. It has been used in groups where numbers range from 5 to 30+. To date applications have included:
- senior management development (8 applications);
- business re-engineering (4 applications);
- student work groups (2 applications);
- family counselling (6 applications);
- project management (6 applications).

4. The Dance Card Technique

Will you, wont you, will you, wont you, will you join the dance?
Lewis Carroll

The Dance Card technique de-constructs conventional groups into five inter-dependent phases. These phases together, and the activities that takes place within them, form a protocol that differentiates Dance Card from any other group management processes. Each phase can facilitate task resolution by reducing the importance of traditional group roles and group work training, replacing them instead with a structure that is both creative and novel. In addition, the technique can reduce pre-existing conflict that may inhibit group effectiveness.

The Dance Card protocol can be seen as a series of phases as below;

Phase one   *Problem Identification and Formulation*

Phase two   *Dyadic Formation*

Phase three   *Implementation*

Phase four   *Iteration and Reflection*

Phase five   *Resolution (or re-formulation) and Reflection.*

Each phase is intra-dependant on each other and the whole constitutes an overall architecture.

Phase 1

Initial formulation and structuring of the event. In this phase the task is identified by both individuals and the group as a whole. Problems can be wide ranging, from the management of a new process through to therapeutic activities. Typical problems have included; interpersonal friction, poor communication and design of management tools i.e. appraisal system. Training tasks have included counselling skills, modifying corporate culture and setting mission statements. This phase also introduces the explicit identification of skills and weaknesses in individual members (this process is explained in the case study). The phase introduces the concept that the group will not be working together as a whole as in, for example, brainstorming, but rather breaking into subgroups each with clearly defined discussion areas. Each group of two people will be self determined but will operate within the overall protocol.

FIGURE 1.
The Dance Card Cycle

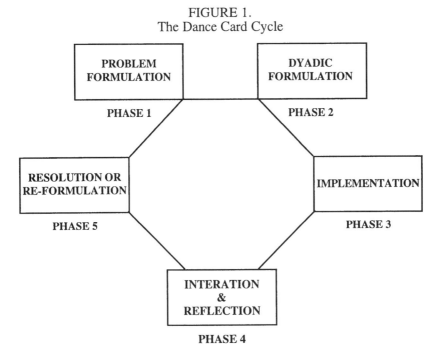

Phase 2

The dyadic formulation phase not only sets the meeting protocol but also identifies rules governing meetings and meeting leaders. The phase is typified by group members identifying who they wish to meet, and completing their personal Dance Card. Each group member has their own Dance Card with provision to book dyadic meetings on (the dances). The Card is divided into time slots (see Figure 1).

Phase 3

Implementation. Dyads or triads meet and notes are taken as appropriate. The convenor of the sub meeting decides the agenda and in effect becomes the leader of the sub meeting. The role of the external facilitator is that of time keeper and moderator . At this point, the group facilitator is subject to the same constraints as other group members and cannot participate in dyads without the consent of the members involved. During this phase, when participants are meeting (dancing), the facilitator has no influence over the various meetings taking place.

Phase 4

The iteration phase requires each dyad to report to the group as a whole its discussions (within the limits of agreed confidentially). Often experience has shown that individuals need time to reflect on the activity or undertake unfinished business caused by the need, during the process, to terminate one dance in order to join another.

Phase 5

At this phase the group reflects on both the outcomes (problem resolutions) and the process. Experience suggests that the group will either pursue a course of action identified in a dyad, or address the issues either by reforming dance meetings or reforming as a whole, as in conventional meetings. This phase will often see the Dance Card moderator leading some reflection in order to allow the group to exploit and make explicit learning outcomes from the activity. Unlike the traditional facilitators role the moderator also learns about the activity rather than leading it.

The operational process of the Dance Card technique has evolved, in practice, to try at least to be straightforward, objective and creative. The initial phase of Dance Card requires individuals to identify both strengths and weaknesses. Operationally, this has been done by giving each participant two blank cards (post-it notes are good!). On the first card, each member of the group is asked to write down three items which they feel are individual and personal areas of strength – these might include organisational ability, analysis and delegation. All the strength cards are then marked „for sale" and with the group members names on and pinned onto a convenient board, where all participants can see them. On the second card, group members are asked to write down three areas of weakness and these are marked „wanted," then also posted on the board. Some time is allowed for participants to scan this data. This activity is important as it not only identifies strengths and weaknesses, but by doing so in a non threatening manner, starts to break down, even partially

FIGURE 2.
A typical Dance Card "blank"

DANCE CARD

NAME ..... *PATRICK*

TIME NOW............ DANCING BEGINS AT...*1.30*..........

> 1.30..........................
> 1.40..........................
> 1.50..........................
> 2.00..........................
> 2.10,,,,,,............... ....
> 2.20..........................

Please insert the name of the person you will be meeting with next to the appropriate time slot. If they have requested the meeting, inset their name in CAPITALS, If you have requested to meet with them, use lower case.

Please remember the following;
1) The person requesting the meeting has the right to determine the issue discussed.
2) Discussions can be confidential if agreed by BOTH dyad members.
3) Keep to the time limits as indicated by your card (a domino effect can happen if only one "dance" goes on too long).
4) You may form a triad (group of three) if this acceptable to both members of the dyad.
5) You may invite the moderator in as either a participant or guest of the dyad, again ONLY if this agreed by all members of the triad.

NOTES. You can use these "dances" to either address issues that are highlighted on the "For Sale" or "Wanted" post-it notes. However you can use the time just to get to know another member of the full group (often chats can be unexpectedly useful!).

There is no requirement to fill up the dance card. If you think it would be helpful, leave a slot empty to allow you to think/talk to yourself.

© G. LEVY 1991

both reserve in individuals and reluctance to participate in what may be seen, at this stage, as a bizarre exercise for those new to the technique.

Dance Card may be characterised by an architecture that encompasses a number of protocols (or rules). Often these will be situational , responding to the needs of the particular group. However experience suggests that there seems to be certain cardinal rules (although like all other rules they improve by being broken from time to time). These include;

– If you request a Dance Card meeting with another member of the group he/she becomes the legitimate leader of the dyad, and as such, controls the meeting AS OF RIGHT, and may dictate the topic of discussion. This is irrespective of their status outside of the dyad. The person to whom the request for inclusion on their Card is made is known as the "leader." The person making the request is the "guest."

– "Dances" are to start and finish within the allotted time. The role of the individual managing or facilitating the event (called the "moderator") is to act as time keeper.

– Outsiders may not "butt in," this includes the moderator. Outsiders from the dyad may, however, be invited in only with permission of the dyad leader and in negotiation with the leader's guest.

– Dyadic groups may maintain confidentiality in phase five of the process. However the dyadic leader will defend the reason for such confidentiality to the rest of the full group.

– The full group have to "sign up" to the idea of Dance Card and its protocol, this includes leaders of the group (legitimate or otherwise). It is this adherence to the "rules" that often gives Dance Card a tremendous ability to deal with both groups in conflict, and groups consisting of members of differing organisational status (Dance Card was used to good effect with a group of 25 people from a University ranging from clerk to Assistant Vice Chancellor).

In order to explain a Dance Card in action, the following case study is offered below. The names of both individuals and the organisation have been changed to offer confidentiality to the participants and protection to the author. However, the description and many of the quotations included are from notes made by the author at the time or from tapes of individual conversations.

5. Case Study: Management At the O.K. Coral

This people hath a revolting and a rebellious heart
Jerimiah 23

Background

JETCO (Japan Electronic Trading Co.) is the British division of a Japanese inward investment company. The factory (based in the Midlands) is a "low tech" assembly plant producing electrical white goods for the European market. At the start of its third year of operation in the UK, directors were exclusively Japanese nationals on a three year posting from the parent company. A recent announcement from the Managing Director advised the senior management team, (who were British), that JETCO intended to make its first board level appointment in the forthcoming year from within this senior management group. However, the Japanese Managing Director had not said which of the group of five managers would be promoted. It was felt, however, that a degree of hostility existed within the SMT group and this was resulting in poor communication and a "lack of tranquillity" in the factory. The Finance Manager, Michael, had been "requested" by the Managing Director to re-establish harmony at the factory as the MD would feel unhappy about making a board level appointment under the existing culture.

As Michael said, "The MD told me that when he was last in Japan, he felt that other members of the main board could not understand such a situation, as it was incomprehensible that it occurred elsewhere in the company." As a result of this request from the MD, it had been decided by the senior British managers group that an external consultant be brought in to "sort us out." Three consultancy companies had tendered and made presentations to this group. The author was offered the contract both because he had previously undertaken work for JETCO, and the British managers thought his approach would not encompass any "flavour of the month "mumbo jumbo." The contracting was the responsibility of Michael, who invited the author for a drink "away from the factory" to offer a full and confidential briefing. The following report of the briefing was compiled from notes made soon after by the author.

The Briefing

"The thing is, Gerald, you need to understand the personalities who will make up the group you will be working with. In the main, they are a difficult bunch ranging from the bloody minded to the downright incompetent. My feeling is that within twelve months none of them will still be employed by us." He went on: "It's important that you and I see eye to eye on this for two reasons. Firstly, I think that I will be made a director of JETCO within the next 6 months and, therefore, if you are to undertake more work with us, and there is likely to be a considerable amount, you need to understand right from the outset who your real client is. Secondly, I may also wish you to support a report that I have been asked to make to the MD on the competence of the existing team. Indeed I may ask you to write and present the report yourself along with a proposed action plan. Of course, you would be paid extra for this additional work. I am sure you fully understand the situation now." Michael now went on to give me his opinion of the group who would be at the two day residential workshop.

The Players

There will be six of us in total. They will be:

Mark is the general manager of the factory, a bit of the old school type. Although he is nominally the most senior of us, he tends to have little to do with the Japanese bosses. He is seen as reliable as an administrator and is very presentable to local VIP's, but there is not much more about him – a bit of an old woman really."

"Alan is in charge of quality control. He is universally disliked by everyone. How he got the job I don't know, our quality rating is the lowest in the entire company world-wide. He thinks he is in the running for the directors job because quality is so important but, I am sure his days are numbered. The only thing he seems to be good at is buttering up the Japs."

"Tom is production manager – a bit of a whiz kid. He joined the company in the last year or so, and is very keen on all these management ideas that seem to come from you people all the time. He got an MBA or something so he knows it all. I don't think he will stay. I hear he is already on the look out for a job elsewhere."

"Paul was an early member of the management team, starting soon after JETCO arrived. As the company has grown, he has rather lost his way. There is little doubt that he will not be with us for long. Pity, a nice chap really."

Myself as you know, I'm a qualified accountant and control all expenditure for the company.

Lastly is Danny.

"Danny is Japanese. He is an engineer and has no management responsibility. He is joining us at the request of the MD who wants him to gain some insight prior to him being appointed to a management position back in Japan. My feeling is that everything said will be reported back to the MD by Danny. I think everyone knows this and will tailor what they say accordingly."

The Problem

Within the first two hours of the first day of the residential programme it became apparent that the lack of esteem that Michael had shown towards his colleagues was not solely unidirectional. The introductory session had been "led" by the author, to try to illicit from the group members. Their individual expectations for the outcomes for the event. Although most of the talking had been done by either Michael or Alan, it was apparent that any views other members of the group may have held they did not wish to share. One comment that seemed to be supported by the remaining three group members was "I don't want to take sides." By the end of the second session (lunch time), what had been barbed derisory banter between Michael and Alan had degenerated into overt hostility. Both the protagonists had made various attempts at leadership of the group. Danny had not said anything at all, but had spent the morning in apparent silent contemplation. Mark, the most senior manager present, had attempted in the early stages to encourage a peace between Michael and Alan and had, after being attacked by both protagonists withdrawn from the group. He had in fact done this by both refusing to take part in discussions and moving his chair and table a few feet from the horseshoe configuration of the seminar room. It seemed that some radical intervention was called for. The author requested that the lunch break scheduled for an hour be extended to two. Participants were asked not to discuss the mornings events with each other but rather to reflect on how their performance as a team was affecting JETCO. The author further announced that the afternoon WOULD be different!

The following is an abstract from notes made by the author over the lunch break which were made in the privacy of his bedroom sanctuary.

"This has got to stop."

"Should I become the leader? (If so how?), will there be anybody in the seminar room this afternoon?"

"The level of hostility is so high it is more like a psychotherapy group than a management group." I am out of my depth.

"Do these people have anything to offer JETCO? How can I find it in the climate of the room?"

"If they cannot even function as a work group, how can I break them down and still maintain control/influence?"

"Drastic times call for drastic measures."

"What is MY power base?"

As a result of both the reflection of the mornings events and a consideration of the above notes, the following desired outcomes were drawn up.

1. The current group structure was destructive and therefore had to be replaced.
2. Participants had to share personal and professional strengths.
3. The leadership bids had to be contained, at least in the short term.
4. Participants had to exit from the event with worthwhile outcomes.
5. A greater awareness of the cost to the company of the present manager/leader conflict had to be made explicit, either to the participants or the MD.

From the above, an action plan was devised as follows:

1. Deconstruct the group into pairs to address issues away from other influences.
2. Establish and agree a code of conduct for all participants.
3. Make explicit strengths and needs.
4. Modify the process fundamentally in order to address the task.

At the commencement of the next session all the participants had reassembled in the seminar room. However, Tom had brought in his packed suitcase and announced his intention of leaving the workshop which he found "distasteful and poorly managed and a waste of his valuable time." Michael intervened advising Tom that he was on company time, and if he wished to remain a member of the senior management team, he would leave when the rest of the group did and not before.

Phase One and Two

The author then made the following comments: *this morning has been something of a blood letting session... in the main for Michael and Alan. Although this can be helpful at times, I do not feel that any good use would come from it continuing. I propose to restructure the next few hours. Instead of continuing to meet as a group, we will break down into pairs, each pair will tackle issues of importance to that pair. At the end of these "mini meetings" we will re-assemble and review progress. Where issues identified in the pairs are seen as important, these will be addressed either in the whole group or again in another cycle of sub-group meetings.*

Each participant was then given two "post-it" sheets and the following instructions: "Please write at the top of one sheet FOR SALE. Underneath list three areas of special expertise that you feel you can offer either the group as a whole or individuals; these can be as wide ranging as you like. On the other "post-it" sheet head it up WANTED. On this sheet write three things that you need help, advice or information about. Make sure your name is on the bottom of each sheet and fix them to the flip- chart paper headed FOR SALE or WANTED. Remember that the purpose of these two days is to develop this SMT, its effectiveness in managing JETCO and improve the competitive advantage of the company. You should in some way orientated your statements with this in mind."

The group members produced the following items for the "FOR SALE" (Figure 3) and "WANTED" noticeboards (Figure 4).

(Authors note: Where delegates produced items of either a technical or specific nature that could identify the company these have been omitted to protect confidentiality.)

Phase Three – Implementation

From the two "noticeboards," participants arranged to meet partners.Each session was scheduled to last 10 minutes. With a total of 7 sessions scheduled, it was possible for every delegate to meet any other delegate. Danny was a more popular choice with other delegates, however, he chose to reserve the last ten minute slot for personal reflection. Paul was the only delegate who had an "empty slot." As the event unfolded there was a degree of interest as to who had elected to meet with who. Perhaps surprisingly, Michael and Alan booked the first session with each other. The author was not invited to attend any of the sessions. From the perspective of the moderator, it was impossible to forecast the outcome of the dyadic meetings. It was a relief, however, to find that a group that had only that morning been locked into a conflict mode, at least now engaged in some type of reasoned activity. From the end of the first session, time keeping became a problem as delegates became immersed in conversation. However the 10 minute rule was more or less

FIGURE 3.

FOR SALE

MICHAEL
1/ Expertise on Finance
2/
3/ JETCO strategy

    TOM
    1/ Up to date management knowledge
    2/ Insights into production
    3/

   MARK
   1/ Information on production planning
   2/
   3/ Age and wisdom!

DANNY
1/ Engineering problem solving
2/ Assistance with line balancing
3/ comparisons with other JETCO plants in Far east and USA

    ALAN
    1/ Managing staff problems
    2/ T Q L and Quality groups
    3/

     PAUL
     1/ Product Distribution
     2/ Sales into E Europe
     3/ Shoulder to cry on

FIGURE 4.

WANTED

MICHAEL
1/ *Personnel Projections*
2/ *Improved Quality*
3/

       TOM
       1/ *A way to improve forward planning*
       2/ *New product information*
       3/ *Better communication*

    MARK
    1/ *A way of working together better*
    2/ *New supplier of quality systems*
    3/ *Age and wisdom!*

DANNY
1/ *Advice on U.K. market*
2/ *An understanding of 5750*
3/ *Learning to be a better manager.*

      ALAN
      1/ *Improvement in communications – internal*
      2/ *Improvement in supplier quality*
      3/

        PAUL
        1/ *A better way of talking to each other!*
        2/ *Managing JIT problems*
        3/ *Early warning of export orders*

---

maintained. At the end of the 7 ten minute meetings the group reformed. Delegates were invited to break for coffee after which we would, as a group, try to make sense of the data from the sessions.

Phase Four – the Iteration

Moderator : Before we start to look back at the last hour and a half, may I remind you that you may, if you so wish, maintain any contract of confidentiality you entered into while meeting in pairs. I should also like to tape this bit of the discussion.

Michael: I am happy for anything I said to be discussed in open session.

(General agreement of group)

Moderator: Again, before we go on to look at specific issues that came out of the sessions, do you feel the time has been well spent?

Alan: I don't think we could have carried on like this morning. I was surprised by the amount that I got done this afternoon. It is much easier to get what you want from a discussion if there is only two of you. We should have started like this this morning.

Moderator: Is that the view of everybody?

(General agreement of group)

Moderator: OK, who wants to go first?

Mark: I found that a point which came up with everybody I met with is, the level of frustration that we all seem to feel with regard to Michael's war with Alan. SMT meetings back at the factory are dominated by their bickering. The question is, do they realise just how pissed off we are with them?

Paul: (quickly) I agree wholeheartedly with Mark. I think that some time over the next two days they (Michael and Alan) should find a quiet corner and get themselves sorted – but not now, we don't want to get tucked up with this right now. Certainly at my meetings, a lot of things have come up which need dealing with.

Moderator: Danny, it would be helpful to me to understand your thoughts on the last two hours.

Danny: It is not for me to comment on the difficulties that have been expressed. I was pleased to learn information from my colleagues and to share some understanding with them. As some will know, it is not normal for us in Japan to have this sort of open argument; it would be considered to be very rude. I would be happy to continue with this form of meeting.

Alan: OK Gerald, you have heard from us, now what do you think. Do we pass your social engineering experiment?

Moderator: Yes, if nothing else we have at least spent some time having some sort of meaningful discussion without bloodshed. It seems to me that this in itself is a worthwhile outcome. But perhaps we should go onto consider the issues that were raised in the sessions. At the end of the day JETCO is paying for us all to be here, and I assume that as they are not a charity, they will want something out of the two days.

Phase Five – Resolution

From the outcomes of the sessions, in excess of ninety separate issues were identified. These were sub-divided into two areas. In the first, seven groups of problem areas were identified as being of medium term strategic importance. These included:
1. Strategic issues (Quality).
2. Operational issues around getting B.S. 5770.
3. Personnel Issues (relating to sales driven operations).
4. Transfer of decision making from Japan to UK.
5. Supplier quality control and liaison.
6. Improving communications.
7. The effects of the U.K. and Japanese economy on the core business.

The second major area of concern to the group members related to the group itself ,and the way it managed its own affairs. These included:
1. Michael and Alan, the relationship as it affected the group.
2. Michael and Alan, the effect of their relationship on staff on the shop floor.
3. The perception of the Japanese directors of the U.K. management group.
4. Balancing the perceived demands of individual careers with the needs of JETCO.
5. Managing ourselves (the SMT group).

The group decided that instead of trying to address all these problems in the available time as a group, they would again break down into subgroups and meet together to update the whole group just before meal times. Where issues were so problematic that they needed input from the whole group, they would be discussed over meals. A second Dance Card Session took place towards the end of the two day workshop with the intention of setting objectives for the SMT group upon return to work. This second session was at the instigation of the delegate group, rather than the author.

6. Reflection on the Process

1. Individual's Thoughts

Members of the group were invited to make observations on the process of de-construction during the rest of the two day workshop. With the exception of Michael, all felt it had been worthwhile. Comments included:

"this is first time in over a year that we have made any headway as a group ... it is pathetic that we need to be separated like arguing school children in the playground in order to move forward."

"Breaking down into pairs allowed me to have a say, most of the time I just let them get on with it."

"It is really good to listen to Danny, I never realised the Japanese had a sense of humour."

"It was strange having a head to head with Michael in a sort of semi-controlled environment. I think we both felt that we were obliged to some how make some progress. The strange thing, of course, was that although we were talking "alone" but being in the same room with the others, and the fact that they were obviously engrossed working, acted as control for our emotions. Michael found it difficult to come to terms with the fact that he was in my meeting, and that I dictated the subject. I don't think he is used to playing second fiddle and not being able to do anything about it!"

"As we talked I was aware of some conversation in the background. I would hear just a snippet of someone else's meeting and think I wouldn't get a word in there!"

"This is the first time I have felt as though I am making progress with the other managers. It is strange that it seems the only way we can work as a group is when we don't meet as a group."

"I accept that we have made some progress through these mini-meetings. However, it is very time consuming, and at the end of the day we still have to learn to work together."

2. Facilitator's Thoughts

"Suddenly there is a sense of hush in the room, not the uncomfortable silence of earlier, but of a group of people working in unison on problems that are real to them. By imposing control and constraints, a new freedom is available."

Some immediate thoughts:

"When the group breaks down I have no control over anything. I am redundant for most of the time.

Roles and leadership are irrelevant to this in a group of two we do not need "chairman, company workers, resource investigators" and all the rest of Belbins roles. Groups of two manage without them.

Although it seems that this method of conducting groups is easy for members as it effectively manages conflict, it is interesting that those members who would have been fairly happy to watch the world go by, seemed to get fully involved. This reduction in social loafing is a useful by-product of the activity.

It is difficult to assess if the apparent success of the methodology is due to the protocol of the process, or the frustration of the group prior to starting. Either way, at least nobody walked out. The question is: Has this process helped these people manage their own affairs or has it just defused a difficult situation? The role of the facilitator is very different from any that I have experienced before. What am I facilitating, other than setting up the thing in the first place? As a moderator you have no option but to be non-directive, there is after all, nobody to direct!

7. Endnote – Three Years Later
and They All Lived Happily Ever After!

The author had occasion to visit JETCO some three years after the workshop. The only member of the old SMT still with the company was Michael – now a director of JETCO UK. He reported that he felt the workshop had been helpful. However, he went on to say: "We needed to clear out the dead wood from the company, therefore there had to be some changes. Most of the others liked the idea of breaking down into small groups, but it did not head off for long the inevitable showdown."

8. A Personal Reflection

The case study reported was the foundation of the Dance Card proto-col. As can be seen, it stemmed not from a considered approach, but rather from necessity. Since this time, the Dance Card Technique has evolved and, as is perhaps common, become contextual in its applica-tion. A continuing concern of the author is: "Can it become a legitimate mechanism for avoiding the issues of conflict or inappropiate leader-ship?" In the intervening years, (five to date), the technique has been applied in a range of applications from basic "ice breaking" for new groups to addressing very complex issues. One area that Dance Card seems to work well in is where groups are too large for conventional small group techniques to function. The largest application of the tech-nique to date has been a "small group" of twenty-eight managers in a six hour dance. Where Dance Card has failed is in circumstances where a group leader has recognised that the protocol would deny power and influence. On this particular occasion the "legitimate" group leader ordered the protocol to be abandoned, as: "There is no point in my people taking part in such an activity. Back at work they are required to either lead or be led, we are not a democratic organisation." Upon reflection this particular application highlighted the importance of the group having a shared common goal. The author recognises that Dance Card seems to perform a function in moving a group on from a frozen state. However, a growing issue is to develop a "post Dance Card" protocol for addressing this and other issues.

References

Allport, F.H. (1924). *Social Psychology*. New York: Houghton Mifflin.

Bales, R.F. (1970). *Personality and Interpersonal Behaviour*. Holt.

Belbin, R.M. (1981). *Management Teams – Why They Succeed or Fail?* Oxford: Heinemann.

Brown, R. (1988). *Group Processes*. Oxford: Blackwell.

Buchanan and Huczynski (1985). *Organisational Behaviour*. London: Prentice Hall.

Campbell, D.T. "Common Fate, Similarity and Other Indices of the Status of Aggregates of Persons as Social Entities." *Behavioural Science* Vol. 3 (1958).

Deeming, W.E. (1986). *Out of the Crisis*. Cambridge Mass.: MIT.

Janis and Mann (1977). *Victims of Groupthink*. New York: Free Press.

Le Bon, G. (1896). *The Crowd, a Study of the Popular Mind*. London: Fisher Unwin.

Lewin, K. "Frontiers in Group Dynamics." *Human Relations* 1 (1947).

Lewin, K. (1948). *Resolving Social Conflicts*. New York: Harper & Row.

Revans, R.W. (1980). *Action Learning – New Techniques for Management*. London: Blond & Briggs.

Ringelmann, M. "Recherches sur les moteurs animes." *Annales de l'Institut National Agronomique 1913*.

Schein, E.H. (1988). *Organisational Psychology*. New York: Prentice Hall.

Learning by Action. The Case of the Polish Environmental Movement

Piotr Gliński
The Institute of Philosophy and Sociology
of the Polish Academy of Sciences,
Warsaw, Poland.

1. The Polish Green Movement in the 1980s

During the communist era (at least untill 1980) there were no truly independent environmental organisations in Poland. A few "official" conservation associations existed within the system and behaved according to its rules. They were fully politically controlled and conformed to a role in the system as set by the authorities.

It was only in the 1980s that independent, spontaneous, and collective proecological actions developed and expanded on a large scale in Poland. Arising from the grass roots, the ecological movement, born as a typical *protest movement*, aimed at provoking specified social change. A particularly important motivation for the development of the ecological movement was the creation, operation and finally – and this may sound paradoxical – the dramatic blocking of the official activity of the independent trade union, "Solidarity." The explosion of genuinely public activity during the sixteen months of the legal operation of the union bore fruit in the form of various social initiatives, including ecological initiatives.

The short history of the Polish ecological movement divides into *two developmental phases*. Each one reflects a different socio-political situation as well as the dominance of specific organizational forms. The first phase coincided with the creation of "Solidarity" in 1980, and the political changes of 1989 launched the second.

Imprinted on the character of the *first phase* were the political conditions of social resistance to the communist authorities. For the environmental movement, it was a time of *demonstrations and protest*. Greens above all engaged in symbolic acts designed to appeal more to emotions than to rational choices and strategies. Typical for this period were spontaneous informal organizations and groups, often arising in response to local conflicts over ecological danger. These were the first independent citizens' initiatives in Poland that sought to pressure authorities from below concerning ecological problems. The level of formal organization among these groups was very low: they possessed virtually no organizational or negotiating skills; and there was little coordination among groups, which made access and exchange of information very difficult.

The liberalizations of the communist system in Poland which took place in the years 1987–88, allowed the first authentic nongovernmental ecological organizations to come into being. The phenomena of independent civil activity, to which I call attention here briefly, due to the character of the totalitarian system of which it was a part, had the nature of resistance movements and were examples of certain *enclaves* of *oppositional civil society*.

By 1989, at the beginning of the transformation period, Poland boated a relatively broad ecological movement, encompassing more than one hundred various organizations and groups, and more than a dozen ecological foundations (altogether 135 independent environmental formal and informal organizations) (Gliński 1996: 155–156).

The movement's fundamental trait was – and remains today – *a pluralism* that brought together various segments of society: young people, religious groups, technical specialists, professionals, local associations, etc. Individual groups differ in their degree of institutionalization, demands, legal status, involvement in societal conflicts, the geographic and social range of their activity, involvement in politics, and their search for alternative cultural models. All of them, however, share *a rejection of all forms of violence*. We should note that – at least until mid-1989 – many ecological groups and organizations, particularly those organized among young people, suffered political harassment. We should also note that the ecological movement primarily attracts members of the intelligentsia and young people. Farmers are less in evidence, while workers are conspicuously underrepresented.

Two general orientations were – and they still exist – present in the movement as a whole. One continues the traditional "preservationist" approach to ecological problems, striving to protect nature mainly out of concern for the consequences of environmental degradation for human beings and contemporary civilisation. This tendency is frequently characterised – especially by its critics – *as the "ecology of fear."*

An alternative orientation consists of groups searching for new cultural values and striving to change "civilizational paradigm." These groups draw on counterculture traditions that challenge consumerism and economism and that stress humanity's unity with nature, which entails the need for people to renounce domination over the environment. Such an "introspective" approach to ecology is congruent with the principles of *"deep ecology"* (Devall and Session 1985).

2. Development of the Green Movement After the System Changes

The second phase of the environmental movement began in 1989. It has contained both the quantitative and qualitative changes in the movement.

The political changes which took place in Poland during the summer of 1989 brought about a dynamic quantitative growth of environmental organizations. The period of the most dynamic growth was in the years 1991–92. In 1995 there were around 700 environmental organizations in Poland (520 associations and informal groups, and 180 foundations).[1]

The internal structure of the movement was also developed during the years 1989–1995. Because of the rather vague group identities, it is more difficult even now than a few years ago to build any typology of the movement participants or organizations. Generally speaking, fourteen groups of participants can be differenciated within the Polish envoronmental movement of the nineties. These are: Polish Ecological Club, League of Nature Protection and other postsystemic organizations, The Green Federation, animal rights activists and vegetarian movement, other youth organizations (students, pupils, scauts, the rest of "I Prefer to Be" Movement and "Freedom and Peace" Movement, etc.), "deep ecology" circles, conservationists, local organizations, educational organizations, specialists and experts (economists, lawyers, organizations of ecological farmers, alternative energy and technology groups etc.), religious and quasi-religious group (catholic, budda, hindi etc.), artistic and para-artistic milieu, service and support institutions, others (quasi-ecological groups both countercultural and quasi – non-governmental, certain foundations, individuals etc.).

The main fields of the movement's activity in this period covers twenty-four problems and campaigns: anti-nuclear actions (mainly in 1989 – against the construction of Żarnowiec nuclear power station), hydro-investments (i.e. Czorsztyn dam), recycling and west management campaignes, "Wilde Life" campaign, traditional conservation and nature protection, animal rigths, "Green Lungs of Poland" project, transport pollution, bicycle promotion, "Vistula Now!" campaign, Carpaty euro-region campaign, local defensive actions, ecological education, cooperation with local self-government, development of ecological agriculture, environment and health problems, ecological friendly food promotion, environmental policy and environmental action plan issues, protection of Baltic See, environmental NGOs and banks, Greenpeace International involvement, attempts to bring about a general change in people's attitude towards nature (i.e. a deep ecology perspective), movement development and support activities, and actions placed at the edge of the movement.

The members of the environmental movement do not all follow the same ideology. The movement in general is quite varied with differences in ideology. However, the processes of "maturation" and "self-education" are leading to the convergence of collective beliefs and common thinking.

The environmental movement in Poland is a community bound by only the most general goals. Specific groups often have very different aims. This is a very natural situation and results from specialization and the free choice groups have in determining their objectives. However, a social movement must be able to recognize a common aim in order to function. Despite the ideologically radical programs of many pro-environmental groups, it can be said that the idea of *environmentally appropriate* development (sustainable or eco-development) serves as a common goal of the movement. There is also a long list of secondary goals more of a symbolic nature, such as: opposition to nuclear energy, opposition to large dam construction, the preservation of ecologically significant habitats (unique ecosystems), energy conservation, the introduction of waste management systems, etc. The problem lies in determining priorities among these goals.

The social composition of the Polish environmental movement's membership only partially reflects the societal structure of Western new social movements. The basic difference lies in the absence of a large *middle class* in Poland, especially the lack of a "new" middle class. (As a result, our case study involves the phenomenon of *the development*[2] of a "new social movement" without a middle class, which automatically limits its scale to a "non-mass" movement, given the Polish context.) The role of the middle class is, in part, assumed by the intelligentsia in the Polish environmental movement. Their involvement presupposes a more rational, pragmatic and self-limiting character of the movement. The ethos of the future Polish middle class will in large part impact on the future of the movement. The former middle class, however, plays no role in the movement. As in the West, youth play a fundamental role in the Polish Greens, especially high school and university students. The movement's counterculture background plays an important role, for it is from the counterculture that many of its participants emerged and its networks were established. This is also a common characteristic held with the West. The list of traits in common with the West continues with the urban character of the movement, predominance of highly educated participants and noticeable lack of the working class, nouveau riches or political elites.

3. The Maturation Process

Besides the *quantitative changes* described above, the Polish environmental nongovernmental organizations sector is also characterized by *qualitative changes* – changes in the form and style of organization's activities. In the eighties and in the initial stages of transformation, environmental organizations took upon themselves primarily resistance activities directed against state administration and engaged in the simplest forms of social group action, such as articulation of the interests of a given group and actions of protest and intervention. At present the dominant forms of activity are more typically civil: monitoring the aims of those in power, participation in the processes of preparation and making decisions (cooperation with the administration mainly at the local level, pointing out problems to be solved, consultation of legal solutions, lobbying, and others), as well as taking over on one's own initiative of non-state social spheres (realization of various undertakings, preparation of alternative solutions of social problems).

Participants in the Polish environmental movement conduct "new" *types* of activities and *methods* of operating, typical of new social movements. In the Polish context, these "new" elements also include using humor of the absurd, distancing oneself from reality, and rejecting all forms of violence in its activities. The movement is characterized typically by "new" *organizational forms*. Lateral structures, networks and a low level of formality dominate. Fundamental features are direct democratic governance, consensus and the close interaction of its members. At the same time, organizations are emerging with more professional structures, similar to the structures found among new social movement groups in the West.

Changes occurred in the organization of the movement's structure and its methods of activity, leading to *a gradual maturation and professionalization.* Rational strategies increasingly guided its activities. More and more, protest actions were supplemented or even replaced by constructive and positive action. Informational networks were set up and non-governmental experts engaged. Movement activists trained themselves to conduct environmental campaigns and programs, to administer non-governmental oraganizations, and to become familiar with legal codes. They learned how to work with state agencies and the mass media and to raise money for ecological activity.

The phenomenon of "maturation" of the Polish environmental movement, which is characteristic of the whole Poland's non-government sector, depends primarily on: 1. Changes in the forms of organizations' activity, as discussed above; 2. Growth of the information and communication network in and outside of the sector (among other the creation of regional and countrywide cooperative institutions – Environmental NGOs Annual Meetings in Kolumna n/Łódź, Regional Environmental Offices, Polish Green Network, Environmental Educational Centers' Network, "List of twenty-one",[3] etc., and growth of the third sector press and e-mail networks); 3. Development of contacts with the local milieu, above all cooperation with local government, regional groups, academic groups; the beginnings of cooperation with the mass media (Wygnański 1995) and the parliament (e.g. "Lobby Facility" Project); 4. Development of the third sector services institutions (Information Bank of Nongovernmental Organizations KLON/JAWOR; Service Bureau of Self-Help Initiatives; Service Office for Environmental Movement, etc.); 5. Process of professionalization[4] of nongovernmental organizations' activities. As can be seen from the above, the maturation process of the third sector in Poland is still in its introductory phase – for example, there is relatively little interest on the part of NGOs in the legislative process – the trend of the changes is, however, clear.

4. Learning by Action: The Self-educational Process

The immediate reasons and causal mechanisms of the discussed changes are: *the influence and help of the western partners*; and – known from the theory of social movements (Eder 1993) – *processes of self-education* of the participants of the environmental movement (which express the phenomenon of *learning by action*).

In the years 1990–1994 foreign foundations and ecological funds turned over to the Polish pro-ecological organizations at least 1.6 million dollars (Gliński 1996). The extent of foreign aid to the third sector in Poland is in reality much greater because a part of government grants for the Polish NGOs comes from foreign aid – principally from the program PHARE. Many of the voluntary organizations, especially Polish nongovernmental institutions supporting the growth of the third sector, are directly financed by PHARE and USAID. Foreign aid to them was especially important in the beginning phases of growth of non-governmental organizations when there were practically no other sources of financing. The private sector was very weak and the people who were creating the third sector in a post-communist Poland had no management skills and no financial know-how.

A very large, and often unappreciated, role in the growth of the nongovernmental sector in Poland is also played by foreign non-financial aid, indirectly tied to the activities of western foundations and aid organizations, for example the American Peace Corps. This role is: 1. providing professional organizational skills; 2. inspiration to a change toward a more professional attitude and maintaining of commitment to volunteer work (building the image of a volunteer); 3. forcing the Polish government organizations to interest themselves in the local third sector problems, as a mechanism which helps promote the environmental protection and the growth of civil society in Poland.

The phenomenon of learning by action can be illustrated by the history of Czorsztyn dam protest. During the years 1988–1993, the ecological movement was involved primarily in *two large protest campaigns*: against the construction of a nuclear power plant in Żarnowiec and against the construction of a dam at Czorsztyn. The first protest, in which the

movement employed tactics such as mass media campaigns, road block-
ades, demonstrations, and even hunger strikes, ended in success: work
on the power plant stopped. The main reason for the Polish government's decision, however, appears to have been economic (the lack of
money to pay for continued construction). Protest against the Czorsztyn
dam, on the other hand, in the form of an annual summer blockade of the
approach roads to the site and a propaganda campaign in the mass media, did not produce the same practical results, although they lent noto-
riety to the problem. Forcing investment for certain ecological installa-
tions – mainly sewage treatment facilities – has been the only
accomplishment. The dam's construction continued despite protests.

In 1991 some of the environmental groups – being aware of a likely
forthcoming defeat of the protest – added other types of activity to their
strategy: direct discussion and contact with the ministry, lobbying par-
liamentary representatives, mobilizing and activating a broad coalition
of non governmental environmental organizations (including experts)
against the dam, and, finally, generating a report of independent experts
on the circumstances and effects of constructing the dam. These were
opposed by some radical youth groups (in particular, Freedom and Peace).
Despite sharp conflicts within the movement over the new activities,
they marked a new level of cooperation with the government and parliament, and increased intra-movement coordination.

As a result of the constant pressure exerted by ecology groups, and
favorable personnel changes in the Ministry of Environmental Protection, contacts between the movement and the Ministry intensified in 1992.
The Ministry established an office responsible for this purpose, which
sponsored monthly meetings between representatives of the Ministry
and participants in the movement. The goal of these meetings was, on
the one hand, to make it easier for ecologists to bring grievances to the
attention of the minister on a regular basis, and to exchange information
regarding concrete ecological problems and the state's ecological policies, and on the other hand, to mobilize the environmental movement in
support of the Ministry's policies. Working together in this way – given
the proper organizational preparation – was intended to lead to permanent forms of participation by non-governmental organizations in the
ecological decision-making process.

This process of *"politicization"* brought with it efforts to change the
ecological movement's internal structure. The Polish ecological movement moved gradually into the second phase of development noted in

this article – the phase of constructing effective, professional non-governmental organizations. Many foundations and ecological groups began to seek financial support for their activities (often from foreign sources) and decided to employ a professional staff. Pre-1989 ecological organizations that used to be mere-communist "fronts" began to function independently. The movement also started to construct an internal information network. Efforts were undertaken to coordinate the activities of different groups and organizations. The majority of the ecological groups participated actively in all of these processes. Attempts at coordination can be traced back to 1988, but it was not until September 1991, that a Service Office for the Ecological Movement was set up, thanks to aid provided by Western sponsors.

The neccesity to solve other ecological problems and crizes has led subsequently to "the process of maturation" described above. Facing the problem and trying to find a practical solution, environmentalists have been forced to look for information and knowledge, alternative solutions and improvements, to be flexible in their tactics, to increase both internal and external cooperation, to establish new, more efective institutions, modes of activity, procedures, etc.

Another characteristic example of "the learning by action process" refers to the searching for any adequate decision-making procedure within the Polish environmrntal movement. The way decisions are made in a social movement or any group without formal membership always causes much trouble to their participants. In such cases we can't routinely use simple voting procedures or consensus agreementst. The same applies to the Polish ecological movement. But practicly there was an urgent need to elaborate any decision-making procedure in the movement: there was a need to coordinate the activity of various groups, to cooperate with government agencies or to speak on behalf of the movement itself. After a seven-year period of attempts and efforts of individuals, groups and movement's institutions, the movement has evetually, at least in part, succeded. A kind of a specific decision-making procedure has been created by the group of the leaders ("List of twenty-one"). The procedure is a specific mixture of "consensus and voting," but first of all refers to the intangible, "magical" atmosphere of confidence shared by people who have been shaped and joined by *the experience of collective, common action* (that's why it's called "magical").

Generally speaking, the process of learning by action in the case of the Polish environmental movement consists in a continual drawing of practical conclusions from action itself. The latter induces the need to improve the efficiency of the activity through the self-reflection process. The need leads to the changes in the movement's activity as described above: both to the maturation (professionalization, institutionalization, etc.) and politicization of the movement (the "trap" of political participation).

Two factors strictly associated with the action itself play the decisive role in stimulating of the learning process. They are: the participants' *self-reflection*, which, to some extend, is created by the action itself (mainly the analysis of defeats and successes of the movement's activities); and the very *interactions* in which participants are involved throughout their activities (both, interactions with internal and external objects).

5. Resistance to the Changes

The changes presented above did not come about without resistance, principally of two kinds.[5]

In the first place it is very difficult to overcome ingrained habits of falling back on easy things, of conducting protest type actions which do not requiring special skills. This happens especially in conditions of new political freedom – when "courage gets cheaper" – and in situations of by and large negative attitude of the governing political elites toward the third sector when the social prestige of the state and political classes is still low – as is shown by public opinion polls. To these circumstances we must ascribe the fact that the positive changes of environmental organizations' activity, which we already discussed, came to pass as if outside the sphere of immediate contact with the world of politics. Studies of the third sector in Poland prove that the predominant type of relationship between NGOs and state administration is simply lack of contact, and between the NGOs and the political parties and the politicians, lack of contact coupled to an unwillingness to even to begin it (Wygnański 1995a).

Secondly, during the time of system transformations characterized by weakness of democratic institutions, the subtler civil forms of activity based on commitment and competence on the part of non-government organizations, sometimes tend to weaken their political position and tend to erode their power. Primitive, demagogic protest actions are often more effective in reaching the interest of a particular group. In this case we have to deal with the classical dilemma of force and competence, which the Polish environmental organizations often have to face (Wygnański 1995).

Despite a functioning informational network within the movement and the coordination and professionalization of some groups, the environmental movement in Poland was still beset with numerous organizational shortcomings that limited its effectiveness. These included: an inability to devise action strategies (for ecological campaigns and above all for campaigns to mobilize public support and recruit new members); the preponderance of defensive and protest-oriented activity; shortages of funds, professional personnel and expert advisors (e.g., in the field of environmental law and economics); and the lack of basic negotiating skills.

During the transformation period the ecological movement in Poland has undergone remarkable changes in terms of its accessible resources. At the beginning of the transition process, the movement lacked almost all of the typical social movement's resources: funds and fund-raising abilities, organizational structures, organizational and managerial skills and knowledge, membership etc. Most of these resources have become accessible for the movement during its professionalization and maturation except for skilled *leaders and membership*. There is still a shortage of recognised leaders of high authority in the movement, who could raise the level of co-ordination and effectiveness of the movement activities. Membership of the movement is still limited in number as a result of the general passivity of the society and inadequate efforts of the movement activists to increase the membership of their organizations, which is caused by insufficient organizational skill and a specific *reluctance toward mass mobilization* or recruiting actions among movement participants. This attitude stems from the communist time when any public mobilization campaign was perceived as artificial and hypocrite.

Notes

1. Without taking into consideration some local branches of PKE (Polish Ecological Club), LOP (League of Nature Protection) and "Animals" Foundation. According to data provided by the Polish Information Bank of Non-Governmental Organizations KLON/JAWOR there is also about 700 NGOs concerned with ecological and other problems (declaring ecological goals among other aims of the organization), and environmental organizations states for 14–17% of the Third Sector in Poland. The whole Polish Third Sector, according to different estimates, accounts for 17 000–47 000 organizations. (JAWOR 95).
2. I understood the intelligentsia as a specific social group characterized by its unique ethos of mission and civil virtues.

3. The group of 21 leaders trying to coordinate the movement's activity.
4. The phenomenon of professionalization of organizations is characterized by: employment of professional organization leaders, accumulation of resources from beyond the sector, a relatively inert member body; aspirations to represent broader public group interest; attempts at political lobbying. (Zald and McCarthy 1990).
5. The general conditions of the environmental activity in Poland (e.g. the economic, cultural, social and institutional barriers and obstacles to the voluntary activity) are presented in my other works (Gliński 1996; 1996a).

References

Devall, B. and Session, G. (1985). *Deep Ecology.* Layton: Gibbs Smith, Publisher.

Eder, K. (1993). *The New Politics of Class. Social Movements and Cultural Dynamics in Advanced Societies.* London: SAGE Publications.

Gliński, P. (1996). *Polscy Zieloni. Ruch społeczny w okresie przemian [Polish Greens: A Social Movement in the Time of Transformation].* Warszawa: Wydawnictwo IFiS PAN.

Gliński, P. (1996a). ''The Polish Greens and Politics: A Social Movement in the Time of Transformation.'' Paper delivered at the Conference "Environmental Protection in Poland," Bloomington, Indiana University Press (in print).

JAWOR 94/95, Informator o organizacjach pozarządowych w Polsce [Polish NGOs Directory], Warsaw: Fundusz Współpracy, Program Dialog Społeczny – N.G.O.S.

Offe, C. "New Social Movements: Challenging the Boundaries of Institutional Polities." *Social Research* 4 (1985).

Wygnański, J. J. (1995). *Raport o organizacjach – Public Policy Oriented [Raport on Public Policy Oriented Organizations].* Warszawa. Mimeographed.

Wygnański, J. J. (1995a). "Czym jest Trzeci Sektor w Polsce? [What is the third Sector in Poland?]." Paper delivered at the seminar "Building Civil Society: Role of Nongovernmental Organizations in Poland," 12 June 1995, Senate, Warszawa. Mimeographed.

Zald, M. N. and McCarthy, J. D. (1990). *Social Movement in an Organizational Society. Collected Essays.* New Brunswick: Transaction Books.

The Intellectual Entrepreneur

Stefan Kwiatkowski
Warsaw University
and Academy of Entrepreneurship
and Management
in Warsaw.

1. The Research. A Broader Perspective

Successful entrepreneurs characterized by extraordinary concentration of intellectual features have been identified by Thomas Dandridge in the USA, Bengt Johannisson in Sweden and Stefan Kwiatkowski in Poland. Between November 1995 and March 1996 intensive interviews were conducted with those individuals. Despite the minuscule size of the sample (thirteen individuals altogether) it was possible to discern these characteristics of intellectual entrepreneurship which are common in a modern world, and those which seem somehow affected by transformation processes.

Such intellectual features as combining information screening and absorption capacities due to diverse knowledge base, and/or ability to see details from different perspectives by approaching reality simultaneously through linear rationality and holistic intuition, are present in any instance of successful entrepreneurship. This we have learned not only from cursory observation of general facts but first of all from much deeper case based analysis made in mentioned above countries. We have also learned, however, that the role these characteristics play as determinants of entrepreneurial success considerably grows as a result of economic, social and technological changes. The ability to see and define emerging patterns, and to reject still dominating modes of behavior, might constitute not only the most intriguing, but also critical factors of entrepreneurial processes. Thus, it might be claimed that entrepreneurship becomes more and more an intellectual endeavour.

Mentioned above phenomena create entrepreneurial chance and challenge for people whom we called intellectuals and who would previously very seldom consider an entrepreneurial venture. The degree to which such a chance is perceived and utilized is considerably bigger under conditions of rapid social and economic changes than in a more stable situation. Hence a decision to base this paper on just three Polish cases epitomizing the essence of intellectual entrepreneurship.

2. The Research Conducted in Poland

During October of 1995 several intellectuals directly engaged in new business enactment were identified. Also, during informal conversations with representatives of business and intellectual communities a detailed plan of a personal interview with intellectual entrepreneurs was elaborated.

Between November 1995 and March 1996 six interviews based on exactly same questions were conducted with:
- the university professor and a leading management authority, who is the founder of two private business schools. One of them, created only few years ago, has already more than 3000 students. It offers both graduate and undergraduate programs;
- the university professor and a leading philosopher, who is the founder of one of the best social science schools within Central Europe;
- the linguist from Wroclaw who founded a non-conventional center of language education called "A journey into intellect." She is a thirty years old mother of two children and while a successful business-woman – an avowed intellectual;
- the film wizard who opened three successful film studios;
- the journalist and commentator who founded the major PR agency in Poland;
- the university professor and a leading mathematician who turned around a family business which became the first franchiser in Poland.

Additionally to the interview proper (lasting from two to four hours each) the background written materials have been collected and cursory discussions conducted with co-workers, friends, clients and suppliers in each case.

Each of the interviewed individuals can be easily identified. They expressed no reservations concerning their names revealed. They not only contributed their time and energy but showed considerable interest in the research by reading all cases and participating in the follow-up session. Three cases resulting from this research were already used in the class situation (with participation of a given entrepreneur) and another one is about to be used in the following academic year. All cases follow exactly same pattern in which identical elements are distinguished and emphasized:

– the business characteristics with special emphasis on enactment,
– the words and symbols with special emphasis on perceptions and categorizations,
– the motivations,
– the credits given to those which contributed to intellectual and entrepreneurial success.

Structural similarity of each case results from exactly same questions asked:

1. Words and symbols to describe an entrepreneur.
2. Words and symbols to describe an intellectual.
3. Do possible linkages/interfaces exist between the world of an entrepreneur and that one of the intellectual?
4. ... and in your case?
5. What do you have to give up as an entrepreneur?
6. What do you gain as an entrepreneur?
7. Your biggest success, your biggest failure?
8. Your personal goals?
9. Suppose your firm goes under ...
10. Can you mention possible contributors to your success?
11. Whom did you learn most from?

Needless to say, mentioned above structural similarity greatly facilitates analysis, allowing concentration on particular aspects of entrepreneurship. It is possible to illustrate the above made general assumptions with material taken directly from particular interviews. Because of this paper length limitations it is rather impractical to draw from all six cases. Each of them is of the length of this very paper! Therefore we confined ourselves to just three cases only. Trying to present them in the most concise form, while preserving a unique climate of the interview discourse, we have been stricken by salient similarities. Hence the title of the following paragraph. Whatever impressions might the Reader have, he should understand that the following text is taken directly from the interviews which were authorized by the interviewed individuals.

3. Similar or Very Unique Stories?

a) Jack – the Film Wizard

When talking with Jacek, a Warsaw film maker, one can recall an old English story about a foreigner inquiring what it takes to have a smooth lawn.

"Nothing special, "the Englishman says," you simply take proper seed and every fortnight you cut your grass."

"For how long?," demands a foreigner.

"Just about three hundred years."

We are talking film making, which is definitely much more difficult an enterprise than lawn cultivation. But for Jacek everything seems to be simple and not worth elaboration.

"If you have a good script, you will have a good film. Good people will come up with good production. True, there is also a question of proper technology. This takes knowledge and money. If you have both, you can be certain to just collect orders and awards."

"So this is why you are called a «lucky award eater»?"

"If you are known and well established, they give you different names. Some people hate you, some like you, some simply respect you. The people I care for are my partners, customers and employees. And they know that my evident success has nothing to do with luck or chance. It is not accidental. If you are good in what you do, if you get fully immersed in what you do, if you devote your full time to do it, if you have enough humility and keep learning, success will come by itself."

"Yyyes, amazingly simple and easy, but ..., but you are not an artist only. Not only an actor, a scrip writer, a director, a producer. YOU ARE AN ENTREPRENEUR, A MANAGER, A BUSINESS PARTNER ..."

"Here again I do not see anything unusual. You should simply know your goals. Be certain of what you are after. You should assemble a group of people who share your goals and your vision. And then comes the most important thing ..."

"The money?"

"No, money will come by itself. But from the very beginning you should BE UTTERLY HONEST to yourself, to your employees, to fiscal authorities. Your financial dealings should be just transparent."

"To invite jealousy?"

"No, rather to prompt you to invest in your employees, to share with them your profits. To incite their interest and identity with what they do."

"How many employees do you have?"

"Fifty-four."

"How many firms?"

"Three in which I am a major partner. And two in which my firms are the major partners."

"What was the value of your sales in 1995?"

"About 8 million US dollars."

"And this year?"

"It will double at least."

"Net return on your investment?"

"About 30%."

"And what do you think about your employees?"

"They are just wonderful, just great. Young, enthusiastic, competent, devoted, loyal, innovative."

"How are they paid?"

"Really well. Much above the average. They are paid what they are worth for. And they are worth a lot."

"Jacek, what does it take to achieve a success like that?."

"YOUR WHOLE LIFE!"

"And how old are you?" I demand recalling a number of generations needed to come up with a good lawn.

"Thirty-eight."

"For how long has your oldest firm been in existence?"

"Just for four years!

It is the middle of March 1996, I have him sitting on a sofa, seemingly relaxed but chain smoking.

"I never relax," he once confessed. "Even while watching a movie, while reading a book, I consider an artistic structure, I ponder the images, the sequence of events, the plot ..."

AN ARTIST in his every inch, how come that he became an entrepreneur. And how come that he is so mature as the one?

In early 1989 he was offered a job of the artistic director of the foreign advertising firm ODEON. Since the owner did not know too much about doing business in Poland, Jacek was practically the chief manager of the firm. In his quest for making it the best firm in Poland he managed to employ the most talented people and proved himself a successful team leader and manager. Then he witnessed the accelerating process of his employer demoralization which threatened the very existence of the firm. Just two years after getting hired he decided to quit. What followed was almost an immediate offer from ODEON's competitor – ITI.

ITI, the first film advertising company in Poland, offered him a position of director of its production studio.

"I just changed my position of the manager of Odeon into position of the manager of ITI." Again a comfortable salary, again a company car, again a pursuit to make his new firm number one in Poland through building a team based on the most able, most talented people. And again an undisputable success measured by increase in sales and the number of prestigious rewards. And finally again a conflict with the owner not willing to stand by his words, promises, and even some written agreements.

Without even considering his possible next steps Jacek quits just overnight. "I really learned, "he says," how not to manage a firm. I learned what should be avoided. My learning process of a hired manager was completed. I did not want to work for anybody any more. For money, I could be selling shoes or cabaret tickets – as I did as a youngster – but my only passion was film production. And my only problem was the lack of money."

Upon leaving ITT Jacek discovers that his two closest colleagues make the same decision. It does not take them long to decide to form a partnership in which they invest about $ 1,000 each. They all have tremendous film knowledge and share a vision of a modern professional studio. As a firm they are quickly joined by five professionals formerly employed by ITT. It takes the three partners quite a long time until they pay themselves some salary. But within six months the firm employs twelve people and looks for new ones in order to cope with a growing number of clients. Actually clients had been the ones responsible for making Jacek's firm viable. Their quickly coming orders were just a verification of his (and his partners') professional position. Their advanced payments, constituting the main (if not the only) source of financing, proved the righteousness of the business concept which was based on the highest quality of the product.

"What plans do you have?"

"In 1997 I will make a musical. This is something I have dreamed about since a long time. A feature film which I am going to direct."

"And produce as well?"

"No, this film will be produced by one of my partners. It is rather impossible to be director and producer simultaneously."

"And then?"

"I am also thinking about two TV serials and about some other feature movies. And then, there is something I kept considering since a long time."

"Yet another film?"

"Once we have started making feature movies, we shall continue. But in order to do it properly, we need a modern studio. Well constructed and very well equipped. As good, or maybe better than those in Holywood. I think we shall have such a studio within free to four years."

"And then?"

"And then I will really have reached my ceiling. I would then like to go searching for the greener pastures. Somewhere where I could be well below the ceiling. Where I could find a new challenge. Perhaps to Australia or New Zealand."

"To do what? Spending your money?"

"No, I think I will never leave film making. And I hope I will always be a partner in my firms. If I go chasing my challenge I will do it only to grow, to do something different, to do it better."

b) Tadeusz – the Journalist

Beginning sometimes in the 1960s as the press agency reporter and eventually foreign correspondent, Tadeusz established himself as one of the most esteemed journalists in Poland. As such he managed to become known to and respected by the viewers of different TV programs, quite often initiated and directed by himself. A sharp commentator of economic, technological, and especially foreign affairs, he suddenly became quite less visible to readers and watchers used to a "cool eye" approach of this eminent journalist often used as a special envoy by Polish different media. The reason has been his direct entry into the world of business. While learning how has it happened one discovers new dimensions of entrepreneurship, and new secrets, if not wonders, of business enactment.

"It had been quite a long time since I became intellectually challenged by what I was learning about business. ... As a foreign correspondent, I was slowly discovering this totally different world, only to learn that it is governed by principles not much different from those which prevail in the world of politics..."

"Really? Are you not exaggerating?"

"Oh no. The essence of business is information and influence over masses of people. Thus business can be understood as a form of politics. And the very heart of some kinds of business is just a technology of getting results. Technology development has always been my field of interest. This was not my devotion to the communist system, but rather my thorough knowledge of technology which facilitated my journalistic career in Poland. Now, I was suddenly discovering the interfaces of world politics, technology development and business behavior. And eventually, if not naturally, I started to play with some ideas of DOING IT, of continuing my engagement in politics in some different form, of jumping into the world of business."

"I registered my firm as its sole partner in my private apartment and with a secretary paid from my own pocket. But from the very beginning it was conceived of as a major PR and advertising agency with a clearly defined mission – TO PROMOTE POLAND."

"From your tiny apartment, with just one telephone line and a secretary paid from your own pocket ...?"

"The firm was registered in June of 1990 and in one month time we wrote our first invoice for reception organized for Arthur Andersen who was opening its office in Warsaw. It was not a big money but a good start. We used this opportunity to establish viable links and connections with several major firms and public institutions. During this very reception I was given an offer to publish a weekly magazine for a major business consortium. The first issue appeared already in September of 1990 and was an immediate success. Quite soon it became our own publication after we had paid a handsome sum of money for the right to use its name. Yes, "he continues," that reception gave us visibility and contacts I previously had as a journalist but not as an entrepreneur. So we decided to go ahead with more ambitious plans."

"We?"

"There were already four of us. Besides the secretary and myself we had another journalist and an art designer. But I knew I could easily mobilize several part-timers. So we rented a small room in the center of town, and ... by the middle of 1991, just one year after we got chartered, I was so engaged in my own business that I left my press agency for good."

"So, you are not a journalist any more?"

"Quite to the contrary. To be a journalist is a life sentence without parole; it is a way of looking at the world around you. You never cease to be one. But I also remain an active journalist in my firm. I am editing our magazine, I write a weekly commentary syndicated to Polish newspapers with a circulation of 4.5 million copies, I am still present in Polish and foreign TV and radio."

"How many employees do you have and what are the main areas of your activity?"

"We have fifty-three people working for us on a permanent basis. And then, there are about 300 co-workers. But when it comes to a particular venture we can easily mobilize new people. Our main areas are promotion, PR, publications, and film and TV production. We are the largest firm of its kind in Poland. In 1995 our total sales exceeded $ 8 million. In September of 1995 we became an affiliate of the firm which is the second largest in the world in the area of PR and promotion."

"What do you gain as an entrepreneur?"

"A FASCINATION coming from GAME PLAYING. In this business, each day and each operation are different. This is not for the people who enjoy order and known configurations. My games are changing. There is a change of situations, of players, of stakes, and of the bets. This is good for somebody who is used to independence. Somehow it resembles the life of a foreign correspondent. The results of the game are almost immediate. And satisfaction is often of much more importance than money. And ... there is also a RESPONSIBILITY."

"Responsibility as a gain?"

"Yes, certainly. This is a responsibility for the people and for their families. A material but also a moral responsibility. One should not do anything which might cause some psychological discomfort on part of your employees."

"This sounds like a Sunday sermon ..."

"I was offered quite good financial terms for a telephone sex parties promotional campaign. I did not do it. And while depriving me of good money this decision had given me a real satisfaction. Simply, I am respected by my employees for making what they consider to be morally proper choices. And this feeling gives me a tremendous satisfaction which I could not otherwise experience."

"Fascination and responsibility. Are these your only rewards for being an entrepreneur?"

"Oh no, there is also a feeling of POLITICAL POWER."

"Inside your firm?"

"I am still a journalist. Not only when I write. Journalism is not a profession only, but also the way one perceives the world. In my approach, in my orientation I will never cease to be a journalist. As an entrepreneur/manager I have some influence over my employees. But for a man of media this influence is much broader. A journalist cannot escape the world of politics. I have it here. And I enjoy it. So this is my important gain. Perhaps a compensation for giving up the stage of macropolitics. The supreme excitement for me is to PROVIDE A LEADERSHIP for my employees and partners, and – if possible – for a wider public. TO TALK SENSE in the environment where sense and reason are not ruling criteria yet."

"And money? Why do you shy away from this aspect of motivation?"

"When Becker or Agassi play the game, they do not think about the money. They concentrate on hitting the ball. I ALSO WANT TO HIT A BALL. It is an exciting feeling when everything combines to produce a PERFECT HIT."

"OK. Let us talk the game. Can you identify your biggest success?"

"Maybe you caught me. Maybe my tennis parallel has not been adequate. There are different measures of success. And the best one seems to be satisfaction for both sides. What we do is not based on a zero sum game principle. We get satisfaction from satisfying our clients."

c) Andrzej – the Mathematician

Fine arts and the art of doing business have always been going hand in hand in Andrzej's family. As a potential successor of the family tradition and business he was destined to marry an artist and carry on as a pastrychef. And so, he married a trained painter and became a successor of the famous Warsaw school of ... mathematics...

By 1978, when his father became terminally ill, and eventually died in 1981, Andrzej was already a very well established and connected mathematician. His pioneering adventure with denotational semantics and with formal methods of software design and specification was just beginning but he had already established a record of publications, invited conference talks, international seminars, tutorials, editorials, etc...

typical for an eminent representative of a Warsaw school of mathematics. Welcome at any corner of the world, he embraced the challenge and opportunity offered by applications of logic to software design. This life of the citizen of the world was exciting and both intellectually and materially rewarding. And strangely enough, it was somehow fostered by his … father who encouraged his son to enter Warsaw Polytechnic and eventually Warsaw University. The motivation was rather obvious – back in the 1950s, under the socialism, one could not be certain about the future of his family business.

Somehow his father managed to persuade the mathematician to practice … pastrycooking. In 1969, three years after receiving his Ph.D., he passed qualifying exams for a journeyman, and in 1975, just one year before becoming a full professor, he managed to successfully complete his pastrychef's examinations. Since then, PROFESSOR, as his father told the people to address him, became an oft visitor of the firm, greatly enriching its color and local charm. But he was still the visitor only and his status did not greatly change with his father's illness and passing away.

The 1980s were quite harsh for both small business and luxury consumption. Professor was just a part of a small family business, a civil law firm with three other partners besides himself. The firm was run by his cousin. His role was confined to public relations. This was taking about one day a week. A lot for a professor of mathematics. Very little for a firm. Especially during revolutionary times which did away with communism and called market forces into full command of Polish economy.

It is the early evening of 3 January 1996. This date has been chosen purposefully. Exactly five years ago PROFESSOR was about to depart Warsaw for a skiing vacation. He took a two-weeks leave of absence from his institute. Not intended as such the leave has been dramatically extended. At 5.30 in the morning on the fourth of January of 1991 greatly surprised employees saw PROFESSOR entering the premises. "There is no snow" was his only explanation. And then, quite unexpectedly for them and for himself he added: "… don't call me PROFESSOR any more. Call me BOSS." And this sudden nomination gave him the right and the obligation to study the firm and to apply a shock treatment to its transformation. "Yes," he answers my immediate question, "there have been many shocks, and initially nothing seemed possible. But with time things started to change. And the firm was on a new track."

From a serious inside perspective his firm looked quite differently than he previously expected. "It was rather primitive. Tradition, work ethos, trademark, and location constituted our main assets. Yet, we had to grow. Otherwise we were doomed to disappear."

One of the largest and seemingly most prestigious small business investors approached Andrzej only two weeks after his aborted ski trip. Andrzej immediately realized he did not have enough knowledge of his financial needs. But he also learned the market value of his goodwill. Within just few weeks he prepared his first business plan based on immediate modernization and expansion of production capacities. The sum of planned investment was $ 450,000. His net worth (excluding the value of his trade mark) was assessed at ... $ 60,000. Despite this glaring disproportion his scheme was met with understanding. He was offered quite favorable terms. So he made immediate plans and contacted potential contractors. But preparation of the final credit contract kept protracting. And when it came to signing, Andrzej saw something dramatically different from what was previously negotiated and agreed upon. He was too wise to sign the arrogantly and unfavorably changed clauses of the agreement. So the previously made investment plans had to be called off. "No," he answers the obvious question, "I did not consider going back to my institute. Instead I decided to correct my mistakes. And besides, I had already learned my real needs and my strengths as well."

"Learning" is probably the most often used word during this interview. But while still learning was he not afraid of a serious failure? "Yes," he answers. "Then, I was really scared. But I am not afraid any more. And since I have learned that absence of development is a beginning of annihilation I am now on the eve of a new revolution."

But this is already a completely new firm. Legally, financially, materially, commercially, personally, and first of all – conceptually.

Legally it is a limited liability company, with Andrzej as the major stock owner, his cousin, his son and a non-family member who in 1992 came to the financial rescue for a minor share of the equity. Along with the money, this last person brought another important factor – a new management culture, which he had mastered due to his Western background. During 5 years the firm has undergone some legal transformations designed to accommodate various forms of strategic investment in its equity. It managed to attract about $ 1 million of investment. Some of its equity shares have been swapped for credit to be repaid by the end of 1998. "But I am not afraid of this debt," says Andrzej. "In fact, I am about to take a new one. If you know how to calculate and whom to deal with, you should not be afraid of debt."

What he took over in 1991 was just one shop in Warsaw with a monthly sales of ECU 30,000. In the meantime he expanded the number of his own shops to 6, and opened an elegant cafe just next door to his original prime location. Besides he became the first Polish private franchisor with 6 franchises around Poland. His monthly sales reached ECU 145,000. The number of his own personnel grew up from forty to 140. Furthermore, there are about twenty-five people employed by the franchisees. His production and administrative area was extended from 250 square meters in 1991 to 1500 in 1995. And although a significant part of production is still manual due to the high quality and assortment of his product, the equipment is totally new and most up-to-date. The same is true for administration. It is fully computerized. "And besides," he adds, "I procured a quite handy overhead projector." AN OVERHEAD PROJECTOR? "Yes, he answers. This is just a symbol of the newest change I am about to introduce. A NEW TECHNIQUE OF MANAGEMENT."

Just two month ago Andrzej was exposed to the work of W. Edward Deming. Although he kept learning since joining the firm for good, no management literature he was reading before made any real impact on him. All legal contracts were drawn by him. Only the final drafts were consulted by practising lawyers who "confined themselves to adding necessary legal phrases." He personally constructed his business plans, computer programs, administrative procedures, personnel development plans. He found time and energy to complete five educational programs run by the French Institute of Management in Warsaw. He thinks he gained a lot. But, as already mentioned above, he was never impressed nor moved by the management literature he studied. His sound mathematical knowledge enriched by practical experience seemed to suffice as the base of effective decision making. What he now discovered was a kind of revelation and intellectual excitement he could only compare with his first exposure to denotational semantics. "Deming," he says, "has been an intellectual turning point for me." Initially his intentions were quite practical. He was only considering introduction of ISO 9,000. But now he is taking Deming as an intellectual and practical challenge to him and to his firm. So he is about to begin a full semester thirty hours course on TQM for twenty of his … key personnel.

The firm will experience quite serious expansion attempt. Since due to exclusiveness of its original product it practically reached the ceiling of market growth, it has to diversify. In order to grow, it needs a high financial volume. So it has to continue to change. This is something his employees have already learned from and with their BOSS. But the most interesting and challenging adventure seems to be implicated in his attempt to co-opt them as fellow students (and consequently practitioners) of a new approach to management. Will this not be perceived as just an intellectual freak?

"No," says he. "I have kept exposing them to such freaks from the very moment I became the BOSS. And each time something which initially looked impractical worked out quite smoothly..."

"Is there really any possible linkage between the world of an intellectual and that one of an entrepreneur?"

He takes this question personally, and answers positively.

"Managing my firm provides me with an intellectual satisfaction. I am creating something concrete and material. It is a great satisfaction for a mathematician. Initially I was not taken by performing simple tasks. But now, when I have developed a lecture as a tool of management, I can grow myself. This is through entrepreneurship that I develop intellectually."

A creative zest in a manufacturing firm! Is a research institute still needed?

4. Conclusions and Implications

Through combining intellectual curiosity and flexibility with non-conventional thinking entrepreneuring intellectuals can identify and tap opportunities which are non-existent for a more conventional mind. The above conclusion offers an important theoretical contribution to the field of entrepreneurial studies. Especially with respect to the mode of learning! But practical implications in the area of education and training might be of a more dramatic importance. The research is still continued, however. It is definitely much too early to draw final conclusions and to speculate about implications.

Notes about the Authors

Airaksinen Timo (Ph.D., Turku, Finland, 1975) is Professor of Philosophy (ethics, social philosophy and philosophy of law) at the University of Helsinki. He is a visiting Professor of Philosophy at the Texas A & M University, Corpus Chricti 1994–96. He is also a Life Member of Clare Hall, Cambridge, England, the Vice-President of the International Society for Value Inquiry, and an Honorary Member of the Learned Society of Praxiology (Warsaw, Poland). He has published extensively on epistemology, history of philosophy (Berkeley, Hobbes and Hegel), and ethics. Some of his books are *Ethics of Coercion and Authority* (Pittsburgh University Press, 1988) and *The Philosophy of the Marquis de Sade* (Routledge, 1995). He is the managing editor of the journal *Hobbes Studies*. His main research interests are the theory of professional ethics, the philosophy of Hobbes, and the philosophy of literature. he is working on an interpretation of H.P. Lovecraft.

Barker Albert had a classics education and went on to read philosophy. He joined Procter and Gamble in 1960 and in 1971 he founded a high tech engineering company. Over the following years he became increasingly sceptical about some aspects of management training and the dubious contributions of non-practising "experts" in business management and social economics. In the 1980s he met Prof. Reg Revans and quickly became convinced of the integrity and efficacy of Action Learning. He has since been collaborating closely with Revans, becoming a firm disciple and friend. He has researched and applied the use of Action Learning precepts in technological development programmes, community projects, and as a means of pursuing the engagement and development of democracy as a natural expression of human nature. He believes that Organisational Development through Action Learning extends to the widest social and community spheres and embodies the moral and spiritual development of the Individual as well as improving our operational effectiveness. It is the means of generating appropriate autotherapeutic change. he has a variety of business interests and engages Action Learning in a voluntary capacity. He believes that if we want a better world – then those engaged in the real here and now practicalities had better get together and get on with it! Action Learning is about Collaborative Deeds, not just Words!

Birchall Greg R.[*] is Director of the MBA International Management Program in the Graduate School of Business at RMIT University. His research interests are in the areas of organisational learning, qualitative research methods and management learning. He is supervising both John and Dean's Doctoral Research.

Botham David. DavidBotham first engaged in the process of action learning during the early 1980s. Prior to this, he worked in the fields of industrial chemistry and higher education. In addition, he spent several years working in a number of British high security prisons during which time he bcame interested in the behavioural sciences.

In the late 1980s he worked alongside Reg Revans and John Morris, pioneering a number of action learning programmes for public and private sectore organisations.

In 1994 he was invited to become the first Director of the Revans Centre for Action Learning & Research based at the University of Salford.

Enderby John E.[*] is Principal Adviser Change Management for the Service Industry Advisory Group. He advises executives on the planning and implementation of change and is a specialist in helping groups, teams and consultative committees to be more output orientated. He is completing his Ph.D. in the area of organisational learning.

Hebron de Winter Chris and Doreen have for the past ten years been respectively Academic Director and Financial Director of H + E Associates, the British higher education development seminar and training consultancy organisation, of which Doreen is the senior partner. Previously, both worked extensively in British technical and higher education and in the UK civil service: Doreen, additionally, had an equally extensive career in business and as a business consultant. In their academic careers, Chris (Ph.D.) specialised in research into the higher education process and Doreen in management and business, while both also worked in the field of communication studies. Both have also extensive experience of working with students from developing countries: indeed it was in their capacity as Overseas Welfare Officers for their respective colleges that they first met.

Gasparski Wojciech W. Professor of Humanities, Dr. S. is a Chairman of the Academic Board at the Institute of Philosophy and Sociology, Polish Academy of Sciences, Warsaw, Poland. He also serves as a Chairman of the Science Studies Committee of the Polish Academy of Sciences. Recently he organized in Warsaw the *Collegium Invisibile* for which he is a Principal; the College is focused on humanities and social sciences gifted students for whom it offers tutorials taught by eminent scholars. He teaches at American Studies Center, Warsaw University, Warsaw University of Technology, and at School of Management. He was a Fulbright Senior Visiting Scholar at the State University of New York and visited universities in other countries and extensively contributed international conferences. Now he is a Consulting faculty of the Saybrook Institute in San Francisco. He published several books and over two hundred articles and conference papers. He is Editor-in-Chief of series *Praxiology: The International Annual of Practical Philosophy and Methodology* (published in the U.S. by Transaction Publishers) and Polish journal *Prakseologia*. His recent publications are: (1) W.W. Gasparski, L.V. Ryan, C.S.V., eds, 1996, *Human Action in Business: Praxiological and Ethical Dimensions* Transaction Publishers, New Brunswick (USA)–London (UK); (2) T. Airaksinen and W.W. Gasparski, eds, 1995, *Science in Society* IFiS Publishers, Warsaw; (3) W.W. Gasparski, 1993, *A Philosophy of Practicality: A Treatise on the Philosophy of Tadeusz Kotarbiński* Societas Philosophica Fennica, Helsinki.

Gliński Piotr received M.A. degree in 1978 in economics (M.A. thesis: "The Relations of Consumption and the Current Model of Consumption in Poland"). Between 1978 and 1982, took a postgraduate doctoral course at the Division of Life Styles Research of the Institute of Philosophy and Sociology of the Polish Academy of Sciences. Doctoral dissertation, entitled: "Economic Conditioning of Life Style. Urban Families in Poland in the 1970s," was completed in 1983. After the imposition of the Marshall law in Poland in December 1981, blacklisted and prohibited from working in research institutes for over two years. During years 1984–86, worked at the Studies Bureau of the Committee for Studies and Prognoses "Poland 2000" as a research worker. At the same time participated in research work of the Division of Life Styles of the Institute of Philosophy and Sociology, Polish Academy of Sciences. From October 1986, has been employed in this Division and undertaken studies on the problems of the environmental movement in Poland as well as of the ecological awareness of the Polish society. In 1989, granted Ford Foundation scholarship and in the first half of 1990 worked as a visiting scholar at Stanford University. He is the author of the book *Polish Greens. Social Movement in the Time of Transformation* (1996), as well as over forty articles in the field of sociology of culture and social movements. Since 1991 he has been working at the Division of Civil Society, Institute of Philosophy and Sociology, Polish Academy of Sciences; acting as the head of this Division (since 1992).

Kline William received M.A. degree in 1993 in philosophy at Bowling Green State University (Ohio, USA) where he is about to complete his Ph.D. (in December 1997). The areas of his current research are Ethics, Political and Social Theory, Philosophy of Economics. He is also interested in Business Ethics, Medical Ethics and Game Theory. Lately he has been cooperating with Budapestian *Invisible College* and with ELTE University (Budapest, Hungary).

Kwiatkowski Stefan, professor of management at Warsaw University. Teaching entrepreneurship and innovation both at Warsaw University and at International Business School/Academy of Entrepreneurship and Management in Warsaw (one of the first and probably the best non-public business schools in Poland, of which he is the Chairman of the Board of Trustees and partner). Over 150 books and articles published in Polish, English, Russian and other languages of the region. Recently engaged in an extensive program of interviewing Polish entrepreneurs and managers of large state owned enterprises. Another research project initiated and performed together with professors Bengt Jonannission and Thomas Dandridge addresses "intellectual entrepreneurship." Also the author of educational entrepreneurship program for small children and v-chairman of the jury of the national competition program for high school students "My school as the school of entrepreneurship." Chairman of the Association of Management Education "forum" and head of its Accreditation Committee. Member of the board of Central and East European Management Development Association CEEMAN.

Levy Gerald M. is a Principle Lecture in Management Learning at Liverpool John Moores University, England and a member of the Revans Centre for Action Learning and Research at Salford University, England. From 1990 until 1995 he was Director of MBA programmes in Liverpool and is currently on sabbatical working on his PhD thesis which is researching Dance Card applications.

Phelan Dean R.[*] is a Corporate Psychologist and Director of the Service Industry Advisory Group, a Network of specialists which assists organisations to achieve their purpose and vision. He is an international speaker and author in the areas of human resources management and organisational change. He is also completing his Ph.D., looking at the relationship between Leadership and organisational learning.

Ulrich Werner is Titular Professor of Social Planning in the Department of Philosophy, University of Fribourg, CH-1700 Fribourg, Switzerland. He holds doctoral degrees in economics and social sciences from the University of Fribourg and in philosophy of social systems design from the University of California at Berkeley. He is a noted pioneer of "critical systems thinking" and is on the editorial boards of three international journals, among them *Systems Practice* and *Systems Research*.

Note

* John E. Enderby, Dean R. Phelan and Greg Birchall are members of the Advisory Board of the "SIAG Applied Research Unit," an organisation dedicated to Research and Development in the fields of Human Resources Management and Organisational Learning. The Service Industry Advisory Group (SIAG) head Office is located in Melbourne, Australia.

  Both John and Dean were invited from Australia by Professor R.W. Revans to participate in the First International Action Learning Mutual Collaboration Congress in London 1995.